The M.E. Sharpe Library of
Franklin D. Roosevelt Studies

Franklin D. Roosevelt
and the Transformation of the Supreme Court

Volume Three

Stephen K. Shaw
William D. Pederson
and Frank J. Williams
Editors

Routledge
Taylor & Francis Group
LONDON AND NEW YORK

First published 2004 by M.E. Sharpe

Published 2015 by Routledge
2 Park Square, Milton Park, Abingdon, Oxon OX14 4RN
711 Third Avenue, New York, NY, 10017, USA

Routledge is an imprint of the Taylor & Francis Group, an informa business

Library of Congress Cataloging-in-Publication Data

Franklin D. Roosevelt and the transformation of the Supreme Court / Stephen K. Shaw, William D. Pederson, and Frank J. Williams, editors.
p. cm.
Includes bibliographical references and index.
ISBN 0-7656-1032-9 (alk. paper)
1. United States. Supreme Court—History. 2. Political questions and judicial power—United States—History. 3. United States—Politics and government—20th century. I. Shaw, Stephen K. II. Pederson, William D., 1946– III. Williams, Frank J.

KF8742.F73 2003
347.73′26′09—dc21

2002066944

ISBN 13: 9780765610331 (pbk)
ISBN 13: 9780765610324 (hbk)

TABLE OF CONTENTS

The M.E. Sharpe Library of Franklin D. Roosevelt Studies

Volume Three

Introduction

Stephen K. Shaw

"No event of twentieth-century constitutional history is better remembered," argues William E. Leuchtenburg, "than Franklin D. Roosevelt's ill-fated 'Court-packing' scheme of 1937; . . ."[1] The president sought authority from Congress to "reform" the federal judiciary by adding a new federal judge, including justices of the United States Supreme Court, for each member of the federal judiciary who did not retire upon reaching the age of seventy.[2] To this day the bombshell that FDR dropped on a largely unexpecting nation yet not completely surprised capital seems scarcely explicable. For whatever (or a variety of) reasons, Roosevelt miscalculated badly, for his judicial reorganization initiative suffered an ignominious defeat at the hands of an overwhelmingly Democratic United States Senate. It was a political and personal debacle from which the president never fully recovered.[3] Even Eleanor Roosevelt, late in her long life, "still would shake her head and say that she could not imagine what had led her husband to follow such a disastrous course."[4] Nonetheless, his largely secretive and ultimately unsuccessful attempt to "pack the Court," appeared to have, according to one leading student of the affair, "an inherent logic and even inevitability."[5]

The United States Supreme Court did not rule on a New Deal statute until 1934, and in the *Blaisdell* ruling,[6] which was decided by a 5 to 4 vote with "The Four Horsemen" dissenting,[7] Chief Justice Charles Evans Hughes opined, "While emergency does not create power, emergency may furnish the occasion for the exercise of power."[8] President Roosevelt, from day one in the Oval Office, clearly and fully subscribed to Hughes's dictum, and aggressively sought to exercise such power in the face of the Great Depression. He believed the Constitution authorized and the U.S. electorate had recently sanctioned such executive power and prerogative. The New Deal Congress largely concurred.

However, the Hughes Court, that "Court of Methuselahs,"[9] had come to regard the New Deal regime as antithetical to "the Court's prevailing habit of mind—the idea that government cannot be left judicially unsupervised in possession of a power that might be abused."[10] Over a period of approximately seventeen months in 1935–36 the high Court invalidated no less than a dozen New Deal statutes, and created deep doubt throughout the Roosevelt administration about other New Deal legislation whose constitutionality was yet to be determined.[11] As Justice Harlan Fiske Stone, later to be named chief justice by FDR, wrote in a letter to his sister June 2, 1936, "We finished the term of Court yesterday, I think in many ways one of the most disastrous in history. At any rate it seems to me that the Court has been needlessly narrow and obscurantic in its outlook. . . . [W]e seem to have tied Uncle Sam up in a hard knot."[12]

No chief executive had ever attempted to change so much so quickly.[13] No institution represented the established order more vividly than "the nine old men."[14] With the beginning of his second term in 1937, Roosevelt found himself in the historically odd and politically unpalatable position of being the first president since James Monroe to serve a full term without a single appointment to the Court. "Little wonder," observes Henry Abraham, "he was convinced the fates were conspiring against him. Death and retirement seemed to have taken a holiday."[15] The president, therefore, felt compelled to act to save the country from those "five stubborn old men [who] had planted themselves squarely in the path of progress."[16] Given the Court's rulings throughout 1935–36, and in part particularly due to the *Humphrey's Executor* decision,[17] Roosevelt "sought a way not merely to liberalize the Court but to chastise the Justices for past misdeeds."[18]

President Roosevelt's March 9, 1937, national radio address, "the only time he used one of his famous fireside chats to ask the public to pressure Congress in behalf of his policies,"[19] entailed a full-fledged, frontal attack on the Court itself, and not just on an allegedly aging federal judiciary. "The Court," Roosevelt contended, "has improperly set itself up as a third House of the Congress . . . reading into the Constitution words and implications which are not there, and which were never intended to be there."[20] Distinguishing between the Court and Constitution, which was an important yet somewhat overlooked distinction in the Constitution's sesquicentennial year of 1937,[21] FDR concluded, "We have, therefore, reached the point as a Nation where we must take action to save the Constitution from the Court and the Court from itself. . . . We must find a way to take an appeal from the Supreme Court to the Constitution itself. We want a Supreme Court which will do justice under the Constitution—not over it."[22]

The president found the temptation to pack the Court, as most presidents do, irresistible.[23] And pack it he did, for even though his Court-packing proposal was defeated, he succeeded, thanks in no small part to the Court following the election return of 1936 and thus conducting the famous "switch in time that saved nine," ultimately "more than any other President in packing the Court."[24] FDR's "transformative appointments,"[25] ranging from Hugo Black in 1937 to Wiley Rutledge in 1943, and including the likes of Felix Frankfurter, William O. Douglas, and Robert H. Jackson in between, constitute "a record of professional approbation attained by no other president."[26] In the words of David M. O'Brien, "He turned a conservative Court into a liberal one and changed the direction of the Court's policy-making."[27] In so doing, FDR changed the direction of the country itself.

Franklin Roosevelt was a regime builder, and even though one can make a plausible case that he had the modern presidency thrust upon him as much as he created it,[28] he did give birth to "the expectation that the chief executive would be a primary shaper of his times—an expectation with which each of his successors has had to deal."[29] His impact on the presidency, which he entered with "transformative ambitions,"[30] and American life itself can be traced in large part to the battle over the Court. "The Court struggle," according to Leuchtenburg, "speeded the acceptance of a substantial change in the role of government and in the reordering of property rights and also had the probably unanticipated result of the appointment of Justices much more solicitous of civil liberties and civil rights."[31] His one particular success in the Court fight was "the legitimation of a vast expansion of power of government in American life."[32] At the center, the "vital center" of that expansion has been the American president. As Theodore White once told us, "All contemporary national politics descend from Franklin Roosevelt."[33]

The essays in this volume derive from the conference "FDR After 50 Years," held at Louisiana State University in Shreveport in September 1995. This collection of essays examines the impact of FDR on American law and politics, primarily through his collision with and influence on the Untied States Supreme Court. In the long history of the American presidency and the high Court, few events, if any, have been of more lasting consequence than the Court battle of the mid-

1930s. As these essays clearly and convincingly demonstrate, this chapter in American politics is still being written. We continue (and will for some time to come) to measure the effects of Roosevelt's exercise of presidential power and his unprecedented efforts to shape national recovery and restoration of the American polis.

Barbara Perry and Henry Abraham examine a defining moment in the history of the United States Supreme Court. The Court was at a crossroads, in terms of its image and its jurisprudence, in the mid-1930s. It had moved into "the marble palace" in October of 1935, and perceptions and expectations of the Court, from within and outside its own halls, were in a state of flux. As Perry and Abraham demonstrate, the Court both sullied and saved itself during this time period, and would emerge as a changed institution.

Roger Corley scrutinizes the "constitutional revolution" of 1937, and the manner in which and the degree to which the Court responded to the Holmesian "felt necessities of the time." The Court *does* follow the election returns, and it *does* adhere to its own calendar and culture. The Court is, as other scholars have argued over the years, a storm center in American law and politics, and as Corley proves in his analysis of the Court's development in the 1930s, the Court is not immune to pressures and realities outside the justice's chambers.

James Duram analyzes the furor caused by the Court-packing plan of 1937 and the reaction in the press, particularly the newspaper industry. While his focus is on the heavily Republican oriented state of Kansas and its print community, his case study is indicative of what happened elsewhere as well. The "fourth estate" was a critical actor in the battle over the Court, and Duram's examination of what transpired in Kansas (a state in fact carried by FDR in his electoral juggernaut of 1936 over Kansas' allegedly-favorite son, Governor Alf Landon) clarifies the press's role in shaping the terms of this Court fight and influencing its outcome.

Kenneth Holland begins Part II with his careful,

insightful treatment of the all-important relationship between two politicos of obvious talent and impressive ambition. Chief Justice Charles Evans Hughes and President Franklin D. Roosevelt were alternately allies and adversaries, and in large measure they reflect Madisonian democracy at work a century and a half after the founding, for each checked the other's political and personal ambitions. Holland's analysis of these two towering figures of American law and politics, one whose presidential aspirations were realized—the other not—sheds new light on the forces at work when such titans both collide and cooperate in our national political theater.

Elaine T. King provides a penetrating perspective on the controversy surrounding the initial appointment that President Roosevelt made to the high Court—United States Senator Hugo Lafayette Black, Democrat of Alabama. Black, native son of the south and political liberal, was a staunch New Deal supporter (the sine qua non for all of FDR's Supreme Court nominations) and political ally of the president's, including his role as one of the crucial advocates for the Court-packing plan in the Senate. Evidence emerged after his nomination (and before his eventual confirmation) of Black's one-time, brief membership in the Ku Klux Klan, an element made even more ironic by Black's later emergence as one of *the* voices for civil liberties and an egalitarian society during his long, memorable tenure on the Court.

William Bader highlights the third of FDR's nominees to the Supreme Court—Harvard law professor Felix Frankfurter. Frankfurter was a critical, central member of the Roosevelt "brain trust," and had a national reputation and years of public service (as did almost all of FDR's nominees to the Court) before joining the Court in 1939. Justice Frankfurter was a person and jurist of great intellect and perhaps even greater enigmatic complexity. However, in Bader's hands he surfaces as a persuasive proponent of both political liberalism and judicial restraint, and his pivotal place in the development of twentieth-century law and jurisprudence in the United States is clearly established.

The final chapter in Part II offers an investigation and evaluation of a side of the Court often overlooked. The members of the Court, especially those who would come to comprise the Roosevelt Court, were persons of no small political experience or ambition, public or private statements to the contrary notwithstanding. William O. Douglas, FDR's fourth nominee to the Court in 1939, was often (and not without reason), as James Moses demonstrates, seen as entertaining thoughts of national elective office. The election of 1944, Roosevelt's last, had more than its share of cunning, cabals, and Machiavellian machinations, and many hoped (or feared) that FDR would tap Justice Douglas as his running mate. Moses illustrates how members of the Court are not necessarily hermetically sealed from affairs of state nor inoculated against Potomac fever.

The third and final part of this anthology moves to the realm of constitutional law as applied politics. Donald Jackson and James Riddlesperger illustrate the centrality of executive leadership within a political system where presidential leadership is both expected and limited. Presidents invariably realize more frustrations than triumphs, and yet essential to the accomplishment of virtually any particular program of national scope and purpose is presidential vision, accompanied by a necessary and proper amount of political bargaining skill in our system of fractured power. The Rooseveltian model of presidential power and leadership, while showing signs of age and stress, still deserves and bears special scrutiny, as this chapter reveals with persuasive lucidity.

Stephen Shaw examines the vital role played by the Roosevelt Court in the genesis and maturation of First Amendment religion clause jurisprudence, especially with respect to the establishment clause. Beginning in the 1940s, particularly with cases concerning fiscal aid and the role of religion in public schools, the Court announced precedent-setting, culture-influencing decisions whose impacts are still felt and often heavily debated today. The Court's understanding of the role of religion in American life, and its development of doctrine and tests regarding the meaning of the establishment clause have guaranteed a crucial place for the Roosevelt Court in the annals of American law and politics, as issues and cases continue to reveal.

The final essay by Harvey Hudspeth provides a fitting conclusion to this anthology. American liberalism both shaped and was shaped by the presidency of Franklin Roosevelt and the jurisprudential work of the Supreme Court, especially following the Court battle of 1937 and "the switch in time that saved nine." The liberal political and legal order that emerged from the Roosevelt presidency and Roosevelt Court entailed an energetic federal presence in our national life, and the expansion of governmental powers in the administrative, welfare state was not (and is not) accomplished without controversy. Hudspeth documents some of the realities and implications of "the changing nature of American liberalism."

In sum, what the reader will find here is a rich assemblage of insightful, idiosyncratic perspectives on a protean even Promethean political figure whose shadow still looms large on the American political and legal landscape, and an institution, the United States Supreme Court, often veiled in secrecy and riddle yet also viewed as having at least quasitalismanic properties essential for the survival of the republic. Both the individual and the institution demand our critical attention as citizens and scholars.

ENDNOTES

1. William E. Leuchtenburg, *The Supreme Court Reborn: The Constitutional Revolution in the Age of Roosevelt* (New York: Oxford University Press, 1995), p. 82.

2. See Michael Nelson, "The President and the Court: Reinterpreting the Court-Packing Episode of 1937," *Political Science Quarterly* 101 (1988): 267; Joseph Alsop and Turner Catledge, *168 Days* (Garden City, NY: Doubleday,

Doran and Co., 1938); Leuchtenburg.

3. See Alan Brinkley, *Liberalism and Its Discontents* (Cambridge, MA: Harvard University Press, 1998); and Stephen Skowronek, *The Politics Presidents Make: Leadership from John Adams to Bill Clinton* (Cambridge, MA: Belknap Press of Harvard University Press, 1997).

4. Frank Friedel, *Franklin D. Roosevelt: A Rendezvous with Destiny* (Boston: Back Bay Books, 1990), p. 228.

5. Leuchtenburg, p. 131.

6. *Home Building and Loan Association v. Blaisdell*, 290 U.S. 398 (1934).

7. Justices Willis Van Devanter, James McReynolds, George Sutherland, and Pierce Butler. They were the dependable conservative bloc on the Hughes Court, most consistent in registering their displeasure with the New Deal.

8. *Blaisdell*, 426 (1934).

9. Leuchtenburg, p. 85. The Supreme Court at this time was the oldest collection of justices in its history. The average age was seventy-two, and six of the nine justices were over seventy.

10. Robert G. McCloskey, *The American Supreme Court*, 2nd ed., revised by Sanford Levinson (Chicago: The University of Chicago Press, 1994), p. 95.

11. See Leuchtenburg; McCloskey; Alpheus T. Mason, *The Supreme Court from Taft to Warren* (New York: W.W. Norton and Co., 1964); Nelson; and cases such as *Railroad Retirement Board v. Alton Railroad Company*, 295 U.S. 330 (1935); *Schechter Poultry Corporation v. United States*, 295 U.S. 495 (1935); *Louisville Joint Stock Land Bank v. Radford*, 295 U.S. 555 (1935); *Humphrey's Executor v. United States*, 295 U.S. 602 (1935); *United States v. Butler*, 297 U.S. 1 (1936); *Carter v. Carter Coal Company*, 298 U.S. 238 (1936); *Ashton v. Cameron County Water District*, 298 U.S. 513 (1936); and *Morehead People of State of New York ex. rel. Tipaldo*, 298 U.S. 587 (1936).

12. Quoted in Mason, p. 92.

13. Roosevelt not only saw himself, as he declared in his 1933 inaugural address, as the people's instrument of change, he also saw himself "in a real sense an anointed agent of Providence." Nelson, p. 280.

14. Drew Pearson and Robert S. Allen, *The Nine Old Men* (Garden City, NY: Doubleday, Doran and Company, 1936). This sensationalized work caused quite a stir when published in the fall of 1936.

15. Henry J. Abraham, *Justices, Presidents, and Senators: A History of the U.S. Supreme Court Appointments from Washington to Clinton*, new and revised edition (Lanham, MD: Rowman & Littlefield, 1999) p. 158.

16. Alpheus T. Mason, *Harlan Fiske Stone: Pillar of the Law* (New York: Viking, 1956), p. 438.

17. *Humphrey's Executor v. United States*, 295 U.S. 602 (1935); see Nelson and Leuchtenburg.

18. Leuchtenburg, p. 109.

19. Samuel Kernell, *Going Public: New Strategies of Presidential Leadership*, 3rd ed. (Washington, DC: Congressional Quarterly, 1997), p. 128.

20. Quoted in Alpheus T. Mason, *Free Government in the Making*, 3rd ed. (New York: Oxford University Press, 1965), p. 801.

21. Michael Kammen, *A Machine That Would Go of Itself: The Constitution in American Culture* (New York: Alfred A. Knopf, 1987).

22. Mason, p. 801.

23. David O'Brien, *Storm Center: The Supreme Court in American Politics*, 5th ed. (New York: W.W. Norton & Company, 2000), p. 55.

24. Ibid. p. 56.

25. Bruce A. Ackerman, "Transformative Appointments," *Harvard Law Review* 101 (1988): 1164, 1165.

26. Abraham, p. 160.

27. O'Brien, p. 63.

28. See Skowronek and Brinkley.

29. William E. Leuchtenburg, *In the Shadow of FDR: From Harry Truman to George Bush*, 3rd ed. (Ithaca, NY: Cornell University Press, 2001), p. ix.

30. Skowronek, p. 301.

31. Leuchtenburg, *The Supreme Court Reborn*, p. 162.

32. Ibid, p. 161.

33. Theodore H. White, *America in Search of Itself: The Making of the President 1956–1980* (New York: Harper and Row, 1982), p. 47.

I

The Supreme Court: Image and Reality

1

Franklin Roosevelt and the Supreme Court
A New Deal and a New Image

Barbara A. Perry and Henry J. Abraham

March 4, 1933, the last presidential inauguration day to be held in late winter rather than the now constitutionally mandated January 20 date, dawned bright and sunny for Franklin Delano Roosevelt's swearing in as the thirty-second president of the United States. As FDR faced the crowd to deliver his stirring inaugural message of hope, one governmental symbol was conspicuously absent from the vista across the east lawn of the Capitol grounds. With the trees still devoid of foliage, Roosevelt would have been able to see clearly to the corner of First Street and Maryland Avenue, N.E., directly behind the Capitol. And just what would he have seen looking east from the stage erected on the Capitol steps? A half-completed structure that we now know as the Supreme Court building. It is indeed remarkably symbolic that the very institution that Franklin Roosevelt would attack after his 1936 reelection did not even have a separate home of its own at the beginning of his first presidential term.

Departing from previous scholarship on FDR and the Court, we focus on the concepts of symbols and images and their explanatory value in understanding the outcome of the clash between the president and the judiciary nearly sixty years ago. We borrow from Barbara Hinckley's 1990 study of "the symbolic presidency" her definition of a political symbol as an object that "has a range of meaning beyond itself" and that conveys an "emotional, moral, or psychological impact. This larger meaning need not be independently true, but will tap ideas people want to believe in as true."[1] Technically, the words image and symbol may be used interchangeably, but in our analysis, symbols contribute to the creation of images. For example, almost half-century ago, Judge Jerome Frank wrote about the traditional judicial wardrobe, which he wanted to see abolished: "The robe . . . gives the impression of uniformity in the decisions of the priestly tribe. Says the uniform black garment to the public mind: Judges attain their wisdom from a single superhuman source; their individual attitudes must never have any effect on what they decide."[2]

Bolstering this priestly image was the erection of the "marble temple," the Supreme Court's first permanent and separate edifice, which was completed in 1935. Arguably, the majesty and solidity of the Court's physical structure was emblematic of the tribunal's ultimately successful emergence from the turbulent Roosevelt years. Moreover, the justices of the U.S. Supreme Court (on both sides of the New Deal battle) had clung tightly to their image of impartiality, fairness, and independence throughout the 1930s—even in their most contentious and politically charged decisions. In addition, the media transmitted that image to the public, whose favorable opinions toward the Court are evident in polling data from the era.

Admittedly, the Supreme Court had begun its life as the "least dangerous" and most obscure branch of the federal government and only gradually developed into its full partnership with the president and Congress. As historian

Michael Kammen's study of the Constitution in American culture relates, the Court was the unknown branch for much of the Republic's first century. Yet when Americans did contemplate the Court, they often saw it inextricably bound with the Constitution—sometimes viewing the Court and Constitution as one in the same. To the extent that Americans developed reverence for the Constitution, they developed reverence for the Court.[3]

Nevertheless, image and reality of the Court collided during the New Deal crisis. The clash between the justices and FDR embodied two competing strands of the Court's modern history. Inserting itself so boldly and obviously into the governmental process is said to have politicized the Court. In addition, the petty rivalries among justices in the 1940s, which were heavily publicized, humanized the Court. As political scientist Herman Pritchett described this phenomenon, the Court was now served by "justices without halos."[4]

Yet if FDR's Court-packing proposal represented the nadir of the Court's sullied image, its rescue by Congress in defeating the plan helped to restore the tribunal's revered status. Congress's salvaging of the independent judiciary—ensuring that it was beyond the reach of the more political branches—was truly a "defining moment" in the Court's history, to quote Chief Justice William H. Rehnquist.

The stories of the "Roosevelt Court," the Court-packing scheme, and the antagonisms among the justices in the 1940s have been chronicled expertly elsewhere.[5] In contrast, our examination of the public image of the Court during the New Deal era evaluates how the Court as an institution portrayed itself, how the justices presented themselves, how the media transferred these images to the public, and how the public perceived the Court at this critical juncture in its history.

How the Court Presented Itself: Edifice as Image

In the first 145 years of its life the Supreme Court of the United States led a truly nomadic existence. As a permanent exhibit at the Supreme Court notes, "Through the years, the Court was like a poor relation, with meeting space arranged almost as an afterthought."[6] In 1790 the Supreme Court met for the first time under the new Constitution in the then seat of the national government—New York City. The Court convened in the Exchange Building, which was a combination marketplace on the ground floor and meeting space on the upper level. At the end of 1790 the federal government's locale moved to Philadelphia, and the Supreme Court's first half of the 1791 term was spent in the Pennsylvania State House, now known as Independence Hall. The Court convened for the second half of its 1791 term in the newly completed Philadelphia city hall. Location was not a crucial issue for the Court, however, because during its first several terms it heard very few cases.

At the turn of the nineteenth century, the peripatetic national government finally settled in Washington, D.C., and a Capitol and executive mansion were the first governmental buildings erected. There were no separate plans for the Supreme Court, however. Architect Benjamin Henry Latrobe's design for the Capitol building included a small room for the Court's use; it would occupy several such niches as it was pushed from one chamber to another in the course of history.

The Court initially occupied a small room in the southwest corner of the Capitol's north wing. Improvements on that wing of the Capitol included a new chamber for the Supreme Court in the building's basement, where it moved for its 1810 term. Just four years later, however, the British stormed Washington during the War of 1812, and the Capitol was severely damaged in one of the many fires set by the invaders. In fact, the British ignited a blaze in the Supreme Court chamber itself. The highest court in the land truly followed the old cliché of moving from pillar to post in the years after the

War of 1812; it took up residence in a number of sites scattered throughout Washington.

With the restoration of the Capitol, the Supreme Court returned to its basement chamber in early 1819, but by 1859 the "Proceedings of the House of Representatives" declared that "[t]his Congress will not allow the Supreme Court of a Government like ours to sit in the cellar of the Capitol, and have strangers, when they come here and ask to be shown the greatest judicial tribunal of the country, to be taken down [into the] cellar." Thus, in 1860 the Court moved upstairs to a more spacious room just vacated by the Senate for its move to the present Senate chamber. The old Supreme Court chamber in the basement then became a law library for the tribunal. Still, there was no room for the justices to have their own offices, and they therefore worked at home. In 1899 the *Wilmington News* reported to its readers in Delaware that a new building for the Supreme Court had been proposed in Washington. Arguing for the construction of such a structure, the newspaper commented, "There is no sound reason why the court should be cooped up in a six-by-nine room in the Capitol. Let the court have a handsome home of its own."

Nevertheless, the Court remained "cooped up" until 1935 when, as if to assert a physical symbol of its presence, it moved into its current majestic home after almost a century and a half of occupying "borrowed" space in the Capitol building across the street. The very idea that the legislative and judicial branches would share quarters was anathema to a system of separated powers. In ways big and small, sharing space with Congress was a humiliation. For example, when rooms were at a premium, justices initially had to robe in public before oral argument; when they finally did procure their own robing room in the Capitol, it was barely large enough for all nine justices and their assistants. In contrast, the present Court building has a spacious robing room for the justices, where they exchange their symbolic collegial handshake before emerging en masse from behind the burgundy velvet curtains to ascend the bench for their public sessions and sit in order of seniority, the chief justice in the center chair.

When Chief Justice Charles Evans Hughes spoke at the laying of the Court building's cornerstone in 1932, he summed up the importance of the Court's separate edifice: "The Republic endures and this is the symbol of its faith." In the depths of the Great Depression, many Americans must have wondered if the country (much less the Court) would indeed endure.

On October 7, 1935, the Court opened the first term in its new home—and a fitting home it was. Cass Gilbert, the architect who had taken on the Court's design as his last major project at age seventy, planned a stunning visual impact from the Court's front plaza and facade. He chose the classical temple style from the Roman adaptation of the Greek building form. Appropriately for the home of the "priestly tribe," Gilbert used Pierre Vignon's La Madeleine church in Paris as a modern source of inspiration for the Court. He then surrounded the building's exterior and filled the edifice's interior with a plethora of symbols to augment the Court's majestic image.

The lampposts are adorned with ram heads and lion paws, both of which are meant to represent strength. A peak under the light standards reveals that they rest on bronze tortoises, reportedly signifying the deliberate pace of justice. Eight relief panels in the bronze doors on the Court's front facade depict the growth of the law from ancient Greece and Rome to the early United States. Designed by sculptor John Donnelly Jr., the doors' style is said to follow that used in the fifteenth century by the Italian artist Lorenzo Ghiberti in his famous "Gates of Paradise" on the baptistery in Florence. Allegorical figures representing the "contemplation of justice" and the "authority of law," carved from a 250-ton slab of marble, flank the Court's front entrance. The figure of Justice is blindfolded as a symbol of impartiality and is holding a pair of scales to represent balance and fairness. Flagpoles on the Court's distinctive plaza depict cherubs also displaying scales and swords representing the strength of justice. Other carved angels hold masks and torches to symbolize the ability of enlightenment to uncover the mask of untruth.

The Court's front pediment displays a classical sculptural group of allegorical figures that depict liberty, justice, order, authority, council, and research past and present. Artist Robert Aitken, who sculpted the figures, impishly included the faces of well-known Americans in his depictions. For example, Chief Justice William Howard Taft, whose personal lobbying for the Court's new building was instrumental in its completion, is portrayed as a student at Yale University, his beloved alma mater, in the figure of "Research Present." Taft had remarked to a member of Congress in 1923, "I shall continue to protest against the fact that you do not allow the Supreme Court to have space enough for its records." Sadly, Taft died before his pet project came to fruition, but it is appropriate that his visage gazes down upon all who enter what can accurately be called "Chief Justice Taft's building."

Those who do enter the edifice after climbing the imposing, broad, white steps and stepping under the soaring Corinthian columns will be equally impressed by the so-called great hall, designed by Cass Gilbert—who also did not live to see his masterpiece—to dramatize the approach to the courtroom of the highest tribunal in the land. The walls, floor, and modified Doric columns that support the hall were constructed of Alabama marble; twenty-two-foot blocks of stone constitute the monolithic pillars. Massive wooden doors, carved with symbolic figures, grace the entrance to the court chamber at the opposite end of the great hall.

In the same year that the Court moved into its new home, it established a public information office. Thus, the Court institutionalized the presentation of itself to the media and public at large. In 1935, the office began giving journalists copies of full opinions as they were announced from the bench. The new procedure made reporting on the Court's decisions easier and presumably more accurate.

How the Justices Presented Themselves: Their Work as Image

The Court's new structure also gave the justices an enhanced space and opportunity to present themselves through the public component of their work—namely, oral argument. Its sparse quarters in the Capitol building had barely allowed room for spectators. When the Court opened its first term in the new building, however, it looked out on a chamber that could hold approximately 300 visitors. Chief Justice Taft had also suggested that adequate space for the press be incorporated into the chamber's architectural plans.

The courtroom's design and appointments were as majestic as the entire structure. Gilbert emphasized that "the location of the chamber itself, in the very heart of the structure, symbolizes the importance of the room in which the Court presides." He imported marble from Spain for the walls and friezes and Italian marble for the Ionic columns that support the room. Gilbert even met with Italian dictator Benito Mussolini to ensure that only the highest quality Italian marble was exported for the project. The courtroom's elaborate ceiling, designed by mural artist Ezra Winter, displays various styles of plaster rosettes all highlighted with twenty-three-carat gold leaf. Bronze gates border the room on either side and separate it from two bright colonnades that face charming exterior courtyards. Each eight-foot gate contains reliefs of lion and eagle heads, torches, and scales of justice. Surrounding the room on all four sides are friezes sculpted by noted artist Adolph Weinman, who depicted a classical procession of "great lawgivers of history," portraying the development of secular law. Hammurabi, Moses, Solomon, Confucius, Mohammed, Charlemagne, Blackstone, John Marshall (the fourth chief justice and only American portrayed in the friezes), and Napoleon are among the historical figures included in the friezes. The carvings directly above the winged Honduran mahogany bench depict allegorical figures representing majesty of law, power of government, wisdom, justice, and the defense of human rights and protection of innocence.

To this day the Court performs at its symbolic best when it convenes for an oral argument session. The courtroom itself, with its marble columns, carved friezes, pews, and velvet curtains, has a church-like quality about it. Spectators speak in hushed tones while they wait for the sessions to begin, and five minutes before the justices enter, the guards "shush" the assembly. At exactly the appointed hour, the silence is broken when the marshal pounds his gavel and utters the famous incantation calling the room to order. Appropriately for our thesis arguing that the Court has successfully maintained its image as a "priestly tribe," the marshal's cry ends with a dramatic flourish, "God save the United States and this honorable Court!"

Because only a small number of Americans ever see the Court in session, the tribunal's release of opinions presents one important method of reaching the public. Again, with so much scholarship already devoted to describing and analyzing the substance of the Court's New Deal jurisprudence, we do not rehash those narratives. Instead, we focus on the images of the Court when portrayed by justices in landmark decisions of the New Deal era.

The very concept of "opinions for the Court," which become the law of the land, indicates that decisions are presented on behalf of the institution. Dissents and concurrences, on the other hand, usually reflect the individuality of the author who refers to himself/herself in the first person. In contrast, opinions of the Court are couched in the language of the third person, similar to the Roman Catholic pope's use of the papal "we." The propensity of the Court to fracture into closely divided five to four and six to three rulings on economic regulatory legislation during the 1930s threatened to destroy the Court's ideal of uniformity.

Two cases in 1934 gave New Dealers hope that a narrow majority of the Court would prevail in upholding at least state legislative efforts to ameliorate the effects of the Great Depression. *Home Building & Loan v. Blaisdell*[7] upheld the Minnesota Moratorium Act, giving homeowners and farmers an extension on their mortgage payments during the economic crisis. In concluding his opinion for the five-person majority that the Minnesota statute did not violate the U.S. Constitution's contract clause, Chief Justice Hughes emphasized the Court's neutral image in the realm of public policy. He wrote, "Whether the legislation is wise or unwise as a matter of policy is a question with which we are not concerned." The "Four Horsemen's" dissent, drafted by Justice George Sutherland for Justices Willis Van Devanter, James McReynolds, and Pierce Butler, also invoked the image of the Court as a neutral arbiter of the constitutionality of legislation. Nevertheless, the minority reached the opposite conclusion from the majority and argued in its dissent that the Minnesota statute violated the contract clause.

Following *Blaisdell*, the Court upheld a New York state milk price control law, again with ominous dissents from the Four Horsemen, in *Nebbia v. New York.*[8] With Justice Owen Roberts writing this time for another close 5 to 4 majority, the Court reiterated its "function" of applying the pertinent provisions of the Constitution (in this instance the due process clause of the Fourteenth Amendment) to determine the validity of the challenged statute.

The Roosevelt Administration's fleeting hopes were dashed, however, at the start of 1935. In early January of that year the Court struck down a portion of FDR's National Industrial Recovery Act (NIRA) on the grounds that Congress had unconstitutionally delegated power to the president to exclude from interstate commerce any oil produced in excess of state regulations.[9] Chief Justice Hughes, who had supported *state* regulatory legislation in the previous year's *Nebbia* case, again made reference to the Court's neutral exercise of judicial review and expanded the image to portray the Court as the guardian of the American constitutional system. As Hughes wrote for a majority that included all but Justice Benjamin Cardozo, "The question is not of the intrinsic importance of the particular statute before us, but of the constitutional processes of legislation which are an essential part of our system of government."

President Roosevelt and his New Deal suffered several more famous blows from the Court before the end of 1935 (most prominently in *Schechter Poultry Corp. v. United States*,[10] which unanimously struck down Section 3 of the NIRA—the very heart of the statute—on the grounds that it unconstitutionally delegated power to the president and ran afoul of the interstate commerce clause), and the new year brought only more judicial defeats for the beleaguered and increasingly frustrated chief executive. During the first week of January 1936, a six-to-three decision by the Court in *U.S. v. Butler* held unconstitutional the essential provisions of the Agricultural Adjustment Act of 1933, which provided government subsidies to farmers for agreeing to reduce crop production.[11] Money for the subsidy was to come from a tax levied on the processor of the commodity. Justice Roberts's opinion for the Court found Congress's statutory plan to regulate and control production to be beyond the powers delegated to the national government and a clear violation of the Tenth Amendment.

Roberts followed Hughes's lead from the "hot oil" case and argued, "We approach [this case's] decision with a sense of our grave responsibility to render judgment in accordance with the principles established for the governance of all three branches of the government." He continued with his now-famous explication of a mechanistic and supposedly neutral approach to judicial review. Roberts asserted: "When an act of Congress is appropriately challenged in the courts as not conforming to the constitutional mandate, the judicial branch of the government has only one duty; to lay the article of the Constitution which is invoked beside the statute which is challenged and to decide whether the latter squares with the former." Reiterating the Court's impartial stance vis-à-vis public policy, Roberts declared, "This court neither approves nor condemns any legislative policy."

Justice Harlan Stone's dissent, joined by Justices Louis Brandeis and Cardozo, also noted, as had the majority opinion, "that courts are concerned only with the power to enact statutes, not with their wisdom." Yet Stone called on his brethren to uphold the challenged legislation in an exercise of judicial "self-restraint." In a book published four years later and just before his own appointment to the Supreme Court, Robert Jackson wrote that "[w]hat Mr. Justice Stone was saying, in measured words, was that the decision of the majority was not a legal judgment, but a political and an economic judgment, which the Court had no constitutional authority to make."[12] On a collision course then were the image of the Court as an impartial, apolitical arbiter and the perception by some that a slim majority of the "nine old men" was engaging in unconstitutional public policy making.

Still to come before the end of the Court's first term in its new building was an invalidation of the Bituminous Coal Act of 1935, which was Congress's attempt to stabilize the coal industry through regulation of prices, methods of competition, and labor relations, and the negation of a New York state minimum wage law for women.[13] President Roosevelt grew more enraged and frustrated as he saw his initial term of office waning without an opportunity to appoint a new member to the highest court in the land. Nevertheless, he was almost completely silent during the 1936 campaign on what he might do in his second term to eliminate judicial opposition to the realization of the New Deal. For years observers have credited FDR's landslide victory over Republican Alf Landon, and the president's subsequent announcement of his Court-packing plan in February 1937, with persuading two members of the Court, Chief Justice Hughes and Justice Roberts, to change their votes to support economic regulatory legislation in *West Coast Hotel Co. v. Parrish*, which upheld a Washington state minimum wage law for women and minors, and *National Labor Relations Board v. Jones & Laughlin Steel Corporation*, which sanctioned the New Deal's National Labor Relations Act.[14] We choose not to repeat previous theories; rather we examine how the media served as a transmitter of the Court's image during this turbulent period.

How the Media Presented the Court: Journalistic Images

Relying primarily on newspapers, magazines, and opinion journals, we gleaned a sense of how the print medium reported on and portrayed the Supreme Court in the 1930s. A survey of this material indicates that journalistic presentation of the justices generally bolstered the Court's hallowed image from early in the Roosevelt administration and through the judicial negations of New Deal legislation and the subsequent Court-packing debates.

To illustrate, an April 7, 1934, article in the popular magazine the *Literary Digest* reflected the dignified image of the Court and its members.[15] Despite its headline, "The Supreme Court—Nine Mortal Men," the article's subtitle was more in keeping with the priestly image of the tribunal. The secondary headline read, "Misty, Omniscient, Living in an Intellectual Super-World, the Slow, Awe-Inspiring, Black-Robed Procession Proves to Be Made Up of Warm, Vital Human Beings."

The opening sentence of the feature story noted that the Supreme Court is "[b]y far the most majestic branch of the Government of the United States." The article then referred to the justices as "half-deified figures" and described the sessions of the Court as "awe-inspiring," especially the "the slow procession of black-robed, white-haired men to the high-back chairs behind the bench in the small, hushed chamber in the Capitol, and the deliberate unperturbed procedure as they read opinions or listen to arguments." Yet as if to foreshadow the intense scrutiny to which the institution would soon find itself subjected, the reporter wrote, "[A]s a matter of cold fact, the public should know as much about these nine men as about any others in the Government."

The *Literary Digest* piece then described the ideologies and personalities of the Court's nine members. The reporter, one Theodore C. Wallen, crawled out onto a predictive limb with about as much success as his magazine would have in prophesying that Alf Landon would win the 1936 presidential election. Wallen wrote that although the Supreme Court had "not passed on a single piece of the New Deal legislation, its five to four decisions on the State statutes in the Minnesota and New York cases clearly marked a swing to the left and established the basis for upholding much of the New Deal." The article also praised Chief Justice Hughes for his endeavors "to achieve a greater degree of judicial harmony in the apparent hope of reducing the number of six to three and five to four decisions which impair the weight of the Court's decisions by reminding the public that the interpretation of the Constitution is far from being an exact science." He labeled Hughes and Roberts as "middle-of-the-road justices" and "practical men who apparently feel that in periods of flux the Supreme Court must go part way, at least, with public opinion and Congress and the Executive."

Wallen concluded that "to the politically minded observer the significant fact is that the Supreme Court is moving with the tide." The reporter erred in his prediction by three years, but at least he did relate a more prescient comment about those who argued that if the Court did not follow the public and its representatives, the justices might face "enlargement of the Court" or "some other action which would permanently injure the power of the Court to act as a check on the legislative excesses."

Our sample of news articles and editorials from the *Wall Street Journal,* the *Washington Post,* and the *New York Times* on the landmark New Deal cases and FDR's Court-packing plan reveals that these national publications, and the regional newspapers they surveyed, were overwhelmingly deferential to and communicative of the Supreme Court's role as an impartial arbiter of the Constitution. The day after the *Schechter* case came down, for example, the *Washington Post* hailed its unanimity and stated that the Court had helped "to restore our government procedure to the orderly and constructive lines mapped out by the framers of the Constitution. . . . Thus the traditional balance of power between the legislative, executive, and judicial arms of our Government is restored."[16] Tying the Court's decision so closely to the Constitution demonstrated how the tribunal's image was still inextricably bound with the founding document.

The *Post*'s primary news story on *Schechter* even linked the Court's actions to the physical symbols of its power, history, and prestige. The paper reported that the Court's stunning announcement of its decision in the so-called "sick chicken" case constituted the penultimate time the high tribunal presided in the Capitol building chamber. Gushed the *Post*'s reporter: "Seated where those momentous events, which left their mark on American life, took place and facing the marble busts of all the Chief Justices who ever presided over the court, the nine black-robed jurists with grim faces and without ceremony proceeded to their work. . . . Holding the judicial scales evenly balanced, the Chief Justice recited the nature of the *Schechter* case."[17]

Reactions from other newspapers also appeared in the *Post*. From the *St. Louis Globe-Democrat* came more praise for the Court, which, the paper declared, "exists primarily to guard" the foundations of our political system "that have sustained it [the United States] for a century and a half and that have enabled us to grow and to prosper beyond any other nation under the sun." The *Philadelphia Inquirer* lauded the justices for countering President Roosevelt's "concept of presidential authority," which so argued the paper, FDR had viewed "as differing widely from those of past executives." Concluded the Philadelphia publication, "[E]mergency or no emergency, Mr.

Roosevelt embarked upon a gigantic career of experimentation, at a cost of billions upon billions of dollars, without any misgivings for the legality of his operations." Likewise, the *Kansas City Star* noted that "[e]ven in the name of emergency it [the Constitution] protects the people and the States as it was designed to do." Moreover, the Kansas City paper hailed the *Schechter* case as proving that "the Constitution is supreme. It can not be made to mean what it does not say or stretched to cover a broad and virtually unrestricted grant of power."[18] The *New York Times* reported similar "editorial satisfaction with the Supreme Court decision on the NIRA" in newspapers throughout the country.[19]

In addition, Raymond Clapper's syndicated editorial in the *Washington Post* following *Schechter* observed that "[t]alk of blackjacking the court by enlarging its membership collapsed when all nine justices joined in the decision. That subterfuge of packing the court, a weak and uncertain one at best becomes ridiculous to think of now."[20]

The newspapers also reported at length on the press conference convened by President Roosevelt three days after *Schechter* came down. FDR's now famous criticism of the Court as taking the country back to "the horse and buggy stage" of constitutional interpretation appeared prominently in all of the national newspapers. (The widespread quotation of Roosevelt's scathing comment resulted, in part, from the fact that the phrase was the only one the president gave permission to the press to report verbatim. In contrast to the relative openness of today's presidential/press relations, the ground rules of FDR's news conferences maintained that the president could "not be directly quoted without his specific permission.")[21]

A *New York Times* editorial was typical in its criticism of Roosevelt's demeanor and message at his May 31, 1935, press conference. Dismayed by FDR's uncharacteristic vitriol, the *Times* editors responded, "One of the things most admired in Mr. Roosevelt, all through his term, has been his calmness and poise of spirit. Modest in victory, he has been cheerful in defeat. No one could have expected him to betray the pique that appears in his remarks yesterday. It is to be feared that the bitterness of his attitude will frustrate the very purposes he has in mind."[22]

On the other hand, the *New Republic*, with its self-admitted socialist vision of government and public policy, was apoplectic in the days following *Schechter*. It explicitly attacked the Supreme Court and its image, asserting: "The legal fiction is that the Court does not, or should not, concern itself with matters of economic policy. . . . Whatever may be the mental processes of the honorable Justices, however, the practical result of their decisions is often to forbid or reverse important economic policies."[23]

A more famous (or infamous) attack on the Court in the journalistic realm came from columnists Drew Pearson and Robert Allen's book *The Nine Old Men*.[24] Published in late October 1936, it quickly found its way onto the bestseller lists, was serialized in newspapers throughout the country,[25] and presumably reached a wider audience than the more elitist *New Republic*. The book began with a snide look at the justices' new home, which Pearson and Allen dubbed "The Taj Mahal." The authors offered not a scintilla of documentation for their observations and judgments on the Court as an institution, its members, and its procedures, and historian William Leuchtenburg has commented that "[e]ven critics of the Justices were disturbed by the book's tone and by its inaccuracies."[26]

Thus, when President Roosevelt announced his plans for restructuring the federal judiciary, including his scheme for enlarging the Supreme Court's membership, on February 5, 1937, even the *New Republic* was lukewarm on the proposal. FDR told the American people in one of his famed fireside radio broadcasts on March 9, 1937, that "[t]he Court has been acting not as a judicial body, but as a policy-making body."[27] Of course, the *New Republic* wholeheartedly agreed with the president's assessment, but its editors noted in a column the following week that "neither the president nor anyone else has any marked enthusiasm" for the court reform plan.[28]

Indeed, the media had expressed virtually no enthusiasm for the plan from its announcement. The *Los Angeles Times* took issue with the president's motives, if not the substance of the reform package, just one day after FDR had sent his plan to Congress. Coming to the aid of the Court, the LA paper wrote about the president's blueprint, "These proposals should not pass, even though, in the ordinary course, there is undeniable merit in some of them. It would be better for the United States to suffer stagnation in its judicial system, a breakdown of court processes through congestion and delay, than that the independence of the judiciary be destroyed."[29] Included in the same edition of that paper was an editorial cartoon entitled, "The Hands of Dictatorship!" depicting two hands of "the Chief Executive," with one squeezing a man labeled "Legislative Branch of Government," and the other groping hand marked, "Grasp for the Judiciary."[30]

Even the papers normally aligned with the Democratic Party in that era opposed FDR's plan for the judiciary. A 1937 survey by the *Christian Science Monitor* of seventy-six leading Democratic newspapers revealed that only twenty papers (with a combined circulation of 3,136,198) endorsed the Court bill, whereas fifty-two papers (with a combined circulation of 13,191,693) opposed the plan. Of the major newspapers that supported President Roosevelt throughout the Court-packing ordeal, the most influential were the *New York Daily News*, the *New York Post*, the *Philadelphia Record*, the *Louisville Courier Journal*, and the *St. Louis Star-Times*.[31]

By the summer of 1937, judicial biographer Merlo Pusey had published a scholarly, yet accessible, rejoinder to Roosevelt's Court-packing plan. Addressed to the "average reader," the book's foreword by Senator Edward R. Burke of Nebraska argued that "only a Supreme Court, independent and unawed, stands guard to protect the rights and liberties of the people. If a million American men and women could receive today the message contained within the two covers of this book, the Supreme Court would be saved from pillage."[32]

Of course, the highest court in the land was spared from the ill-conceived Roosevelt scheme when the legislation was ultimately removed from consideration by the full Senate on July 22, 1937. Yet, in the meantime, good fortune had finally shown on the New Deal when Chief Justice Hughes and Justice Roberts cast their votes to support state and federal economic regulation and Justice Van Devanter, one of the Four Horsemen, announced his retirement from the Court in May 1937.

How the Public Perceived the Court: Images in the American Mind

Throughout the clash between FDR and the Court, the president vowed to take his fight to the people, who he thought would undoubtedly support his position. Public opinion polls of the era, however, reveal less backing for Roosevelt's stance than he assumed. According to William Leuchtenburg, "[m]ost of the nation in 1935 was still either indifferent to the Court question or outrightly opposed to tethering the Court."[33] In fact, the newly established Gallup Poll asked the following question in the fall of 1935: "As a general principle, would you favor limiting the power of the Supreme Court to declare acts of Congress unconstitutional?" The response of those polled was: yes, 31 percent; no, 53 percent; and no opinion, 16 percent. The Gallup organization discovered the strongest anti-Court sentiment among those respondents who believed they had been harmed by a particular decision. For example, one man complained bitterly that the Court had "turned down" his railroad pension (a reference to the Court's declaring unconstitutional the Railroad Retirement Act of 1934[34]). "But many more thought the justices wise, the system of checks and balances sacred, and Congress mercurial, although their conception of these institutions was sometimes primitive. Asked his view, an Ohio relief recipient said: 'If they didn't know more than the other courts, they wouldn't be called the Supreme Court.'"[35]

Even after Roosevelt's momentous landslide win in the 1936 presidential election, public opinion showed little variation on its support for the Supreme Court's power. Asked virtually the same question by the Gallup Poll as the organization had posed in 1935, namely, "As a general policy, are you in favor of limiting the power of the Supreme Court to declare acts of Congress unconstitutional?" 34 percent of respondents answered yes, 49 percent no, and 17 percent no opinion.[36]

On the issue of FDR's proposal to enlarge the Supreme Court's membership, Gallup Polls indicate that from just after the president announced his plan in February 1937 to the early summer of that year, the highest percentage of respondents favoring the legislation was 45.9 percent.[37] The president's plan reached that public opinion highpoint (although still short of a majority) immediately after Roosevelt's March 9 fireside chat.[38] In that radio address, FDR had compared the Court to the third horse on a team pulling in the wrong direction a plough guided by the American people; the other two horses (the Congress and the president) were pulling in the direction determined by the popular will.[39]

The low water mark in the Gallup Poll (only 31 percent responding favorably toward Roosevelt's scheme) occurred just after Justice Van Devanter announced his retirement from the bench in May 1937. Although the plan regained some support over the next month, the final Gallup Poll taken on the issue during the second week of June 1937 reflects that less than 38 percent of those polled responded affirmatively to the proposal.[40] Obviously, President Roosevelt, despite his electoral popularity, never commanded the allegiance of a majority of Americans in his struggle against the Supreme Court.

Conclusion

Miraculously, the "priestly tribe" had escaped the most direct attack on its independence that it had faced in its history. By 1935, the Court could retreat into the most obvious symbol of its bolstered stature—the "marble temple" at 1 First Street, N.E. in Washington, D.C. Yet even before the justices took possession of their new accommodations, the *New York Times* displayed a photo of the new Court building's east pediment just above the preamble of the U.S. Constitution and placed around the pictures photographs of Chief Justice Hughes and President Roosevelt squared off against each other.[41] Thus, the Court's permanent home and the nation's founding document were already linked as a symbol of the Court's role in interpreting and defending the Constitution.

The struggle between FDR and the highest court in the land revealed a tension inherent in the American system, which inevitably observes its hallowed judges descending into the political fray through their exercise of judicial review, but which chooses to perpetuate the image of a Supreme Court above politics. We have examined that tension in the context of the struggle over the New Deal, and have concluded that the symbols and images of the Court's impartiality, fairness, independence, and dignity survived the battle and allowed the Court to fight another day.

ENDNOTES

1. Barbara Hinckley, *The Symbolic Presidency: How Presidents Portray Themselves* (New York: Routledge, 1990), pp. 4–7.

2. Jerome Frank, *Courts on Trial: Myth and Reality in American Justice* (Princeton, NJ: Princeton University Press, 1949), pp. 256–57.

3. Michael Kammen, *A Machine That Would Go of Itself: The Constitution in American Culture* (New York: St. Martin's Press, 1994).

4. C. Herman Pritchett, *The Roosevelt Court: A Study in Judicial Politics and Values, 1937-1947* (Chicago: Quadrangle Books, 1969), p. ix.

5. Ibid. See, for example, William E. Leuchtenburg, *The Supreme Court Reborn: The Constitutional Revolution in the Age of Roosevelt* (New York: Oxford University Press, 1995).

6. This quote, as well as the balance of information on the Court's

buildings, originates in the script of the Court's exhibit entitled, "The Supreme Court of the United States: Its Form and Function." Unveiled in 1994, the display is the first permanent exhibit in the Supreme Court building. We are grateful to the Court's Curator Gail Galloway for generously sharing the script with us.

7. *Home Building & Loan v. Blaisdell*, 290 U.S. 398 (1934).

8. *Nebbia v. New* York, 291 U.S. 502 (1934).

9. *Panama Refining Co. v. Ryan*, 293 U.S. 388 (1935).

10. 295 U.S. 495 (1935).

11. 297 U.S. 1 (1936).

12. Robert H. Jackson, *The Struggle for Judicial Supremacy: A Study of a Crisis in American Power Politics* (New York: Octagon Books, 1979), p. 136.

13. *Carter v. Carter Coal Co.*, 298 U.S. 238 (1936) and *Morehead v. New York ex rel. Tipaldo*, 298 U.S. 587 (1936).

14. 300 U.S. 379 (1937) and 301 U.S. 1 (1937).

15. The following material is derived from Theodore C. Wallen, "The Supreme Court—Nine Mortal Men," *Literary Digest* (April 7, 1934): 9, 45–47.

16. "More Haste, Less Speed," May 28, 1935, 8.

17. "All Codes Suspended as Supreme Court Scraps NRA," May 28, 1935, 14.

18. "Press of Nation Gives Opinions on NRA Ruling," May 28, 1935, 15.

19. "Press Generally Sees Ruling as a Victory for Fundamental Law," May 28, 1935, 12.

20. "Glee Over NRA's End May Be a Bit Premature," May 29, 1935, 2.

21. "Roosevelt Sees Social Setback of 50 Years in Court Decision; Calls on People to Face Crisis," *Washington Post*, June 1, 1935, 1, 4.

22. "An Imprudent Speech," June 1, 1935, 14.

23. "Social Control vs. the Constitution," June 12, 1935, 117.

24. New York: Doubleday, 1936.

25. Leuchtenburg, p. 119.

26. Ibid.

27. Franklin D. Roosevelt, "Reorganizing the Federal Judiciary," March 9, 1937, as quoted in Alpheus Thomas Mason, *Free Government in the Making: Readings in American Political Thought*, 3rd ed. (New York: Oxford University Press, 1965), p. 800.

28. "The President Faces the Court," March 17, 1937, 154.

29. "Packing the Supreme Court," February 6, 1937, 4.

30. Ibid.

31. E. Kimbark MacColl, "The Supreme Court and Public Opinion: A Study of the Court Fight of 1937," unpublished dissertation, UCLA, June 1953, 224–25.

32. *The Supreme Court Crisis* (New York: The Macmillan Company, 1937), p. vi.

33. Leuchtenburg, p. 94.

34. *Railroad Board v. Alton R. Co.*, 295 U.S. 330 (1935).

35. Leuchtenburg, p. 94.

36. Kammen, p. 325.

37. Lee Epstein et al., *The Supreme Court Compendium: Data, Decisions, and Developments* (Washington: Congressional Quarterly, 1994), p. 605.

38. Gregory A. Caldeira, "Public Opinion and the U.S. Supreme Court: FDR's Court-Packing Plan," *American Political Science Review* 81 (December 1987): 1139–46.

39. As quoted in Mason, p. 799.

40. Epstein, p. 605.

41. "End of NRA," June 2, 1935, Sec. 4, 1.

2

Was There a Constitutional Revolution in 1937?

Roger W. Corley

A standard work in constitutional history found that the revolution of 1937 "had been in the making for some years,"[1] and a widely used text mentions "an abrupt reversal of outlook."[2] A survey of texts used twenty years ago noted terms such as "strategic retreat," "change," "shift," and "switch in time." About half used some form of the word "sudden."[3] A more recent survey disclosed that Franklin Roosevelt had "lost a battle but won a war," or that there was a switch or sudden change.[4]

Thus there seems to have been and still is a consensus that there was a dramatic shift on the Supreme Court in 1937 and that the "Court-packing" proposal somehow brought about that change. The thesis presented here is that it was the deaths of Chief Justice William Howard Taft and Associate Justice Edward Sandford, and their replacement, in 1930, by Charles Evans Hughes and Owen J. Roberts, which began a slow but significant trend. This modification was not always consistent, there were ups and downs and reversals, but when one contrasts the Court in the decade of Taft's leadership with its performance under Hughes, there are stark differences.

Most of this thesis concerning a "constitutional revolution" focuses on the Court's treatment of national legislation affecting the economy, that is, the New Deal. But much of the background of that era involved state and local legislation and litigation over that legislation. As far as national legislation is concerned, there was a revolution in 1937, but this is inapplicable where states and localities are involved.

The method was to read all the Supreme Court decisions from 1921 to 1937 and choose all those involving state and local activity affecting the economy. Some of the findings were statistical; thus only opinions that dealt substantially with the merits of a case were tabulated. If cases were lumped together for decision, they were counted as one; if similar cases had separate opinions, they were considered separately; and *per curiam* or memorandum decisions that did not discuss a case were not evaluated.[5] The study wound up with 732 cases over sixteen terms. The cases were broken down by Court term, according to all cases and split decisions, and by percentage favorable to state authority. The findings are reproduced in Table 1.

Essentially the table is the thesis; using all cases, Hughes and company upheld a greater percentage in every term except that of 1923 for Taft and his brethren. Overall the difference was almost 10 percent; 58.4 versus 68.1. In split decisions, the ups and downs are more striking, but the overall difference is again almost 10 percent; 37.3 to 46.6.

The cases were divided into three areas: taxes, regulation, and social welfare. This is perhaps arbitrary; the criterion was the intent and effect of the legislation, but this is not exact; a tax on factories employing children is effectively a social welfare measure, and a fee for motor vehicle operation, a tax in form, is probably regulatory. However, in either case, if the revenue were too high, it could be considered a tax.

With this methodology, the cases involving taxes presented the largest number. It would be difficult to explain why but the fact that state expenditures rose by 60 percent in the 1920s explains part of it. Education costs and highway construction accounted for most of these increases and as governments enlarged already overburdened property taxes, they sought additional sources of revenue. After 1929, the tax base shrank and more increases and innovations were required

Table 1

Percentage of Decisions, All Cases and Split Favorable to States, by Term

Term	All cases		Split decisions	
	Percentage	Number of cases	Percentage	Number of cases
1921	62.5	48	53.8	13
1922	61.2	67	40.0	5
1923	69.0	58	60.0	10
1924	52.2	46	37.5	8
1925	45.8	48	14.1	7
1926	58.9	56	33.3	12
1927	62.3	53	36.4	11
1928	52.7	55	33.3	15
[a]WHT	53.8	13	00.0	4
CEH	65.4	25	00.0	4
1930	70.6	34	57.1	7
1931	69.4	36	50.0	8
1932	87.9	33	60.0	5
1933	71.7	46	62.5	8
1934	65.1	42	37.5	8
1935	68.6	35	25.0	8
1936	74.3	35	60.0	10
TAFT[b]	58.4	444	37.2	86
HUGHES	68.1	288	46.6	58

[a]WHT refers to that portion of the 1929 term while Taft was Chief Justice; CEH refers to the portion when Hughes presided.

[b]TAFT refers to the entire period of Taft's Chief Justiceship; HUGHES refers to the Court he headed up to June 1937.

merely to sustain schools and roads, much less assume new depression-caused burdens.[6] The Supreme Court had established some guidelines for taxation prior to 1920: It had to be for a public purpose, the object taxed had to be within the taxing power's jurisdiction, there had to be a relationship between burden and benefit, a tax could not violate a contract or burden interstate commerce, and a state could not tax an agency of the federal government.[7]

The Taft Court did not establish much new doctrine, but did spell out a few limits to the standards. They allowed a mining company operating on an Indian reservation exemption from property tax on the ground of federal agency,[8] disallowed franchise taxes that discriminated against corporations,[9] were limited to $3,000 but were imposed on companies engaged in interstate commerce,[10] effectively included income from federal securities as a measure,[11] or involved gross receipts which included as little as 5 percent from interstate commerce.[12] In dealing with levies on income, the 1920s saw the demise of using the value of United States bonds as a measure,[13] and the defining of royalties based on a copyright as exempt as a federal instrumentality.[14] Inheritance taxes were rejected where a statute had defined the transfer of any property within six years of death as being in contemplation of death,[15] and where a state which issued bonds attempted to levy on a nonresident decedent.[16] Gasoline taxes were declared unconstitutional as applied to sales to the Coast Guard[17] and to an interstate ferry which bought its fuel in another state.[18] Overall the taxing power was upheld in 55.5 percent of all cases and in 19.2 percent of the split decisions.

The Hughes Court changed this to 65.1 and 31.0 percent, an increase in each case of about 10 percent. But they developed some new doctrines as they reconsidered old issues and heard others anew. Corporate domicile was established as the jurisdiction to tax rather than place of incorporation,[19] the possibility of double taxation of intangibles was allowed,[20] the federal instrumentalities doctrine was narrowed as far as property was concerned,[21] and a nondiscriminatory tax on the property of a firm engaged solely in interstate commerce was accepted.[22] In the field of franchise taxes, measuring a tax by items immune from taxation was allowed,[23] and although in 1931 the Court had paralleled its limitation of a property tax on copyrights as federal instruments with a bar to a franchise tax,[24] in 1932 the Chief Justice reversed that decision.[25] A federal license to a cotton gin did not prevent state taxation,[26] and a foreign corporation was held to have a commercial domicile and therefore could be taxed,[27] but a radio station which transmitted across state lines could not have its burden measured by all its income.[28]

A tax with a social purpose, peculiar to the 1930s, was upheld in a number of cases. This was a franchise tax, graduated according to the number of outlets, known popularly as the "chain-store" tax. In the *Jackson* case in 1931,[29] Roberts upheld the general concept, but in 1933 he refused to allow discrimination against out-of-country chains,[30] and in 1935 a graduated gross sales tax was refused.[31] However, in May 1937, a tax from Huey Long's Louisiana which discriminated against national chains and in favor of local enterprisers was upheld.[32]

Wisconsin was forbidden to require married couples with separate incomes to file joint returns at higher rates,[33] Ohio could not tax income from the rental of land outside the state,[34] and Vermont was denied a higher rate on income from money loaned outside the state.[35] The doctrine of federal instrumentality was held a barrier to taxing an employee of the Panama Railroad Company,[36] but previous cases, including the income tax case of 1895,[37] were distinguished away and another levy on rents beyond a state's borders was allowed.[38] A gasoline tax imposed on an interstate airline was upheld, as it was the storage of fuel that was burdened,[39] and in other cases the use of gasoline in a state could be taxed if it were a charge for the use of the roads. Curiously, the sales tax, the major new revenue source for states in the 1930s, was not tested, but a use tax was upheld.[40]

The Hughes Court made inroads into the doctrine of reciprocal immunity, limited federal instrumentality, lessened interstate commerce as a barrier to taxation, and was generally more favorably disposed to state power. One gathers that the Taft Court would prefer no taxation to the possibility of double taxation, whereas in the 1930s, the risk might be acceptable as long as there was no discrimination. There were still restrictions, and some of the opinions in these cases read like Mr. Herbert Spencer's *Social Statics*, but there were strong dissents by Justices Oliver Wendell Holmes Jr., Louis D. Brandeis, and Harlan F. Stone, and these became the rule of the Court by World War II.

Regulation, the second area to be considered, is here defined as that part of the police power which limits activities, as opposed to social welfare which benefits selected groups. Definitions and limits are difficult, here, though, as what limits A may benefit B and vice versa. The Tenth Amendment seemingly reserved this authority to the states and the Court had confirmed a broad "public interest" domain, and even allowed state action in the field of interstate commerce if Congress had not acted.[41] This concept was severely weakened in the late nineteenth century, as the due process clause of the Fourteenth Amendment was erected as a barrier to protect private property interests.[42] Later, Taft, speaking for the Court in *Wolff Packing Company v. Court of Industrial Relations*,[43] a case that involved wage setting, stated that only utilities such as railroads, professions, and businesses devoted to the public use could be regulated. This turned out to be a narrow measure.

In the 1920s, prohibiting the use of "shoddy," previously spun or woven material, in mattresses was forbidden,[44] as was requiring state licenses for grain elevators,[45] even if the people readopted the law by initiative.[46] Requiring a two ounce per pound tolerance in bread weights was unreasonable,[47] although the national government had decreed one ounce in World War I. Theater ticket sellers could not be required to obtain a license,[48] but the resale price could not be limited.[49] It was an interference with foreign commerce to require a license of those selling tickets for trans-Atlantic travel,[50] and setting fees for employment agencies,[51] setting prices for gasoline,[52] or requiring drug stores to be owned by pharmacists[53] were all forbidden. However, rent control,[54] requiring establishments selling eyeglasses to have a doctor in attendance,[55] and state legislation for enforcement of prohibition, even if more stringent than federal law,[56] were all acceptable. In numerous utilities cases the Court found established rates confiscatorily low and voided them; it generally seemed that at least a 7 percent return on a friendly rate base was required. Also, the Interstate Commerce Commission was found to have virtually unlimited powers over intrastate rates and operations of railroads.

Legislation from California and Washington that limited ownership and leasing of land by Asians was acceptable,[57] as was a statute requiring the destruction of cedar trees to prevent infestation of apple trees,[58] and a law licensing oyster fishermen and making them return 10 percent of the shells for restoration of beds.[59] On the other hand, interstate commerce was a barrier to a Washington quarantine of alfalfa,[60] and to Louisiana's attempts to limit export of shrimp[61] and oysters.[62] The Fourteenth Amendment barred prohibiting dairies from paying more for milk in one region than in another.[63]

Motor vehicle legislation produced a curious response. If regulation were for safety or conservation of the highways, it was acceptable, but if a law did not explicitly state such a purpose, it might be voided even though its effects were identical to an approved measure. Thus insurance could be required for taxicabs,[64] a nonresident could be sued for an accident by making a state official his agent,[65] and an interstate carrier could be required to obtain a state certificate of public convenience and pay a graduated fee.[66] But, because they were not conditioned on safety, a Washington[67] and a Maryland statute[68] that were very similar in operation were disallowed. When states attempted to regulate contract carriers this was held to amount to converting them to common carriers and was forbidden, whether interstate commerce was involved,[69] or not.[70] In forbidding mining that might cause destruction of surface dwellings, Pennsylvania found that it went too far[71] as did West Virginia in prohibiting the export of natural gas,[72] but Marysville, Kansas was allowed to require that gasoline storage tanks be underground.[73]

The Taft Court accepted regulatory legislation in 54.4 percent of all cases and in 35 percent of the split decisions. Hughes and company dramatically increased these figures to 75.5 and 58.8 percent. In the first case considered, however, a law forbidding stock insurance companies from using salaried agents was overturned.[74] Oklahoma's ice law which required licenses of those selling that then vital commodity met a similar fate.[75] After Congress had authorized states to prohibit sales in interstate commerce of convict-made goods, there were suits contesting laws which banned such items, but the laws were upheld.[76] In one of these contests, the Court virtually eliminated the century-old "original package" doctrine. Chicago could require that all coal sold in the city be weighed on its scales,[77] and South Carolina could demand a content analysis of fertilizer for sale.[78]

When they dealt with utility regulation, the Court in the 1930s advanced some new ideas. In a number of cases they allowed procedural errors in rate setting as long as the result was correct or profits were high.[79] They positively upheld a rate of return of 6.5 percent,[80] and rejected rates only when the return was as low as 4.5 percent.[81] In matters of food, Washington was permitted to prohibit oleomargarine by a tax,[82] and Nebraska could now set standard bread weights, but with a tolerance of three ounces per pound,[83] rather than the previously disallowed two ounces. A very notable decision, especially since it seemed to augur a positive future for New Deal legislation before the Court, upheld New York's milk control act.[84] This seemed to directly countermand the direction the Court had taken in the 1920s and there were strong dissents by

Taft's former cohorts, for price control in an area excluded by the *Wolff* criteria had been accepted. Further cases from New York upheld a price discrimination against advertised brands[85] but denied it as it applied to new dealers,[86] and rejected the denial of a permit to a dairyman who imported milk from Vermont where he paid less than the price set in New York.[87] A similar statute from Virginia was accepted as far as its price setting features were concerned.[88]

In the area of motor vehicles, the Hughes Court reversed a six-year-old decision as to regulation of motor carriers, and it was George Sutherland who wrote both decisions. In 1931, Hughes had followed the precedent,[89] but after allowing state regulation of truck size and weight on the rationale of safety,[90] contract carriers were effectively converted into common carriers on the same ground.[91] This case attracted as much attention in the law reviews as the *Nebbia* case later did in the general press. The Court rejected requiring railroads to pay for the elimination of grade crossings, since this enhanced their competitors, truckers, who paid relatively little.[92] A New Mexico law that charged a fee for "caravans" was upheld[93] but a similar California statute was overturned because the fee was excessive.[94]

Conservation and a desire to protect small independent producers led a number of oil producing states to restrict production. This had long been upheld but after 1930 the reason was to raise prices and there were objections: These laws were sustained.[95] When an attempt to conserve a particular type of gas discriminated against a producer, so as to deprive him of his market and reward others, this was forbidden,[96] but when a particularly wasteful manufacture of carbon black from petroleum was restricted that was acceptable.[97] In a notable case restricting fees paid to insurance agents, a divided Court upheld a New Jersey statute over protestations of liberty of contract.[98]

The Hughes Court achieved new results and overruled recent precedent in the regulation of motor vehicles, justifying this on the rationale of safety. Price regulation was allowed in the area of insurance commissions and milk, in dynamic contrast to the *Wolff* case, and bread weights could be limited. For utilities, much lower rates of return were accepted and results were more important than methods. Convict-made goods could be prohibited even if in original packages. Again there was division; most of the cases dealt with here involved dissents. However at least one majority opinion was written by each justice except the pen-paralytic Willis Van Devanter, and there were some curious reversals of the stereotyped liberal-conservative roles.

The question of social welfare legislation involved concepts that had recently been enunciated by the Taft Court, and as will be seen, brought similar reversals of form after 1929. The linchpin "liberty of contract" had been explicitly stated in the 1890s as the unhampered use of all of one's "faculties, to be free to use them in all lawful calling; . . . and for that purpose to enter into any contracts which may be proper, necessary, and essential."[99] Some inroads had been made into this notion by the early part of the twentieth century,[100] but as Taft is reputed to have said to his brethren in their first conference together, he "had been appointed to reverse a few decisions," and he "looked right at old-man Holmes."[101] With that one could well expect limitations on what states might do.

National banks were governed both by state and federal law. Generally cases involving them turned on what Congress had said; thus you could not forbid them to be executors,[102] unless that power were achieved by taking over a state bank,[103] but branch banking could be prohibited.[104] Bankruptcy is an exclusive federal concern, but both jurisdictions may engage in cheaper, easier, and simpler operations called liquidations, and either procedure might involve claims based on previous or ongoing state actions. So, in liquidation of a bank, a federal claim to Indian funds had no priority because the assets of the bank were sufficient.[105] Cars repossessed from a buyer just before his bankruptcy could not be returned to other creditors;[106] in a receivership, state courts had priority if they had begun action first;[107] or in a federal court, prior state actions had to be considered,[108] but bankruptcy superseded a prior insolvency action.[109] For insolvent banks it was acceptable to assess all stockholders the full value of their shares,[110] or to assume that all directors knew that their banks were distressed and make them liable for deposits,[111] but you could not automatically find them guilty of fraud.[112] As for mortgages, extending the period of redemption after a foreclosure from twelve to fifteen months affected only a remedy and was allowed.[113]

A zoning law for a village in Ohio was upheld although it severely restricted the free use of private property.[114] The ordinance not only divided the area into districts of various classifications: residential, business, factory, etc., but set various height limitations. Later an ordinance which required the agreement of two-thirds of the abutting property owners before a home for the aged could be constructed was disallowed,[115] as was restricting part of a property to residential use when no relation was shown to health, safety, or welfare.[116]

Workmen's compensation insurance had previously been accepted but there were questions of jurisdiction, especially if there was a possible conflict between a state law and interstate or maritime commerce. There was state jurisdiction on an interstate locomotive in a shop,[117] or on a dock,[118] or if one were pushing a boat into the water,[119] but not if one drowned while working at sea on a pleasure boat.[120] In two Utah cases, each involving deaths on the way to work, it was held that recovery was due even though the accident occurred before work,[121] and in a case involving trespass across railroad tracks.[122] Features of New York's law that required payments to special funds for rehabilitation of the disabled were sustained,[123] as were limitations on attorneys' fees in compensation cases,[124] allowing foreign corporations to be sued anywhere in the state but domestic only in the country of their offices,[125] requirements for keeping records as to wages and employees,[126] and including all employers with as few as five employees.[127]

In suits involving injuries to persons not covered by compensation acts, or damage to goods, a number of suits arising out of the period during and after World War I, when the federal government ran the railroads, or issues developed from the Transportation Act of 1920, came to the Court. These suits were disallowed on the ground that federal power had suspended or superseded state jurisdiction.[128] In other injury cases, the decisions were unanimous; reasonable (to the Court) restrictions, such as a statute of limitations,[129] or the requirement of a flagman at intersections[130] were acceptable, but assuming negligence because of the employment of an underaged youth,[131] or if the railroad failed to prove otherwise was not.[132]

Injury cases could often merge into another problem—access to the courts and comity between jurisdictions. A party could not be compelled to come to trial in a state,[133] nor, although constructive service on a state officer was permissible, be sued if the state officer failed to notify.[134] Someone could be sued if he had an office in the state,[135] but a corporation could not bring suit unless it was registered in the state.[136] In two causes involving federal issues it was held that a Master's fees for work done for the United States Supreme Court could not be set by a state tribunal,[137] and a breach of contract involving a patent was properly dealt with locally.[138]

In a famous case involving a locality, the *Adkins* decision,[139] the Court struck down a minimum wage for women in the District of Columbia. This federal statute's demise is not included in the statistics here, but this is a classic statement of liberty of contract, and provided the rationale for numerous instances of striking down state laws, including two minimum wage acts.[140] Prior to this decision the Court had disallowed an Arizona statute that forbade injunctions in labor disputes on the grounds of denial of due process and equal protection.[141] In four cases dealing with Kansas's Court of Industrial Relations, the

Taft brethren first held that compulsory arbitration to end a labor dispute over wages in the food industry violated liberty of contract.[142] It was also too much when the Kansas court merely attempted to set hours of work,[143] or to intervene in a coal strike.[144] However, the legislation was valid when used to prevent union organizers from inducing others to join in a strike.[145] In a slightly different area it was permissible to sterilize the feeble minded.[146] Although they may have figuratively emasculated labor, the Taft Court accepted 64.7 percent of welfare cases and 65 percent of the split decisions; their highest rating in any area.

Curiously, the Hughes Court accepted more of the total of cases, 75 percent, than their Taft Court brethren and again about ten points higher, but at 58.3 percent were somewhat lower in split decisions. But they heard many fewer cases in this area, and in some terms heard none that resulted in divided courts. The overall figures are statistically valid, that is the comparison between the Taft and Hughes Courts, in any manner, or from year to year as in Table 1, shows significant contrast of split decisions in the areas used does not necessarily reproduce difference.

Banks, bankruptcies, mortgages, and contracts provided much difficulty for the justices; perhaps this explains their inconsistency. Although banks and the then relatively new savings and loan institutions had experienced problems throughout the 1920s, after the 1929 Wall Street crash failures and foreclosures multiplied. In spite of the fact that many institutions were sound on paper, their assets were often immediately uncollectible. States responded to this situation with legislation to try and aid all interested parties, but these new laws necessarily touched upon established rights. In an attempt to preserve its banks, South Carolina's governor declared a bank holiday in 1933. Subsequently the state legislature legitimized this action and when state courts disallowed the action, they passed more legislation to purify the process. The Court found this acceptable as it was merely a change in contract remedies, not in the contract itself.[147] Similarly when Louisiana changed the rules for removal of deposits from thrift institutions from a first-come, first-served system to a rotating partial payment, these were upheld.[148]

In bankruptcy versus state insolvency proceedings, the federal jurisdiction was held to have exclusive control over assets,[149] but if a state acted first, a federal court could not supersede in liquidation proceedings.[150] Yet, when a national bank was involved, federal rules involving assets had to be followed in state courts.[151] When, after two years of liquidation actions had ensued, a state tried to rescue a bank and others similarly situated, this was allowed although new remedies were created.[152] As in the 1920s increased liability against stockholders was allowed.[153]

These cases were intricate and they provided one of the more striking examples of interference with contractual remedies. Minnesota's mortgage moratorium law changed an absolute right to possession within a year in case of default to the possibility of a three-year period, although under rigid restrictions. In a highly controversial decision that, along with the *Nebbia* case, seemed to indicate a disposition friendly to federal experimentation, Chief Justice Hughes, protesting there was no emergency power, allowed the emergency to justify this heretofore impermissible interference.[154] When Arkansas exempted proceeds of insurance policies from judicial attachment, this was rejected as the prohibition was absolute.[155] An equally severe change in remedies was upheld though because the mortgage involved had a clause which included any subsequent changes in the law.[156] When Arkansas tried to extend redemption periods after a tax sale, without any of Minnesota's qualifications, they again overstepped the line,[157] but if a mortgagee bought property at a foreclosure sale, it was permissible to deny him any further claim against the debtor.[158] In a case involving contracts, and especially interesting to educators, salary could be reduced regardless of tenure.[159]

In questions of workmen's compensation, federal-state

conflict continued; thus working on a ship as a blacksmith's helper was interstate commerce and federal,[160] and a general worker who unloaded a ship was involved in maritime work,[161] but working in a navy yard specifically covered by a state law, because of a permissive federal statute, was governed by state jurisdiction.[162] Yet no claim arose under a state law from a railroad's failure to observe federal safety regulations.[163] A worker residing in and performing most of his duties in Vermont was bound by that state's law although he was injured in New Hampshire,[164] and a Mexican alien, hired in California, could sue in that state and did not have to return to Alaska where he was injured.[165]

Two cases involving minimum wages were taken up by the Hughes Court. Their response stirred up a hornets' nest and is usually made a key part of the "switch in time that saved nine." The first concerned a New York statute wherein the legislature had very carefully added to the standard of health and morality, rejected in the *Adkins* case, the criterion of the fair value of the work performed. This was not sufficient grace to be saving; on June 1, 1936, the law was struck down.[166] On March 29, 1937, ten months later, a 1913 enactment of the state of Washington, based solely on health and morality, was upheld.[167]

In between these two decisions there was the presidential election of 1936 and FDR's Court-packing proposal. Did either of these have any effect on the switch? The Court reform proposal definitely did not; the well-hidden "bomb" was dropped in February 1937, and the critical votes by the justices were taken in December 1936. Justice Roberts, the crucial fifth man in each case, later maintained that he had not switched. Rather, as New York had tried to justify its law by pointing out its dissimilarities from the District of Columbia statute, he ruled against it as he could find no meaningful differences, but when the state of Washington asked for a direct overruling of the *Adkins* precedent, he went along. Incidentally, Chief Justice Hughes also switched, for at first he was for distinguishing the Washington law from the District of

Columbia statute, but after the November 1936 election he was for overturning precedent. In both cases Brandeis, Cardozo, and Stone were for reversal. Roberts maintained that as he voted to accept jurisdiction in the second case in October 1936, the election had no effect, yet merely accepting a case for argument does not indicate how one might vote.[168] Also, he probably voted against rehearing the New York case, on the direct ground of overruling *Adkins*, on the same day the Washington law was placed on the docket.[169]

One other decision throws some light on Roberts's actions: unemployment compensation. The major case involved an Alabama statute, alleged to violate the Tenth Amendment, the due process clause, and the equal protection clause of the Fourteenth Amendment. The law was sustained on May 24, 1937.[170] A similar New York statute was accepted for hearing in June 1936, was argued on November 11, and decided on November 14, eleven days after the election.[171] Stone was severely ill and took no part in this case; thus, when the law was upheld by an equally divided Court there was no opinion and no record of the justices' votes. It seems impossible that Roberts voted to negate the law, but this decision occurred after the Democratic triumph at the polls.

One last novelty treated by the Hughes Court was fair-trade laws. These were unanimously upheld.[172] They certainly were not earthshaking, and can in no way compare to the mortgage moratorium, minimum wage, or unemployment compensation legislation, but they were another innovation approved by the Court before 1937. Overall, we again find an acceptance of legislation involving liquidation of banks, although there remained an insistence on federal supremacy in matters of bankruptcy. Not only was a mortgage moratorium allowed, but other changes in contractual remedies and an antideficiency statute was accepted. In workmen's compensation cases a parallel to commercial domicile was established.

Examining Table 1 again, one can see the statistical

significance of these cases. This established that 1937 is not the year of the revolution but rather the culmination of the evolution. We have contrasted the 1920s and the 1930s, Taft and Hughes. Although more change occurred after January 1930, some of the change began before that date under Taft and there was some denial of state power after then.

To wit: The Taft Court allowed rent control, compulsory automobile insurance, compulsory underground storage of fuels, zoning, and an expansion of workmen's compensation coverage and requirements. The Hughes Court denied higher taxes on out-of-state loan income,[173] taxing the income of a federal employee,[174] the regulation of ice manufacture, prohibiting salaries to certain insurance agents, and, in the first instance, minimum wages.

On the positive side, the 1930s saw the establishment of corporate domicile, the possibility of double taxation, the narrowing of the doctrine of federal instrumentality, the allowance of taxes on firms engaged in interstate commerce, the use of nontaxable items as a measure of a tax, a tax on income from a copyright, a tax on gasoline used in interstate commerce, and a use tax. In the realm of regulation, goods could be barred, errors in utility rate setting and lower returns were allowed, bread weight tolerances and price setting for milk were permitted, contract carriers could be regulated, as could caravans and oil production, and insurance commissions could be limited. A state could declare a bank holiday, or change priorities for withdrawal of savings, the first stay law since 1789 was upheld, as was an antideficiency statute, domicile was established for workmen's compensation, a minimum wage law was sustained, unemployment compensation was accepted, and so were fair trade laws. In all this, substantive due process, liberty of contract, and what was unreasonable to a particular judge finally were removed as barriers to state economic activity.

Decisions involving these issues were handed down at every Court term from 1929 through 1936. Of the concepts, doctrines, or principles involved in this change, there were thirty-six cases. Nine were decided in 1937, but there were also nine in the 1933 term, and six in the 1931 term. Obviously many of these decisions involved divided courts; the classic blocs were very apparent.[175] However every justice except Van Devanter wrote at least one majority opinion in these cases.

It is true that some early New Deal legislation was poorly written and this helps explain why it failed in court tests. How then can we explain that state legislators, paid as little as $4 a day and operating without staff, could draft legislation better than the national Congress? Quite clearly, there was a real shift in 1937, but it was not marked by the minimum wage decision. The turning point is the *Jones and Laughlin*[176] decision. Moreover, this apparent shift obscures the fact that in much less dramatic fashion, and with much less attendant publicity, since 1930 the Hughes Court had been accepting new exercises of state power. An evolution had long been underway. And the major difference after Taft's death was the presence on the Court of Hughes and Roberts, both appointed by the forgotten progressive, Herbert Hoover.

ENDNOTES

1. Paul L. Murphy, *The Constitution in Crisis Times, 1918-1969* (New York: Harper and Row, 1972), p. 154.

2. Alfred H. Kelly and Winfred A. Harbison, *The American Constitution: Its Origins and Development* (New York: W. W. Norton, 4th ed., 1970), p. 765.

3. John M. Blum et al., *The National Experience* (New York: Harcourt, Brace & World, 2nd ed., 1968) pp. 694–95; Samuel E. Morrison, Henry Steele Commager, and William E. Leuchtenburg, *The Growth of the American Republic* (New York: Oxford, 6th ed., 1969), pp. 512–16; Robert Kelley, *The Shaping of the American Past* (Englewood Cliffs, NJ: Prentice-Hall, 1975), p. 766; John A. Garraty, *The American Nation* (New York: Harper and Row, 3rd ed., 1975), pp. 11, 734; Richard N. Current, T. Harry Williams, and Frank Freidel, *American History: A Survey* (New York: Knopf, 4th ed., 1975), p. 686; Carl N. Degler et al., *The Democratic Experience* (Glenview, IL: Scott, Foresman, 3rd ed., 1973), p. 463; Thomas A. Bailey, *The American Pageant: A History of the Republic* (Boston: D.C. Heath, 3rd ed., 1966), p. 852; John D. Hicks, George E. Mowry,

and Robert E. Burke, *The American Nation* (Boston: Houghton Mifflin, 4th ed., 1963), p. 603; Richard Hofstadter, William Miller, and Daniel Aaron, *The United States* (Englewood Cliffs, NJ: Prentice-Hall, 3rd ed., 1972), p. 728.

4. Thomas A. Bailey and David M. Kennedy, *The American Pageant: A History of the Republic* (Lexington, MA: D.C. Heath, 10th ed., 1994), p. 816; James K. Martin et al., *America and Its People* (New York: Harper and Collins, 2nd ed., 1993), p. 864; John M. Blum et al., *The National Experience: A History of the United States* (Fort Worth: Harcourt Brace Jovanovich, 8th ed., 1993), p. 713; James A. Henretta et al., *America's History* (New York: Worth, 2nd ed., 1993), p. 795; John M. Faragher, *Out of Many: A History of the American People* (Englewood Cliffs, NJ: Prentice-Hall, 1994), p. 780; Winthrop D. Jordan and Leon Litwack, *The United States: Brief Edition* (Englewood Cliffs, NJ: Prentice-Hall, 1994), p. 344; James T. Patterson, *America in the Twentieth Century* (San Diego: Harcourt Brace Jovanovich, 3rd ed., 1994), p. 840; and Gary B. Nash et al., *The American People: Creating a Nation and a Society* (New York: Harper and Collins, 3rd ed., 1994), p. 840.

5. John D. Sprague, *Voting Patterns of the United States Supreme Court: Cases in Federalism, 1889-1959* (Indianapolis: Bobbs-Merrill, 1968), pp. 151–52. With few exceptions I have followed Sprague's methodology.

6. James T. Patterson, *The New Deal and the States: Federalism in Transition* (Princeton: Princeton University Press, 1969), pp. 7–9, 14–15, 26–27; President's Research Committee on Social Trends, *Recent Social Trends in the United States* (New York: McGraw-Hill, 1933), pp. iv, xi–xii, lx–lxii; Leonard D. White, "Public Administration," *Recent Social Trends,* 1835-37; and "The Search for New Sources of Revenue," *Harvard Law Review*, 47 (1934), pp. 503–9.

7. U.S. Congress, Senate, *The Constitution of the United States of America: Analysis and Interpretations. Annotations of Cases Decided by the Supreme Court to June 22, 1964*, Document No. 39, 88th Cong., 1st Sess., 1964, pp. 1149–77 (hereafter referred to as *Annotated Constitution*); Kelly and Harbison, pp. 537–41; and Loren P. Beth, *The Development of the American Constitution, 1877-1917*, (New York: Harper and Row, 1971), pp. 184–85.

8. *Jaybird Mining v. Wei*, 271 U.S. 609 (1926).

9. *Quaker City Cab Co. v. Pennsylvania*, 277 U.S. 389 (1928).

10. *Cudahy Packing Co. v. Hinkle*, 278 U.S. 460 (1929).

11. *Macallen v. Massachusetts*, 279 U.S. 620 (1929).

12. *New Jersey Bell Telephone Co. v. State Board*, 280 U.S. 338 (1930).

13. *Northwestern Mutual Life Ins. Co. v. Wisconsin*, 275 U.S. 136 (1927).

14. *Long v. Rockwood*, 277 U.S. 142 (1928).

15. *Schlesinger v. Wisconsin*, 270 U.S. 236 (1926).

16. *Farmers' Loan & Trust Co. v. Minnesota*, 280 U.S. 204 (1930).

17. *Panhandle Oil Co. v. Mississippi*, 277 U.S. 218 (1928).

18. *Helson v. Kentucky*, 279 U.S. 245 (1929).

19. *Wheeling Steel Corp. v. Fox*, 298 U.S. 193 (1936).

20. *First Bank Stock Corp. v. Minnesota*, 301 U.S. 234 (1937).

21. *Trotter v. Tennessee*, 290 U.S. 354 (1933); and *Taber v. Indian Territory Illuminating Oil Co.*, 300 U.S. 1 (1937).

22. *Virginia v. Imperial Coal Sales Co.*, 293 U.S. 15 (1934).

23. *Pacific Co. v. Johnson*, 285 U.S. 480 (1932).
24. *Educational Films v. Ward*, 282 U.S. 379 (1931).
25. *Fox Film Corp. v. Doyal*, 286 U.S. 123 (1932).
26. *Federal Compress and Warehouse v. McLean*, 291 U.S. 17 (1934).
27. *Southern Natural Gas Corp. v. Alabama*, 301 U.S. 148 (1937).
28. *Fisher's Blend Station v. Tax Comm.*, 297 U.S. 659 (1936).
29. *State Board v. Jackson*, 283 U.S. 527 (1931).
30. *Liggett v. Lee*, 288 U.S. 517 (1933).
31. *Stewart Dry Goods v. Lewis*, 294 U.S. 550 (1935).
32. *Great Atlantic and Pacific Tea Co. v. Grosjean*, 301 U.S. 412 (1937).
33. *Hoeper v. Tax Commission*, 284 U.S. 206 (1931).
34. *Senior v. Braden*, 295 U.S. 422 (1935).
35. *Colgate v. Harvey*, 296 U.S. 404 (1935).
36. *New York ex rel. Rogers v. Graves*, 299 U.S. 401 (1937).
37. *Pollock v. Farmers' Loan & Trust Co.*, 157 U.S. 429 (1895).
38. *New York ex rel. Cohn v. Graves*, 300 U.S. 308 (1937).
39. *Eastern Air Transport v. Tax Comm.*, 285 U.S. 147 (1932).
40. *Henneford v. Silas Mason Co.*, 300 U.S. 577 (1937); and *Annotated Constitution*, pp. 222–26.
41. *Munn v. Illinois*, 94 U.S. 133 (1877).
42. *Chicago, Milwaukee & St. Paul R. Co. v. Minnesota*, 134 U.S. 418 (1890).
43. 262 U.S. 522 (1923).
44. *Weaver v. Palmer Bros. Co.*, 270 U.S. 402 (1926).
45. *Lemke v. Farmers' Grain Co.*, 258 U.S. 50 (1922).
46. *Shafer v. Farmers' Grain Co.*, 268 U.S. 189 (1925).
47. *Burns Baking Co. v. Bryan*, 264 U.S. 504 (1924).
48. *Weller v. New York*, 268 U.S. 319 (1925).
49. *Tyson & Brother v. Banton*, 273 U.S. 418 (1927).
50. *DiSanto v. Pennsylvania*, 273 U.S. 34 (1927).
51. *Ribnik v. McBride*, 277 U.S. 350 (1928).
52. *Williams v. Standard Oil Co.*, 278 U.S. 235 (1929).
53. *Liggett Co. v. Baldridge*, 278 U.S. 105 (1928).
54. *Levy Leasing Co., v. Siegel*, 258 U.S. 242 (1922).
55. *Roschen v. Ward*, 279 U.S. 337 (1929).
56. *Vigliotti v. Pennsylvania*, 258 U.S. 403 (1922); and *Hixson v. Oakes*, 265 U.S. 254 (1924).
57. *Porterfield v. Webb*, 263 U.S. 225 (1923); *Terrace v. Thompson*, 263 U.S. 197 (1923); *Webb v. O'Brien*, 263 U.S. 313 (1923); and *Frick v. Webb*, 263 U.S. 326 (1923).
58. *Miller v. Schoene*, 276 U.S. 272 (1928).
59. *Leonard v. Earle*, 279 U.S. 392 (1929).
60. *Oregon-Washington R. Co. v. Washington*, 270 U.S. 87 (1926).
61. *Foster-Fountain Packing Co. v. Haydel*, 278 U.S. 1 (1928).
62. *Johnson v. Haydel*, 278 U.S. 16 (1928).
63. *Fairmont Creamery Co. v. Minnesota*, 274 U.S. 1 (1927).
64. *Packard v. Banton*, 264 U.S. 140 (1924).
65. *Hess v. Pawloski*, 264 U.S. 352 (1924).

66. *Clark v. Poor*, 274 U.S. 554 (1927).

67. *Buck v. Kuykendall*, 267 U.S. 307 (1925).

68. *Bush and Sons Co. v. Maloy*, 267 U.S. 317 (1927).

69. *Michigan Public Utilities Comm. v. Duke*, 266 U.S. 570 (1925).

70. *Frost v. Railroad Commission*, 271 U.S. 583 (1926).

71. *Pennsylvania Coal Co. v. Mahon*, 260 U.S. 393 (1922).

72. *Pennsylvania v. West Virginia*, 262 U.S. 553 (1923).

73. *Standard Oil Co. v. Marysville*, 279 U.S. 582 (1929).

74. *Hartford Co. v. Harrison*, 301 U.S. 458 (1937).

75. *New State Ice Co. v. Liebman*, 285 U.S. 262 (1932).

76. *Alabama v. Arizona*, 291 U.S. 286 (1934); and *Whitfield v. Ohio*, 297 U.S. 431 (1936).

77. *Hague v. Chicago*, 299 U.S. 387 (1937).

78. *National Fertilizer Assoc. v. Bradley*, 301 U.S. 178 (1937).

79. *Los Angeles Gas & Electric v. Railroad Comm.*, 289 U.S. 287 (1933); and *Lindheimer v. Illinois Bell Telephone Co.*, 292 U.S. 151 (1934).

80. *Dayton Power & Light Co. v. Pacific Utilities Comm.*, 292 U.S. 290 (1934).

81. *West Ohio Gas Co. v. Public Utilities Comm.*, 294 U.S. 63 (1935); and *West v. Chesapeake & Potomac Tel. Co.*, 295 U.S. 662 (1935).

82. *Magnano Co. v. Hamilton*, 292 U.S. 40 (1934).

83. *Peterson Baking Co. v. Bryan*, 290 U.S. 570 (1934).

84. *Nebbia v. New York*, 291 U.S. 502 (1934).

85. *Borden's Farm Products Co. v. Ten Eyck*, 297 U.S. 251 (1936).

86. *Mayflower Farms Inc. v. Ten Eyck*, 297 U.S. 266 (1936).

87. *Baldwin v. Seelig*, 294 U.S. 511 (1935).

88. *Highland Farms Dairy v. Agnew*, 300 U.S. 608 (1937).

89. *Smith v. Cahoon*, 283 U.S. 553 (1931).

90. *Sproles v. Binford*, 286 U.S. 374 (1932).

91. *Stephenson v. Binford*, 287 U.S. 251 (1932).

92. *Nashville, Chattanooga & St. Louis R. v. Walters*, 294 U.S. 405 (1935).

93. *Morf v. Bingamin*, 298 U.S. 407 (1936).

94. *Ingels v. Morf*, 300 U.S. 290 (1937). When California reduced its fees the law was sustained, *Clark v. Gray*, 306 U.S. 583 (1939).

95. *Champlin Refining Co. v. Corporation Comm.*, 286 U.S. 210 (1932).

96. *Thompson v. Consolidated Gas Utilities Corp.*, 300 U.S. 55 (1937).

97. *Henderson Co. v. Thompson*, 300 U.S. 258 (1937).

98. *O'Gorman & Young v. Hartford Fire Ins. Co.*, 282 U.S. 251 (1931).

99. *Allgeyer v. Louisiana*, 165 U.S. 578, 589 (1897).

100. *Muller v. Oregon*, 298 U.S. 412 (1908); and *Bunting v. Oregon*, 243 U.S. 426 (1917).

101. Alpheus Thomas Mason, *The Supreme Court from Taft to Warren* (New York: W.W. Norton & Company, 1964), p. 50, citing Judge George M. Bourguin in *Investor's Syndicate v. Porter*, 52 F 2d 189, 196 (1931).

102. *Missouri ex rel. Burnes National Bank v. Duncan*, 265 U.S. 17 (1924).

103. *Ex Parte Worcester County National Bank v. Duncan*, 265 U.S. 17 (1924).

104. *First National Bank. v. Missouri*, 263 U.S. 640 (1924).

105. *United States v. Oklahoma*, 261 U.S. 253 (1923).

106. *Finance & Gurantee Co. v. Oppenheimer*, 276 U.S. 10 (1928).

107. *Harkin v. Brundage*, 276 U.S. 36 (1928).

108. *Riehle v. Margolis*, 279 U.S. 218 (1929).

109. *International Shoe Co. v. Pinkus*, 278 U.S. 261 (1929).

110. *Coffin Bros. Co. v. Bennett*, 277 U.S. 29 (1928).

111. *Ferry v. Ramsey*, 277 U.S. 88 (1928).

112. *Manley v. Georgia*, 279 U.S. 1 (1929).

113. *Conley v. Barton*, 260 U.S. 677 (1923).

114. *Euclid v. Ambler*, 272 U.S. 365 (1926).

115. *Washington ex re. Seattle Trust Co. v. Roberge*, 278 U.S. 116 (1928).

116. *Nectow v. Cambridge*, 277 U.S. 183 (1928).

117. *Industrial Accident Comm. v. Payne*, 259 U.S. 182 (1922).

118. *Industrial Accident Comm. v. Nordenholt Corp.*, 259 U.S. 263 (1921); and *Smith & Son v. Taylor*, 276 U.S. 178 (1928).

119. *Smith-Porter Ship Co. v. Rohde*, 257 U.S. 469 (1922).

120. *London Accident & Guarantee Co. v. Industrial Accident Comm.*, 276 U.S. 467 (1928).

121. *Cudahy Packing Co. v. Parramore*, 279 U.S. 109 (1929).

122. *Bountiful Brick Co. v. Giles*, 276 U.S. 154 (1928).

123. *Sheehan v. Shuler*, 265 U.S. 371 (1924).

124. *Leiser v. Dysart*, 267 U.S. 540 (1925).

125. *Power Manufacturing Co. v. Saunders*, 274 U.S. 490 (1927).

126. *Sultan Ry. Timber Co. v. Department of Labor*, 277 U.S. 135 (1928).

127. *Ward & Gow v. Krinsky*, 259 U.S. 503 (1922).

128. *North Carolina Railway Co. v. Lee*, 260 U.S. 16 (1922); *Davis v. Wechsler*, 263 U.S. 22 (1923); *Davis v. O'Hara*, 266 U.S. 314 (1924); *Davis v. Cohen & Co.*, 268 U.S. 638 (1925); and *Virginian Railway Co. v. Mullins*, 271 U.S. 220 (1926).

129. *Louisiana & W. R. Co. v. Gardiner*, 273 U.S. 280 (1927).

130. *Nashville, Chattanooga & St. Louis Ry. Co. v. White*, 278 U.S. 456 (1929).

131. *Chesapeake & Ohio Ry. Co. v. Stapleton*, 279 U.S. 587 (1929).

132. *Western & Atlantic Railroad v. Henderson*, 279 U.S. 639 (1929).

133. *Kentucky Finance Corp. v. Paramount Auto Exchange Corp.*, 262 U.S. 544 (1923).

134. *Wuchter v. Pizzutti*, 276 U.S. 13 (1928).

135. *Hoffman v. Missouri*, 274 U.S. 21 (1927); *Louisville & Nashville Railroad Co. v. Chatters*, 279 U.S. 320 (1929); and *Douglas v. New York, New Haven & Hartford R. Co.*, 279 U.S. 377 (1929).

136. *Hemphill v. Orloff*, 277 U.S. 537 (1928).

137. *In re Gilbert*, 276 U.S. 294 (1928).

138. *Becher v. Contiure Laboratories*, 279 U.S. 388 (1929).

139. *Adkins v. Children's Hospital*, 261 U.S. 525 (1923).

140. *Murphy v. Sardell*, 269 U.S. 530 (1925); and *Donham v. West-Nelson*

Mfg. Co., 273 U.S. 657 (1927). These were both memorandum decisions, without opinion, and are not reflected in the table or in the statistics.

141. *Traux v. Corrigan*, 257 U.S. 312 (1921).

142. *Chas. Wolff Packing Co. v. Court of Industrial Relations of Kansas*, 262 U.S. 522 (1923).

143. *Chas. Wolff Packing Co. v. Court of Industrial Relations of Kansas*, 267 U.S. 552 (1925).

144. *Dorchy v. Kansas*, 264 U.S. 286 (1924).

145. *Dorchy v. Kansas*, 272 U.S. 306 (1926).

146. *Buck v. Bell*, 274 U.S. 200 (1927).

147. *Gibbes v. Zimmerman*, 290 U.S. 326 (1933).

148. *Treigle v. Acme Homestead Assoc.*, 297 U.S. 189 (1936).

149. *Taylor v. Sternberg*, 293 U.S. 470 (1935).

150. *Pennsylvania v. Williams*, 290 U.S. 176 (1935); *Gordon v. Ominsky*, 294 U.S. 186 (1935); *Penn General Casualty Co. v. Pennsylvania*, 294 U.S. 189 (1935); and *Gordon v. Washington*, 285 U.S. 30 (1935).

151. *Jennings v. United States Fidelity & Guaranty Co.*, 294 U.S. 216 (1935).

152. *Doty v. Love*, 295 U.S. 64 (1935).

153. *Shriver v. Woodbine Bank*, 285 U.S. 467 (1932); and *Stockholders v. Sterling*, 300 U.S. 175 (1937).

154. *Home Building & Loan Assoc. v. Blaisdell*, 290 U.S. 298 (1934).

155. *Worthen Co. v. Thomas*, 292 U.S. 426 (1934).

156. *U.S. Mortgage Co. v. Matthews*, 293 U.S. 232 (1934).

157. *Worthen Co. v. Board of Commissioners*, 205 U.S. 56 (1935).

158. *Richmond Mortgage & Loan Co. v. Wachovia Bank*, 300 U.S. 124 (1937).

159. *Phelps v. Board of Education*, 300 U.S. 319 (1937).

160. *Baizly Iron Works v. Span*, 281 U.S. 222 (1930).

161. *Employers' Liability Assurance Corp. v. Cook*, 281 U.S. 233 (1930).

162. *Murray v. Gerrick Co.*, 291 U.S. 315 (1931).

163. *Gilvary v. Cuyahoga Valley Ry. Co.*, 292 U.S. 57 (1934).

164. *Bradford v. Clapper*, 286 U.S. 145 (1932).

165. *Alaska Packers' Assoc. v. Industrial Accident Comm.*, 294 U.S. 532 (1935).

166. *Morehead v. New York ex rel. Tipaldo*, 298 U.S. 587 (1936).

167. *West Coast Hotel v. Parrish*, 399 U.S. 379 (1937).

168. Felix Frankfurter, "Mr. Justice Roberts," *University of Pennsylvania Law Review* 104 (1955): 311–17; and John W. Chambers, "The Big Switch: Justice Roberts and the Minimum Wage Cases," *Labor History* 10 (1969): 44–73.

169. 299 U.S. 619 (1936).

170. *Carmichael v. Southern Coal & Coke Co.*, 301 U.S. 495 (1937).

171. *New York Times*, June 20, 1936; 20; October 20, 1936, 13; October 27, 1936, 10; November 12, 1936, 5; and November 15, 1936, 22; and *Chamberlain v. Andrews*, 299 U.S. 515 (1936).

172. *Old Dearborn Distributing Co. v. Seagram Distillers*, 299 U.S. 183 (1936); and *Pep Boys v. Pyroil*, 299 U.S. 198 (1936).

173. This was reversed in *Madden v. Kentucky*, 309 U.S. 83 (1940).

174. This was reversed in *Graves v. New York*, 306 U.S. 466 (1939).

175. C. Herman Pritchett, *The Roosevelt Court* (New York: Macmillan, 1948).

176. *N.L.R.B. v. Jones and Laughlin Steel Corp.*, 301 U.S. 1 (1937).

3

The Battle to Save the Court
The Kansas Press and the Court Packing Fight of 1937

James C. Duram

This chapter examines the historical context surrounding the editorial response of forty-six selected Kansas newspapers to President Roosevelt's Court-packing plan of 1937. This study illustrates the nature and uses of constitutional argumentation in the 1930s, which was a period of great controversy stimulated by the impact of the New Deal with its demands for activist government and economic experimentation.

One of the most sustained partisan defenses of the United States Supreme Court's restrictive interpretation of national economic regulatory powers appeared in the editorial columns of the American daily press. From 1934 through 1937, the overwhelming majority of American newspaper editors expounded their definitions of conservative constitutionalism in the context of a vigorous attack on the spirit, legislation, and impact of the New Deal. Often masked in patriotic, nonpartisan terms, this hostile response was an expression of the basic attitudes and values of the American business community, of which the newspaper industry was a significant part.[1] Recognition of the business-oriented perspective of the editors is essential for understanding the dynamics and significance of the constitutional debates of the New Deal era.

Previous research into the personal backgrounds and organizational affiliations of these editors suggests that the editorial response of the Kansas press to the New Deal was the product of their Republican backgrounds and probusiness attitudes. A composite picture of the Kansas editors (often editor/publisher) constructed from, among other sources, a survey by Eleanor A. Duram, proves conclusively that the alliance between the editors and the Republican party in the 1930s was, with few exceptions, a firm one (see Table 1).[2]
All but two of the editors regarded themselves as Republicans. Furthermore, the survey illustrates that the nature of that relationship in the 1930s went far beyond mere editorial deference to the pervasive climate of opinion reflected in the long established Republican domination of the Jayhawk State. Many of the editors were, in fact, members of the power structure that shaped the party's policies in Kansas. Among their group, the editors counted Senator Arthur Capper, several who had served as Republican National Convention delegates, two former congressmen, one former secretary of the Republican State Committee, two former governors, and a number of former state legislators. In addition, several served on various state boards as appointees of Governor Alfred M. Landon and previous Republican governors.[3]

Evidence of the probusiness orientation of the editors comes from many sources. Many, because of the small size of their newspapers, were directly involved in the managerial as well as the editorial aspects of the newspaper business.[4] In addition, most belonged to the social and fraternal organizations dominated by members of the business community in their respective towns and cities. Many also held positions as directors of banks and other businesses, and still others were

Table 1

Fact Sheet Regarding the Kansas Newspapers Used in this Study

Newspaper	County	Editor	Circulation in 1936
Abilene Daily Reflector	Dickinson	Charles M. Harger	1,832
Arkansas City Daily Traveler	Cowley	Oscar Stanley Stauffer	5,502
Atchinson Daily Globe	Atchinson	Gene A. Howe	6,344
Augusta Daily Gazette	Butler	Chester K. Shore	
Burlington Daily Republican	Coffey	John Redmond	2,216
Caldwell Daily Messenger and News	Sumner	Harold A. Hammond	1,296
Chanute Tribune	Neosho	Clarence Moody	4,675
Cherryvale Republican	Montgomery	Will R. Burge	
Clay Center Dispatch	Clay	Ray Breitweiser	1,700
Coffeyville Daily Journal	Montgomery	Hugh J. Powell	7,208
Columbus Weekly Advocate	Cherokee	L. M. Knock	757
Concordia Blade-Empire	Cloud	Raymond S. Green	3,024
Council Grove Republican	Morris	J. B. Lawrence	2,031
Dodge City Daily Globe	Ford	Jess C. Denious	5,739
El Dorado Times	Butler	Rolla A. Clymer	5,280
Emporia Weekly Gazette	Lyon	William A. White	
Fort Scott Daily Tribune-Monitor	Bourbon	George W. Marble Jr.	4,050
Garden City Daily Telegram	Finney	Robert B. Reed	
Goodland Daily News	Sherman	Charles L. Bigler	1,263
Great Bend Tribune	Barton	M. D. Spencer	3,606
Hiawatha Daily World	Brown	Ewing Herbert	3,164
Hutchinson News	Reno	John P. Harris	15,107
Independence Daily Reporter	Montgomery	Charles Spencer	5,119
Iola Daily Register	Allen	Charles F. Scott	2,941
Junction City Union	Geary	Harry Montgomery	3,838
Kansas City Kansan	Wyandotte	William A. Bailey	17,942
Lawrence Daily Journal-World	Douglas	Wilford Collins Simons	5,338
Leavenworth Daily Times	Leavenworth	D. R. Anthony, III	5,884
Lyons Daily News	Rice	Paul A. Jones	2,269
McPherson Daily Republican	McPherson	William J. Krehbiel	2,150
Manhattan Mercury	Riley	Fay N. Seaton	2,298
Manhattan Morning Chronicle	Riley	Fay N. Seaton	1,960

Table 1 cont.

Neodesha Daily Sun	Wilson	C. C. Bunger	1,490
Newton Evening Kansan-Republican	Harvey	Mrs. J. C. Mack	3,500
Ottawa Herald	Franklin	Sidney F. Harris	4,808
Parsons Sun	Labette	Clyde M. Reed, Sr.	5,957
Pittsburg Headlight	Crawford	F. W. Brinkerhoff	5,223
Pittsburg Sun	Crawford	F. W. Brinkerhoff	6,826
Salina Journal	Saline	Roy F. Bailey	12,953
Topeka Daily Capital	Shawnee	Arthur Capper	44,678
Topeka State Journal	Shawnee	Arthur Carruth, Jr.	22,144
Wellington Daily News	Sumner	H. L. Woods	2,503
Wichita Beacon	Sedgwick	William Shanklin	78,888
Wichita Democrat	Sedgwick	Molly W. Wilcox	1,500
Wichita Eagle	Sedgwick	Victor Murdock	47,735
Winfield Daily Courier	Cowley	W. G. Anderson	4,923

Compiled from *N. W. Ayer & Son's Directory of Newspapers and Periodicals, 1936* (Philadelphia: N. W. Ayer & Son, 1936) pp. 311–40

investors in oil and agribusiness enterprises as shown in Table 2.[5] Congruence between the editors and the complaints in their editorial columns indicate that they chafed under what they regarded as the onerous regulations of the National Recovery Act's newspaper code prior to its destruction by the U.S. Supreme Court in May 1935.[6] The editors also consistently condemned what they regarded as the reckless experimentation of the fiscal policies pursued by the Roosevelt administration.

One of the clearest manifestations of the symbiotic relationship between the economic and political interests of the Kansas editors appeared in their enthusiastic support for the policies of Republican Governor Alfred M. Landon, a graduate of the University of Kansas Law School who had prospered in the oil business prior to his election in 1932. Once in office, he created an administration that emphasized a businesslike, "no nonsense," pay-as-you-go approach to

Table 2

Survey of Kansas Newspaper Editors in 1936

Ages in 1936:

In their 20s	2
In their 30s	6
In their 40s	6
In their 50s	15
In their 60s	9
In their 70s	5
Unknown	1

Average age: 53 Range: 26-76

Place of birth:

Kansas	27
Midwest	11
East	4
Southwest	1
Unknown	1

Religious affiliation:

Protestant	41
Catholic	0
Jewish	0
None	2
Unknown	1

Military experience:

No	29
Yes	9
Unknown	6

Editors' personal political affiliation:

Republican	36
Democrat	1
Independent-Republican	1
Independent-Democrat	1
Independent	2
Unknown	3

Newspapers' political affiliation

Republican	23
Democratic	1
Independent	17
Independent-Republican	5

Highest level of educational achievement:

Grade school	3
Attended high school	3
High school graduate	5
Attended college	11
College graduate	18
Unknown	4

In addition to this (included in "college graduate" total):

Attended graduate school	3
Master's degree	2
Law school degree	1

Memberships of editors in social-fraternal organizations:

Masons	25
Rotary	13
Elks	10
Woodman	3
Kiwanis	2
Lions	2
Oddfellows	2
Eagles	1
Knights of Pythias	1
Moose	1

Memberships of editors in organizations emphasizing the business and professional aspects of journalism:

Kansas Press Association	14
Sigma Delta Chi	8
Kansas Editorial Association	4
American Society of Newspaper Editors	4
Inland Daily Press Assoc.	4
National Press Association	3
American Newspaper Publishers Association	3
AP Managing Editors Assoc	1

state government.[7] His oft-repeated belief that American business and agriculture could work their way out of the depression without extensive government controls and economic experimentation struck a responsive chord with the hard-pressed editors. Such statements, his strict fiscal policies, and the close personal ties that Landon established with many of the newspaper people translated into enthusiastic editorial support in their newspapers.[8]

Rolla A. Clymer of the *El Dorado Times* exemplified the depth of that support in a letter to a fellow editor written shortly after Landon's reelection in 1934: "Will Beck [Republican state chairman] and I were in accord on this all along. We had Landon's fine record to expound and we had the most loyal support by Kansas newspapers I have ever seen."[9]

Additional evidence supporting the argument that the probusiness mentality of the editors played a major role in the shaping of their subsequent attitudes toward constitutional issues is found in the timing of the emergence of opposition to the New Deal in the Kansas newspaper editorials. The crystallization of the anti-New Deal position in the Kansas press occurred in the five months following the 1934 congressional elections, the same period when strong organized business opposition to the New Deal was developing nationwide.[10] Writing two days after the 1934 election, the editor of the *Abilene Daily Reflector* presented a classic expression of the assumptions that lay at the heart of that opposition: "Business recovery will not come from more wild-eyed legislation. The depression cannot be licked unless experiments in business are put in the discard."[11] Buoyed by their long-established probusiness political and economic sympathies, the Kansas editors joined their brethren throughout the country in mounting an attack on what they characterized as excessive regulation of business, wild spending, socialist concepts, dangerous experimentation, and hastily drafted legislation from the Roosevelt "brain trust."

One of the major themes in this on-going critique in

both the Kansas and the national press was a scathing indictment of the constitutional infirmities of the New Deal. Such criticism was greatly stimulated by the U.S. Supreme Court's invalidation of numerous pieces of New Deal legislation from January 1935 through May 1936 in what one scholar described as a "carnival of unconstitutionality."[12] The editorials in the Kansas press thus exemplify the process whereby the American business community used its defense of constitutionalism to advance its political and economic goals.[13]

The Kansas editors laid a solid groundwork for their 1937 barrage in their editorial comments on the constitutional aspects of the New Deal during the three years prior to the eruption of "the Court Fight."[14] Many of the editors were frustrated and angry that their previous efforts had come to naught. Their vociferous support for Governor Landon's 1936 presidential bid ended in failure, with Landon even failing to carry his home state. Small wonder many of them seized the opportunity presented by Roosevelt's court-packing proposal to blast the president with editorial broadsides.

The editors were further encouraged when it became apparent almost immediately after Roosevelt introduced his judicial reorganization plan, just months after his landslide 1936 reelection, that he was politically vulnerable and the plan was in dire straits in spite of overwhelming Democrat majorities in each chamber of Congress. The plan sharply divided his own party in a manner that no critical issue had since Roosevelt came to power in 1933. In addition to his traditional opponents, the president's plan collided head on with one of the most well-established myths in modern American politics—the idea that the U.S. Supreme Court was an apolitical, neutral tribunal that stood above the clamor of partisan American politics.[15]

The introduction of Roosevelt's judicial reorganization bill on February 5, 1937, brought forth two different types of editorial responses in the Kansas newspapers: first, editorials of a general nature that attacked it; and second, editorials on the specific events of the struggle over its passage.

The general editorials continued throughout the struggle and served to keep reader attention focused on the contest. The overwhelming majority of these editorials contained vehement attacks on Roosevelt and what they frequently referred to as the "Court packing plan."[16] Early in the struggle the editors accused the president of seeking to gain control of the Supreme Court as the final step on the way to his complete control of the federal government. Seeking to take advantage of growing American concern about the rise of fascism in Europe, many of the editors then repeated an earlier charge that the New Deal leadership and its accompanying ideology possessed their own authoritarian tendencies. As the emotional appeal of this argument subsided, the editors emphasized the clear and present danger to the nation in granting Roosevelt such powers, even if he were well intended, that would be inherited by future presidents.[17] Moreover, the editors contended that the plan was fraught with danger even without the threat of dictatorship that it allegedly posed. If the Court were restricted now for liberal reasons, could it not be restricted later for conservative ones? Such a development, they insisted, would lead to a loss of legitimacy for the Court and the Constitution it was supposed to defend. [18]

The editors emphatically rejected the argument that Roosevelt's historic landslide victory in 1936 gave him an unprecedented mandate to reform the Supreme Court. They accused him of deliberately avoiding the question during the campaign in order to prevent the people from expressing their opinion on the Court issue. As the editor of the *Neodesha Daily Sun*, thundered: "Do you think that President Roosevelt himself did not realize his unfrankness when he carefully concealed from the voters his intention touching the gravest effort he or any other president has made to change the pattern of the government?"[19] The editors continued to emphasize Roosevelt's strategic deceit throughout their critique of his judicial reform proposal.

During the extensive discussions of the bill by the

United States Senate Judiciary Committee, the editors characterized the pressure Roosevelt was putting on Democratic senators as overzealous and unparalleled in presidential history. The administration's supporters in Congress were accused of putting party loyalty above the good of the nation, while the papers characterized the opposition as brave, patriotic individuals who were willing to sacrifice their political careers for the country's well-being; clearly, the editors attempted to take advantage of traditional American sympathy for the underdog.[20]

The editors condemned the administration for dealing with the Court through legislative enactment rather than by constitutional amendment. The editors insisted that the latter technique was the most democratic way to address the argument for according increased powers to the federal government. However, they were purposely vague about the type of amendment they wished to support. That vagueness symbolized the editors' attempts to join forces with the liberal opponents of the court plan, many of whom were advocating an amendment that would restrict the powers of the Court.[21]

The editors persistently reminded their readers of their responsibility to defend the Court *and* the Constitution. It was, they argued, the people's business to decide whether they would allow the American system of government to be radically modified. If the people expressed opposition to the plan, Congress, "the people's branch," would take heart and defeat it. To help the people make a "wise decision," the editors hammered home the idea that the Supreme Court was the last bastion standing between them and a likely Roosevelt dictatorship. Contrary to their high praise for the Republican Party as the defender of constitutionalism prior to the struggle, the papers made little mention of the Republicans during the Court fight, preferring to keep their readers' attention focused on what was presented as a nonpartisanship issue.[22]

Editorial references to the Senate Judiciary Committee hearings on the court plan centered on two events. Several of the editors commented favorably upon the letter Chief Justice Charles Evans Hughes sent to the committee refuting the idea that the Court was behind in its docket. They contended that the letter exploded administration arguments about the necessity for reform.[23] The committee vote recommending rejection of the plan also evoked considerable response. Emphasis in the editorials was on the strong language in the majority report stressing the dangers of the proposal. The editor of the *Manhattan Mercury* typified the enthusiasm of this response when he noted: "The language in the report was so direct and vigorous that the President's ears must have burned when he read about it."[24] After the adverse committee vote many predicted the defeat of the measure.

Editorial response to the Court's dramatic shift, "the switch in time that saved nine," in the spring of 1937 to a favorable attitude toward the socioeconomic legislation of the New Deal differed in several respects from their response to earlier aspects of the Court struggle. Caught by the strength of their earlier argument that the Court made decisions solely on the basis of what the Constitution required, the editors made the best of what to them, to say the least, was a perplexing situation. A number expressed surprise and disappointment that the Court had upheld the Wagner Labor Act, the Social Security Act, and state minimum wage legislation, suggesting that they were based on unsound, unworkable premises, or that the Court's shift was not a permanent one.[25] However, most were quick to add that the decisions proved the Court was not hostile to current social legislation, thereby negating the need to pack the Court.[26] The editor of the *Ottawa Herald* exemplified the editors' newly discovered respect for the Court's flexibility: "Yesterday's decision took all the wind out of the sails of the Roosevelt proposal to inject new blood into the Court. Nothing can be accomplished by enlarging the Court."[27]

The recommittal of the Court plan to the Senate Judiciary Committee on July 22, 1937, caused expressions of delight in the editorials. The editors hailed the defeat of the bill as a great victory for democracy, proclaiming that the threat of a dictatorship by Roosevelt or some future autocrat had disappeared.[28] Many of the editors praised the American people for their role in defeating the Court plan. As the editor of the *Coffeyville Journal* contended, the recommittal "was a triumph for our form of government . . . even more significant is that the real opposition came from the people."[29] Several of the editors urged the president to abide by the people's decision and cease his attempts to gain control of the Court by legislative means. Despite the Court's shift (or perhaps belatedly because of it), the editors were convinced that President Roosevelt had been dealt a crushing blow, one that left his party divided, and the American people highly distrustful of his motives.

The Kansas editors had scarcely concluded their victory celebration over the demise of the court bill when President Roosevelt unintentionally handed them an opportunity to extend their criticisms of his "cavalier" attitude toward the Court and Constitution. The resignation of conservative Supreme Court Justice Willis Van Devanter in March 1937 finally gave Roosevelt his first opportunity to fill a seat on the high court. Numerous observers, in and outside of Washington, were appalled at FDR's selection of Senator Hugo L. Black of Alabama, an intensely loyal New Dealer with a strong proregulatory stance toward business. Many of the editors' initial comments regarding the president's nomination and the rapid confirmation of Black, emphasized Black's lack of significant judicial experience and judicial temperament, two of the strengths, they pointed out, of retiring Justice Willis Van Devanter.[30]

When news of Black's association with the Ku Klux Klan surfaced in mid-September, the editors took full advantage of the opportunity, calling for Black's resignation and condemning Roosevelt for ignoring the charges when they were first raised. The president was accused of debasing the Court, of using the Black appointment as revenge for his defeat in the Court fight. The fact that Black had accepted Klan support and later resigned was cited as evidence of his political opportunism and lack of character.[31] One of the most succinct statements of this position appeared in the *Iola Daily Register* after Justice Black attempted to explain his beliefs in a radio address: "No satisfactory speech is possible. Either he was not serious when he took the Klan oath or he is not now. His character is painfully lacking in traits necessary to be a justice."[32]

The editorial treatment of the Court fight in the Kansas press represents the culmination of the sharply critical attitude that the editors had expressed about the constitutional shortcomings of the New Deal since its very inception. This period in American politics reminds us that the major constitutional debates that have been such a persistent part of our political landscape have not occurred in political or economic vacuums. Moreover, what we see here is a superb example of the way interest groups in American society create a perception of what constitutes "correct" constitutional interpretation that fits quite comfortably with their economic, political, and social goals. Conservative constitutionalism proved to be one of the most convenient and thus frequently invoked defenses of the American business community as it faced the shocking, sometimes staggering changes in the American economy of the 1930s.

This brief characterization of the Kansas editorial treatment of the Court-packing fight should not be regarded as proof that constitutional controversy is locked in a rigid economic determinism; rather, it underscores the truism of James Madison's remarks in the *Federalist* No. 10 concerning the natural affinity between a group's economic desires and its political practices.[33] It should not seem surprising, then, if the Kansas editors' attempt to save the American people from themselves during the constitutional struggle of 1937 also sought to cripple the fountainhead of excessive regulation and taxation that Franklin D. Roosevelt and the New Deal had come to symbolize to many segments of the American business community.

ENDNOTES

1. See, for examples of this orientation, the editorials in *Editor and Publisher*, the official journal of the American Newspaper Publishers' Association during the New Deal era. Especially relevant are the following editorials: January 5, 1935, p. 24; August 31, 1935, p. 18; September 7, 1935, p. 22; September 12, 1936, p. 26; November 14, 1936, p. 24. For a discussion of its causes: James Duram, "Editorial Attitudes towards the Constitutional Issues of the New Deal," (Partially published Ph.D. dissertation, Wayne State University, Detroit, 1968), pp. 173–6. S. Alexander Ripa, "Constitutionalism: Political Defense of the Business Community During the New Deal Period," *Social Studies* 56 (October, 1965): 187–90.

2. See Table 1 for a list of the forty-six newspapers and their editors used in this study. Criteria for selection included geographic distribution, membership in the Kansas Daily Newspaper Association, and availability of back copies of the papers either in their local communities or in the Kansas State Historical Library, Topeka (hereafter cited as KSHS). Table 2 was compiled from mailed questionnaires, obituaries, personal interviews, *N.W. Ayer & Son's Directory of Newspapers and Periodicals, 1936* (Philadelphia: N.W. Ayer & Son, 1936), pp. 311–40, and *Who's Who in America, 1936-1937* (Chicago: A. N. Marquis Co., 1937). See Table 2 for a summation of more of its important findings. For an example of a typical Republican editor, see James D. Callahan, ed., *Jayhawk Editor: A Biography of A.Q. Miller, Sr.* (Los Angeles: Sterling Press, 1955).

3. See Table 2.

4. Callahan, *Jayhawk, Editor*, p. 253; Rolla Clymer interview with the author March 8, 1974, in El Dorado, Kansas. Rolla A. Clymer Papers and Jess C. Denious Papers, pp. 1934–37 passim, KSHS.

5. See Table 2.

6. For an excellent analysis of the bitter opposition of the editors to the National Recovery Act's newspaper code, see J. K. Ohl, *Hugh S. Johnson and the New Deal* (De Kalb: Northern Illinois University Press, 1985), p. 15. See, for example: Rolla A. Clymer to Ellina C. Murdock, January 16, 1934, and Roy F. Bailey to Clymer, February 2, 1934, Clymer Papers, KSHS; *Abilene Daily Reflector*, November 9, 1934; *Columbus Weekly Advocate*, January 10, 1935; *Independence Daily*, January 14, 1935; *Iola Daily Register*, January 19, 1934.

7. Donald R. McCoy, *Landon of Kansas* (Lincoln: University of Nebraska Press, 1966), see especially chapters 7 and 8. Alfred M. Landon and Oscar Stauffer interview with the author, June 7, 1974, in Topeka, Kansas.

8. McCoy, *Landon of Kansas,* p. 220; Rolla A. Clymer to Mrs. Buist, February 5, 1934; Alfred M. Landon to Rolla A. Clymer, March 20, 1934; Rolla A. Clymer to Alfred M. Landon, May 4, 1934; Rolla A. Clymer to F. W. Brinkerhoff, November 26, 1934; Clymer Papers, KSHS; Jess C. Denious to Alfred M. Landon, April 2, 1935, F. W. Brinkerhoff to Jess C. Denious, April 4, 1935; Alfred M. Landon to Jess C. Denious, April 6, 1935; Jess C. Denious to R. T. Anderson, August 16, 1935, Denious Papers, KSHS; see also: *Arkansas City Daily Traveler*, August 28, 1934; *Atchison Daily Globe*, January 14, 1935; *Concordia Blade-Empire*, January 17, 1935; *Garden City Daily Telegram*,

November 7, 1934; *Independence Daily Reporter*, January 12, 1935; *Manhattan Morning Chronicle*, November 8, 1934.

9. Rolla A. Clymer to F. W. Brinkerhoff, November 26, 1934, Clymer Papers, KSHS.

10. William E. Leuchtenburg, *Franklin D. Roosevelt and the New Deal* (New York: Harper & Row, 1963), pp. 146–47.

11. *Abilene Daily Reflector*, November 9, 1934.

12. Landon-Stauffer interview, R. G. McCloskey, *The American Court* (Chicago: University of Chicago Press, 1960), pp. 160–64.

13. Ripa, *Social Studies* 56 (October, 1965): 187–90.

14. James C. Duram, "Constitutional Conservatism: The Kansas Press and the New Deal Era as a Case Study," *Kansas Historical Quarterly* (Winter, 1977): 432–47.

15. Leuchtenburg, *Franklin D. Roosevelt* p. 255; Melvin I. Urofsky, *A March of Freedom* (New York: Knopf, 1988), pp. 686–87.

16. *Augusta Daily Gazette*, February 11, 1937; *Dodge City Daily Globe*, February 2, 1937; *El Dorado Times*, February 9, 1937; *Fort Scott Tribune-Monitor*, February 6, 1937; *Great Bend Tribune*, February 11, 1937; *Goodland Daily News*, February 6, 1937; *Hutchinson News*, February 6, 1937; *Lyons Daily News*, February 8, 1937; *McPherson Daily Republican*, February 6, 1937; *Neodesha Daily Sun*, February 6, 1937; *Newton Evening Kansan-Republican*, February 8, 1937; *Pittsburg Sun*, February 7, 1937; *Salina Journal*, February 6, 1937; *Topeka Daily Capital*, February 6, 1937.

17. Typical responses appeared in the *Garden City Daily Telegram*, February 12, 1937; *Goodland Daily News*, March 1, 1937; *Lyons Daily News*, February 18, 1937.

18. Typical responses appeared in the *Goodland Daily News*, February 6, 1937; *Manhattan Mercury*, February 13, 1937.

19. *Neodesha Daily Sun*, February 11, 1937. Typical responses appeared in the *Emporia Weekly Gazette*, February 11, 1937; *Newton Evening Kansan-Republican*, February 15, 1937.

20. Typical responses appeared in the *Garden City Daily Telegram*, February 10/12, 1937; *Goodland Daily News*, February 12, 1937; *Great Bend Tribune*, March 22, 1937.

21. Typical responses appeared in the *Council Grove Republican*, February 6, 1937; *Hutchinson News*, February 6, 1937; *Lyons Daily News*, March 29, 1937; *McPherson Daily Republican*, April 7, 1937.

22. Typical responses appeared in the *Dodge City Daily Globe*, February 17, 1937; *Great Bend Tribune*, March 22, 1937; *Neodesha Daily Sun*, February 6, 1937; *Pittsburg Sun*, February 7, 1937; *Topeka Daily Capital*, February 5, 1937.

23. Typical responses appeared in the *Dodge City Daily Globe*, April 24, 1937; *El Dorado Times*, March 31, 1937; *Great Bend Tribune*, April 10, 1937; *Iola Daily Register*, March 23, 1937.

24. *Manhattan Mercury*, June 16, 1937. Typical responses appeared in the *Goodland Daily News*, June 15, 1937; *Winfield Daily Courier*, June 16, 1937.

25. Typical responses appeared in the *Coffeyville Daily Journal*, May 26 and June 9, 1937; *El Dorado Times*, April 5, 1937; *Iola Daily Register*, May 25, 1937; *Newton Evening Kansan-Republican*, April 14, 1937; *Winfield Daily*

Courier, May 25, 1937.

26. Typical responses appeared in the *Fort Scott Daily Tribune-Monitor*, April 13, 1937; *Iola Daily Record*, April 4, 1937.

27. *Ottawa Herald*, May 25, 1937.

28. Typical responses appeared in the *Goodland Daily News*, July 23, 1937; *Hutchinson News*, July 23, 1937; *Junction City Union*, July 22, 1937.

29. *Coffeyville Daily Journal*, July 31, 1937.

30. Typical responses appeared in the *Coffeyville Daily Journal*, August 13, 1937; *Great Bend Tribune*, August 13, 1937; *Junction City Union*, August 23, 1937.

31. Typical responses appeared in the *Council Grove Republican*, September 6, 1937; *Coffeyville Daily Journal*, October 2, 1937; *Dodge City Daily Globe*, October 9, 1937; *El Dorado Times*, October 6, 1937; *Great Bend Tribune*, September 14, 1937.

32. *Iola Daily Register*, October 2, 1937.

33. James Madison, *The Federalist Papers* (New York: New American Library, 1961), p. 77.

II

The Roosevelt Court, Law, and Politics

4

FDR and Charles Evans Hughes
President Versus Chief Justice

Kenneth M. Holland

The Importance for Constitutional Development of Conflict Between Chief Justices and Presidents

"Nearly every forceful President in American history," observes historian Arthur Schlesinger Jr., "ha[s] come at one time or another into a collision with the Court."[1] This chapter is an examination of the relationship between Franklin Delano Roosevelt, considered one of this country's greatest presidents, and Charles Evans Hughes, conceded to be one of its most significant jurists. This study identifies the various issues of constitutional interpretation over which they disagreed and posits some explanations for these differences but at the same time reveals some rather surprisingly large areas where they shared a common reading of the basic law. Finally, this work documents the extent to which the Hughes-Roosevelt dialectic has shaped contemporary constitutional law and legitimated the role of the Supreme Court as the final arbiter of constitutional disputes.

It is well that we analyze such relationships, for an important source of the stability and health of the American democracy is dialogue between the judicial and executive branches. This interbranch conversation significantly eases the task of articulating and resolving both contests between powerful competing interests and conflicts over fundamental moral questions. The constitutional dialogue between Roosevelt and Hughes lucidly illustrates this peculiar strength of the American political system—the role of rational discourse in the resolution of fundamental disputes over public policy and the distribution of power. Unlike the ideal city in speech crafted by Socrates in *The Republic* or Karl Marx's classless society, the American political system is filled with contradiction, traceable to incongruity among the principles on which it is founded. Among the inherently conflicting goals informing the Constitution are equality, liberty, majority rule, and competent government.[2]

In accordance with the principle of separation of powers, each branch of the national government is designed to act as the principal champion of one of these constitutional goals. The energy and effectiveness of the executive branch make the president responsible for providing competent government, the mode in which members of Congress are elected and reach decisions on the floor of their chambers means that the legislature embodies the principle of majority rule, while the Supreme Court, armed with judicial review, serves as the champion of individual liberty and equality.[3] American constitutional history is nothing less than the story of how these tensions have played themselves out in discrete crises ending in particular resolutions, only to give rise to new controversies, for the irreconcilable can never be fully reconciled. Although a president may not be a constitutional scholar by training or interest, conflict with the judiciary over his legislative program will force him and his advisers to become experts on discrete constitutional issues and to develop a broader constitutional vision. Constitutional reasoning is "a language through which we can debate the rightness and wrongness of what our community is and what we want it to become," a language for "preserving [judges' and politicians'] authority and trustworthiness."[4] The Court thus forces the president to justify legislative programs using constitutional rhetoric. The "rhetorical presidency" that characterizes the United States is in sharp contrast to the practice of most nations' chief executives, who govern largely by fiat.

The Supreme Court is a worthy opponent of the president because of the unprecedented power conferred on the judiciary in the United States by the system of separation of powers, federalism, judicial review, and a constitutionally entrenched bill of rights. The nature of the judicial process means that these contests over basic principles must be articulated as arguments, presentable by the parties in briefs to the court. Even if the disputes that give rise to landmark constitutional decisions arise from clashes between religions, social classes, or economic interests, they are transformed into opposing readings of the Constitution's language, in principle separable from the underlying material interests. The conflict is thus expressed in a form—a reasoned disputation over fundamental issues—which invites the participation of the attentive public and the people themselves, who, according to democratic theory, constitute the ultimate audience and decision maker. Such a national debate can engage the patriotism and intelligence of the citizenry, educating them in the principles of their regime and making them more capable of self-government.

Presidents also enjoy a number of weapons in their battles with chief justices. Thomas Jefferson retaliated against the Supreme Court by urging successfully the House of Representatives to vote articles of impeachment against Justice Samuel Chase. Andrew Jackson, displeased with the Court's decision in *Worcester v. Georgia*[5] prohibiting the state of

Georgia from reneging on a land agreement with the Cherokee Indians, refused to comply, declaiming, "Well, John Marshall has made his decision, now let him enforce it."[6] Abraham Lincoln refused to obey a writ of habeas corpus issued by Chief Justice Roger Taney, who ordered the president to bring John Merryman, a prisoner in Fort McHenry during the Civil War, to his circuit court and state the legal basis for Merryman's detention.[7] Theodore Roosevelt, in keeping with the Progressive spirit, proposed the use of popular recall against unacceptable decisions of the Supreme Court. Woodrow Wilson attempted to influence the policy agenda of the Court by altering its membership through the appointment process, and Franklin Roosevelt tried to nullify the influence of opposing justices by enlarging the size of the Court and reorganizing its work into panels of less than nine.

In accordance with James Madison's design, the heads of the executive and judicial branches are motivated by a desire to aggrandize their respective departments of government. The Constitution fuels this competition for power by making the presidency and the judiciary largely independent of each other. Although members of the president's cabinet, lower-ranked administrators, the associate justices of the Supreme Court and lower court judges all become engaged in constitutional disputes, the dialogue between the chief justice and the chief executive is often the most decisive. The chief is more than a primus inter pares. He has the potential of being both the taskmaster and the intellectual leader of the Court. It is the responsibility of the chief to define issues at the weekly conference of justices, to lead off the discussions of petitions for review and of cases following oral argument, to assign the writing of opinions in cases where he is in the majority and to control the intellectual atmosphere of debate. As William Howard Taft put it, the chief justice has the power "to mass the Court" in favor of particular policies or interpretations. Under the leadership of Marshall and Taney, two particularly effective chief justices, between 1801 and 1863, the Supreme Court vetoed only two acts of Congress. By contrast, under the leadership of Taft and Hughes, between 1920 and 1932 the Court struck down twenty-two congressionally enacted statutes.

Examples from the nineteenth century of constitutional conversations between the president and chief justice that produced major constitutional progress include the dialogue between Jefferson and Marshall and that between Lincoln and Taney.[8] Executive-judicial tension produced such landmark judgments as *Marbury v. Madison*[9] and *The Prize Cases*[10] and such critical political actions as the impeachment of Justice Chase and the Civil War. The most fruitful of these executive-judicial contests in the twentieth century was that between the eleventh chief justice and the thirty-second president. The character of Hughes and Roosevelt insured that the struggle in the mid 1930s over the Constitution's meaning would be a clash of giants. Schlesinger writes of Hughes, "Always aware, always disciplined, always resourceful, always urbane, he bent all his private charm, all his driving energy, all his ruthless genius toward the vindication of the Court as an institution and himself as a Chief Justice."[11] Franklin D. Roosevelt, the "lion and the fox," in James Macgregor Burns's depiction inspired by Machiavelli's advice to princes, was the only president to be elected to four terms.

The principal issue between Hughes and Roosevelt was the constitutionality of the New Deal. The tenure of Hughes as chief justice produced opinions that in importance up to that time exceeded those of every other chief except Marshall.[12] In the end, the president succeeded not by coercion but by persuasion. Hughes came to see national governmental regulation of the economy as within the scope of Congress's and the executive's constitutional powers, following a protracted conversation that commenced on March 4, 1933, when Hughes administered the oath of office to the newly elected former governor of New York, and concluded on March 29, 1937, when Hughes delivered the Court's opinion reversing its previous decision and finding the Washington minimum-wage law to be constitutional.[13]

Roosevelt's and Hughes's Constitutional Differences

Between January 1935 and June 1936, Hughes voted against the administration in seven out of twelve cases considered vital by Roosevelt to his economic recovery plan. Six of the cases involved differences over constitutional interpretation. Justice Harlan Fiske Stone laid principal responsibility for the Court's attempt to destroy the New Deal on Chief Justice Hughes.[14] Hughes cast his vote against the New Deal position on:

(1) limitations on oil production by executive order under the National Industrial Recovery Act of 1933 (in dispute, Article 1, section 1: "All legislative Powers herein granted shall be vested in a Congress of the United States")[15];

(2) relief to farm mortgage debtors under the Frazier-Lemke Act of 1934 (in dispute, Article 1, section 8, clause 4: "The Congress shall have Power . . . to establish . . . uniform Laws on the subject of Bankruptcies throughout the United States")[16];

(3) prohibition of sale of diseased chickens and setting of minimum wages and maximum hours in the poultry industry under the National Industrial Recovery Act of 1933 (in dispute, Article 1, section 8, clause 3: "The Congress shall have Power . . . to regulate Commerce . . . among the several States")[17];

(4) regulation of wages and hours of employees and the fixing of prices in the mining industry, under the Bituminous Coal Conservation Act of 1935 (in dispute, Article 1, section 8, clause 3: "The Congress shall have Power . . . to regulate Commerce . . . among the several States")[18];

(5) limitations on agricultural production under the Agricultural Adjustment Act of 1933 (in dispute, Article 1, section 8, clause 1: "The Congress shall have Power . . . to lay and collect Taxes . . . to pay the Debts and provide for the common Defense and general Welfare of the United States")[19];

(6) presidential removal of a member of an independent regulatory commission (in dispute, Article 2, section 1: "The President . . . shall take Care that the Laws be faithfully executed")[20]; and

(7) refusal by the Securities and Exchange Commission to permit a registrant to withdraw a false statement in order to escape penalty (in dispute, an Act of Congress).[21]

Legislative Power

The doctrine of non-delegation of legislative power. In a message to Congress on May 17, 1933, requesting passage of the National Industrial Recovery Act, Roosevelt said that it would provide "the machinery necessary for a great co-operative movement throughout all industry in order to obtain wide reemployment, to shorten the working week, to pay a decent wage for the shorter week, and to prevent unfair competition and disastrous overproduction." He sought to protect labor through code provisions abolishing child labor, setting maximum work hours and minimum pay rates, and arranging for collective bargaining. In signing the bill, he commented, "history probably will record the National Industrial Recovery Act as the most important and far-reaching legislation ever enacted by the American Congress."[22] In *Panama Refining Co. v. Ryan*[23] and *Schechter Poultry Corp. v. U.S.*[24], Hughes held the National Industrial Recovery Act (NIRA) as invalid because Congress had delegated lawmaking powers to the executive. *Panama Refining* was the first case testing the New Deal to come before the Court and the first case in American history in which the Court invalidated an act of Congress as involving an unconstitutional delegation of legislative power.

In *Schechter*, Hughes admonished, "Congress is not permitted to abdicate or to transfer to others the essential legislative functions with which it is thus vested."[25] Hughes said Congress may not "delegate legislative power to the President to exercise an unfettered discretion to make whatever laws he thinks may be needed or advisable for the rehabilitation and expansion of trade or industry."[26] "Such a delegation of legislative power," he observed, "is unknown to our law and utterly inconsistent with the constitutional prerogative and duties of Congress."[27] In *Carter v. Carter Coal Co.*,[28] Hughes joined Justice Sutherland's position that the wage and hour provisions of the Bituminous Coal Conservation Act of 1935 amounted to an illegal delegation of legislative power. The decisions in these cases were surprising, because the non-delegation doctrine had not once before been taken seriously by the Court in the testing of federal law.

Scope of the commerce power. Roosevelt read Article 1's delegation to Congress of the power to regulate commerce among the several states broadly. Commerce included, he said, not only buying, selling, and transportation but also production, labor relations, construction, agriculture, and mining. He read the residual category of "intrastate commerce," which is out of Congress's reach, very narrowly.

Hughes, on the other hand, limited the definition of interstate commerce to goods in transit. "Building," he said, "is as essentially local as mining, manufacturing, or growing crops."[29] In a concurring opinion in *Carter Coal Co.*, Hughes said, "production—in this case mining—which precedes commerce, is not itself commerce—and that the power to regulate commerce among the several States is not a power to regulate industry within the State."[30] The regulation had to be of an activity that had a direct effect on interstate commerce. The chief justice found the transactions in *Schechter* to be "in" intrastate commerce with only an "indirect effect" on interstate commerce. Hughes denied that indirect effects on interstate Congress even of great magnitude would justify congressional regulation. The distinction between intrastate and interstate commerce was, said Hughes, "a fundamental one, essential to the maintenance of our constitutional system." Otherwise, he feared, there would be virtually "no limit to the federal power and for all practical purposes we should have a completely centralized government."[31] This fear of centralization was crucial to an understanding of the Constitution's confinement of Congress's power to the regulation of commerce among the states and with foreign countries. Hughes's sharp distinction between "direct" and "indirect" effects on interstate commerce, however, is hard to reconcile with his earlier opinion in the *Shreveport Rate Cases*,[32] in which he affirmed federal power to control local commerce even when effect on interstate commerce seemed tenuous.

In *Schechter*, Hughes said, obiter dicta, that a national law governing wages and hours would be unconstitutional, since it would be a regulation of working conditions only indirectly affecting interstate commerce. He abandoned this view, however, when in 1941, following Roosevelt's introduction of the Court-packing plan, he joined the Court's unanimous opinion upholding the Fair Labor Standards Act in *United States v. Darby Lumber Co.*[33] Forsaking the distinction between direct and indirect effects, Justice Stone's opinion legitimated Congress's power to regulate all activities, including production and terms of employment that affect commerce among the states.

The scope of taxing power. Roosevelt believed that Congress was free to use its power to raise taxes to regulate behavior, even in ways that did not generate much revenue. Use of taxation to regulate marked a number of New Deal programs, including the Agricultural Adjustment Act.

Hughes, on the other hand, held that Congress could only use the taxing power for the purpose of raising revenue. Every tax must carry with it an expectation of revenue, not just changes in behavior. In his concurring opinion in the *Carter Coal Co.* case, the chief justice said the Bituminous Coal Conservation Act was not an appropriate exercise of the taxing power of Congress—that the so-called tax was actually a penalty on producers for not submitting to the price-fixing and labor provisions of the act. Hughes joined Justice Roberts's opinion for the Court in *United States v. Butler*,[34] that Congress may not use the taxing power to regulate agricultural production, a matter reserved to the states by the Tenth Amendment. More than any other previous decision, the *Butler* case, said Attorney General Robert H. Jackson, "turned Roosevelt toward the impending necessity of curbing the Court."[35]

Hughes, however, following the introduction by President Roosevelt of his Court-packing plan, changed his position on the scope of the taxing power. He joined Justice Cardozo's opinion for the Court in *Steward Machine Co. v. Davis*[36] upholding the unemployment and old-age features of the Social Security Act. Cardozo ruled that Congress's power to tax is not limited by the reserved powers of the states as Justice Roberts had said in *Butler*.

The general welfare clause. According to Roosevelt, Article 1's language, "Congress shall have Power To lay and collect Taxes, Duties, Imposts and Excises, to pay the Debts and provide for the common Defense and general Welfare of the United States," meant that Congress could pass laws "to provide for the general welfare." In other words, the general welfare clause was a substantive grant of power to Congress, not a limitation upon the taxing power. In *Carter v. Carter Coal Co.* Hughes held that Congress had no independent power to provide for the general welfare.

Executive Power

Doctrine of emergency power. Roosevelt took a number of actions during the Great Depression and the Second World War that were of doubtful constitutionality. The president's actions suggested that he accepted the validity of the view that during times of emergency the president, as chief executive with the power to marshal the country's resources, must act to protect the public interest even if such actions were not legally authorized or even prohibited by law. This was also the opinion of John Locke, who in *The Second Treatise of Government* described the prerogative power enjoyed by whoever exercises the executive power in a government.

Hughes rejected the notion of emergency power. In *Schechter*, he agreed, "Extraordinary conditions do not create or enlarge constitutional power. The Constitution established a national government with powers deemed to be adequate . . . both in war and peace."[37]

Roosevelt never explicitly accepted Locke's view that the executive is empowered to act in the absence of or even against the law to protect the public interest. In public Roosevelt joined Hughes in supporting the myth of the adequacy of the Constitution for all exigencies. In his first inaugural speech, Roosevelt declared, "Our Constitution is so simple and practical that it is possible always to meet extraordinary needs by changes in emphasis and arrangement without loss of essential form."[38] And in 1935, the president stated, "We have undertaken a new order of things, yet we progress to it under the framework and in the spirit and intent of the American Constitution."[39] This myth is important to our theme, because it makes possible constitutional dialogue between the Supreme Court and the president even when the president is in truth exercising prerogative power—the power of a chief executive to do whatever the public interest requires.

In the Minnesota moratorium case Hughes had to choose between nullifying the highly problematic Minnesota statute for sound constitutional reasons or stretching the words of the Constitution to embrace a policy which Article 1, section 10, seemed explicitly to prohibit. There is difficulty in reconciling Hughes's statement in the Minnesota moratorium case with his reasoning in *Schechter*. In 1934 Hughes permitted Minnesota to stretch the contract clause in response to an emergency but in 1935 prohibited Congress from enlarging the commerce clause in response to a similar emergency. Hughes, said Roosevelt, only approved the emergency doctrine when it was used to benefit business interests.

Removal power of the president. Roosevelt, exercising his executive powers, attempted to remove without cause members of independent regulatory commissions. His view was that he could not carry out his campaign promises or the will of Congress if he could not dismiss commissioners who disagreed with the president's policy goals. Unity in the government and responsibility to the voters mandated, he opined, an unlimited power of removal of executive officers in the hands of the president.

Hughes regarded such an unrestrained power of dismissal as tyrannical. In *Humphrey's Executor v. U.S.*,[40] the Court held unanimously that the president could not remove a member of the Federal Trade Commission (FTC) except for cause, because the FTC is an *independent* regulatory commission.

Powers of the States

Dual federalism is the view that the powers reserved to the states by the Tenth Amendment are absolute limits on Congress's powers, analogous to the way in which the First Amendment prohibits Congress from abridging freedom of speech. In his 1927 lectures on the Supreme Court, Hughes declared that one of the principal justifications for judicial review was to maintain "our dual system with its recognition of local authority in local concerns."[41] In *U.S. v. Butler*, Hughes joined Roberts's opinion, holding the Agricultural Adjustment Act of 1933 to be an invasion of the reserved powers of the states, regardless of whether it was a valid exercise of Congress's powers to tax and spend to promote the general welfare. Justice Stone's dissent in *Butler* reflected Roosevelt's opinion that the doctrine of dual federalism was inconsistent with the intention of the framers and the logic of the Constitution, as well as his view of the broad scope of Congress's power to tax and spend for the general welfare.[42] The Tenth Amendment only reserves to the states those powers not delegated to the federal government. It in no way restricts those delegated powers. The fact that Roosevelt did not present the Court-packing plan to the states in the form of a constitutional amendment is testimony to the strong support that Hughes had for his understanding of the scope of state power from the state legislatures.

Hughes, however, became uncomfortable with the dual federalism doctrine during the fight over Roosevelt's Court-packing scheme. The decision of the unanimous Court in *Kentucky Whip and Collar Co. v. Illinois Central R.R.*[43] was that Congress could use a delegated power to serve a purpose not intimately connected with the nature of the specific delegation. Hughes affirmed the authority of Congress to close the channels of interstate commerce to the products of convict labor on the basis of its own policy with regard to the general welfare. This reasoning struck a devastating blow to the doctrine of dual federalism insofar as the doctrine suggested that the rights of the states over local production limited Congress's power to regulate interstate commerce. In this sense, Hughes's opinion represented a rejection of *Hammer v. Dagenhart*[44]—the quintessential expression of dual federalism—and Justice Sutherland's reasoning in *Carter Coal Co.*, acquiesced in at the time by Hughes in a separate concurring opinion.

In *National Labor Relations Board v. Jones & Laughlin Steel Corp.*,[45] sustaining the Wagner Act, Hughes returned to a principle he first enunciated in the Shreveport rate cases: "Although activities may be intrastate in character when separately considered, if they have such a close and substantial relation to interstate commerce that their control is essential or appropriate to protect that commerce from burdens and obstructions, Congress cannot be denied the power to exercise that control."[46] Because a strike at a steel mill would adversely affect interstate commerce, Congress was empowered to regulate labor relations.

Jones & Laughlin dealt a mortal blow to dual federalism, although the doctrine was only specifically repudiated four years later in *Darby*, where Hughes joined Stone's rejection of the argument that a federal minimum wage law was unconstitutional because, even if it were a valid exercise by Congress of its power to regulate commerce among the states, it intruded on the regulation of production, a subject reserved to the states by the Tenth Amendment.

Judicial Power

Judicial review of administrative agency decisions. The nondelegation doctrine limits the scope of executive discretion. If administrative discretion cannot be eliminated, then it must, thought Hughes, be subject to review by the courts. Hughes regarded the separation of powers as indispensable to liberty. He was concerned not only with congressional delegation of legislative power to the executive but also with executive usurpation of the judicial power. Because the "alphabet soup" of administrative agencies that emerged during the New Deal exercised rulemaking, enforcement and dispute resolution functions, there was the danger of the emergence of a "headless fourth branch of government" without adequate congressional and judicial supervision. Hughes's solution was twofold: force the agencies themselves to operate more like courts and allow appeals from agency decisions to the judiciary.

In a 1932 decision, *Crowell v. Benson*,[47] Hughes expressed the fear that to vest authority in administrative agencies to make final determinations on all questions of fact would be "to establish a government of a bureaucratic character alien to our system." In *St. Joseph Stock Yards v. U.S.*,[48] Hughes expressed alarm at the multiplication of administrative agencies, each of which claimed that its findings of fact may be made conclusive and not subject to judicial scrutiny. Hughes sought to "judicialize" administrative proceedings by requiring that the one who decides disputes must also be the one who hears evidence or argument by the disputants. In *Morgan v. U.S.*,[49] Hughes interpreted "full hearing" to embrace "not only the right to present evidence but also a reasonable opportunity to know the claims of the opposing party and to meet them."[50] He thus imposed the traditional elements of due process—notice and hearing—on administrators. The administrator, said Hughes in a public address reprinted in the *New York Times*, must act in "the spirit of the just judge."[51] Hughes's contribution to the law of procedure before administrative tribunals has proved to be one of his most important contributions to public law.[52]

For his part, Roosevelt and his cabinet believed that judicial review of every major agency decision would produce undue delay and contribute to the defeat of the president's program. Roosevelt's views were expressed by Justice Louis Brandeis in a concurring opinion in *St. Joseph Stock Yards*, where Brandeis said, "Responsibility is the great developer of men."[53] He feared that transferring ultimate responsibility for administrative decisions to the courts would emasculate or demoralize administrators and would unduly burden the courts. As noted above, Secretary of Agriculture Wallace discussed Hughes's opinion in *Morgan v. U.S.* over the radio and expressed the hope that the courts would guard against "legalistic, destructive and expensive delay." He also criticized Hughes in a letter to the *New York Times*.[54]

The size of the Supreme Court. In his Court-packing plan, Roosevelt requested Congress to increase the Court's complement of justices from nine to fifteen. He suggested that the Court could work in divisions, in the same way that the U.S. appellate courts operate in three-judge panels.

Hughes opposed tampering with the Court's structure. He said that the Supreme Court would not and could not work in panels as the highest appellate courts in most democracies do. He refused to apportion petitions for certiorari among the justices, requiring all justices to review them. The Constitution, thought Hughes, prohibited the justices from working in panels, as the chief justice expressed in a letter to the Senate Judiciary

Committee. Hughes was ready to testify in person before the committee but Justice Brandeis objected.[55]

Mandatory retirement age for judges. Roosevelt's Court-packing plan would have added one new justice for every justice over the age of seventy on the ground that the advanced age of many of the justices was impeding the efficient operation of the Court. This argument could also be used to justify a mandatory retirement age for federal judges. This could perhaps have been achieved by statute rather than a constitutional amendment. One could argue that "good behavior" was consistent with an age cap, on the assumption that an elderly judge's "behavior" or performance was necessarily inferior to that of a younger magistrate. Hughes vigorously challenged the assumptions about age on which Roosevelt's plan was based. He believed that lifetime tenure for federal judges was an essential bulwark for individual freedom and the rights of the states.

Supreme Court as final arbiter of the Constitution's meaning. Since the presidency of Thomas Jefferson, presidents and chief justices have differed over the role of the Court in making final determinations of constitutional issues. Jefferson wrote to an early supporter of the Supreme Court, "You seem to consider the judges as the ultimate arbiters of all constitutional questions; a very dangerous doctrine indeed, and one which would place us under the despotism of an oligarchy."[56] "The opinion of the judges," said Andrew Jackson, "has no more authority over Congress than the opinion of Congress has over the judges, and on that point the President is independent of both."[57] Lincoln declared, "If the policy of the government, upon vital questions affecting the whole people is to be irrevocably fixed by decisions of the Supreme Court, the instant they are made, in ordinary litigation between parties in personal actions, the people will have ceased to be their own rulers, having to that extent practically resigned their government into the hands of that eminent tribunal."[58] Looking back on thirty years of judicial decisions preventing "measures for social and industrial betterment which every other civilized nation takes as a matter of course," Theodore Roosevelt warned, "one way or the other it will be absolutely necessary for the people themselves to take the control of the interpretation of the Constitution."[59] Wilson predicted "a revulsion against judicial authority" by the common people if the Supreme Court continued "to repudiate liberal courses of thought and action."[60]

Franklin Roosevelt, like his great predecessors, believed that the president sometimes understands the Constitution better than the Supreme Court and that he should have the power to act on his own constitutional understanding, contrary Supreme Court opinions notwithstanding. Roosevelt could not accept the fact that the Court would decide whether the federal government had control over national economic problems. He said, "If we accept the [Court's] point of view . . . the Federal Government must abandon any legislation [aimed at economic recovery]." He called the question of whether the states would control all economic conditions, both local and national, "the biggest question that has come before this country outside of time of war."[61]

By contrast, Hughes argued that the Supreme Court is the final interpreter of the Constitution. As he said while governor of New York, "We are under a Constitution, but the Constitution is what the judges say it is, and the judiciary is the safeguard of our liberty and of our property under the Constitution."[62] As Justice Stone said in *Butler*, "the only restraint [on the judges] is self-restraint."[63] Governor Hughes made an unqualified defense of the authority of the Supreme Court to act as the final arbiter of all constitutional issues. He recognized that reasonable people could disagree about the appropriate spheres of state and federal authority, but thought "we secure our peace and confidence by loyal acceptance of the decisions of our umpires."[64] During the swearing in ceremony during Roosevelt's first inauguration, it is reported that Hughes read the oath with slow and growing emphasis as he came to the words "promise to support the Constitution of the United States." Roosevelt repeated the words with equal force.[65]

Reasons for the Disagreements

Background Characteristics

There are a number of variations in the background of Roosevelt and Hughes, including age, party affiliation, and work experience, which potentially shed light on the opposing positions they took on certain constitutional issues. In the first place, Hughes belonged to an earlier generation, having been born in 1862, twenty years before Roosevelt's birth. Hughes was a Republican and Roosevelt a Democrat. Hughes was first appointed to the Supreme Court in 1910 by Republican president William Howard Taft and left the Court in 1916 to campaign for the presidency as the nominee of the Republican Party, narrowly losing to incumbent Democrat Woodrow Wilson. After his defeat, Hughes began a law firm that specialized in representing large business corporations and appeared many times before his former colleagues on the Supreme Court in defense of the interests of big business before his selection in 1921 by Warren Harding as secretary of state. He returned to his corporate law practice in 1925, where he remained until his designation as chief justice by President Herbert Hoover in 1930. Liberals in the Senate, such as George Norris, William Borah, and Burton Wheeler, opposed his confirmation as chief justice because of his engagement in Republican politics and corporate law practice. Hughes won confirmation by the vote of fifty-two to twenty-six.

While Hughes was closely associated with corporate interests, Roosevelt was strongly supported by organized labor and agrarian interests. As governor of New York from 1928 to 1932, Roosevelt had supported old-age pensions and unemployment insurance and had obtained a law limiting the working hours of women and children.

A closer examination of their respective backgrounds reveals, however, that they had much in common. Natives of upstate New York, both graduated from Ivy League colleges and studied law at Columbia University. Hughes established his public reputation in 1905 as an investigator of public utilities and was a progressive governor of New York when Roosevelt entered politics for the first time as a New York state senator. During his successful 1910 campaign, Roosevelt allied himself with "good" Republicans, denouncing the Republican incumbent in the senate, John F. Schlosser, for having blocked the reform measures of Governor Hughes. The young Democratic senator supported efforts begun by Hughes to enact a public service law permitting state development of water power and to extend state control of forestation in the face of intense opposition from the state bar association, the banks, and the lumber interests.[66] Hughes's voting record during his six years as an associate justice (1910-16) qualified him as the most liberal member of the Court. Both men had gubernatorial and federal executive experience prior to 1933, Wilson having appointed Roosevelt assistant secretary of the navy in 1913.

Ideology

In the cases that divided the justices along a liberal-conservative line between 1930 and 1937, Hughes voted with the liberal position as often as he did with the conservative position.[67] It is thus difficult to characterize Hughes as a liberal or a conservative. What appears to have been vacillation on Hughes's part, in fact, is partially explained by his role as chief justice. In order to maintain any prospect of future influence, Hughes found it expedient to throw his weight now to the liberals and at other times to the conservative side. This moderation on his part enabled him to lead a Court bitterly divided during Roosevelt's first term between a liberal bloc of three and a conservative bloc of four. Hughes's concern with task leadership limited his ability to serve as the intellectual leader of the Court—roles played by Benjamin Cardozo for the liberals and George Sutherland for the conservatives. Hughes's moderation, however, did not prevent him frequently from taking positions on issues of constitutional interpretation directly opposite those of Roosevelt. In the end, background characteristics and ideology provide little help in explaining the disagreements between Roosevelt and Hughes. A more satisfying explanation lies in the different weights they assigned to the Constitution's goals—liberty being of more importance to Hughes and equality receiving greater weight from Roosevelt—and their views on the role of government in sustaining liberal democracy.

Areas of Constitutional Agreement

There was agreement between the president and the chief justice on several constitutional issues, however, even before Roosevelt introduced his Court reform proposal in February 1937. Between January 1935 and June 1936, Hughes voted with the Administration in five out of twelve cases considered vital by Roosevelt to his economic recovery plan. Each involved a question of constitutional interpretation. He agreed with the president's position on:

(1) abrogation by Congress under a 1933 joint resolution of gold clause provisions in private contracts (in dispute, Article 1, section 8, clause 5: "The Congress shall have Power . . . to coin Money [and] regulate the Value thereof")[68];

(2) abrogation by Congress under a 1933 joint resolution of gold clause provisions in public contracts (in dispute, Article 1, section 8, clause 2: "The Congress shall have Power . . . to borrow money on the credit of the United States")[69];

(3) providing pensions for retired railroad employees under the Railroad Retirement Act of 1934 (in dispute, Article 1, section 8, clause 3: "The Congress shall have Power . . . to regulate Commerce . . . among the several States")[70];

(4) the federal government's power to construct a hydroelectric dam under the National Defense Act of 1916 and to sell the electricity generated by it to the general public by contract (in dispute, Article 1, section 8, clauses 3 and 11 and Article IV, section 3, clause 2: "The Congress shall have Power . . . to regulate Commerce . . . among the several States," "to declare War" and "to dispose of . . . Property belonging to the United States.")[71];

(5) a state's power to set minimum wages for women (in dispute, Fourteenth Amendment, section 1: "No State shall . . . deprive any person of . . . liberty . . . without due process of law.").[72]

The Gold Standard

Public and private contracts in the 1930s routinely granted a right to the creditor to demand payment in gold or its equivalent in U.S. dollars. During the depression, such redemptions would have had a catastrophic effect on debtors and creditors since there was not enough gold in the country to satisfy these demands. In three five to four decisions in 1935, Hughes supported Roosevelt's abrogation in 1933 of gold clause provisions in public and private contracts. Private contracts and contracts made by states and municipalities were subject to Congress's power under Article 1, section 8, to establish a monetary system. Because the contract clause in Article 1, section 10 applies only to state laws, congressional abrogation of contracts was governed by the due process clause of the Fifth Amendment. *Perry v. United States*,[73] thus, required Hughes to determine whether the abrogation was unjust and arbitrary. In his opinion he criticized the Congress and president for violating the terms of federal contracts—an act he considered unjust—but refused to order damages be paid to the plaintiff on the ground that he had failed to show any harm from the abrogation. Hughes's opinions in these cases provoked Justice Stone's contempt for the chief justice's talent at facing both ways—the rights of property as well as the powers of government.

Railroad Regulation

In *Railroad Retirement Board v. Alton Railroad Co.*,[74] the majority held the Railroad Retirement Act of 1934, which established a compulsory retirement and pension system for all carriers subject to the Interstate Commerce Act, unconstitutional. The act fell afoul both of the ban on deprivation of property without due process of law contained in the Fifth Amendment and the prohibition on congressional regulation of intrastate commerce implied in Article 1, section 8. Caring for the social welfare of the worker, said Justice Roberts in the opinion for the Court, was remote from the regulation of commerce. Hughes, in his dissenting opinion, rejected the use of the substantive due process doctrine and pointed out that Congress was correct in concluding that the lack of a pension system had lowered morale among railroad employees, thereby diminishing the efficiency of railroads, an industry vital to the health of interstate commerce. Industry, admonished Hughes, had an obligation to care for "its human wastage," through both workers' compensation and pension plans. He found all but one detail of the act as reasonable and therefore consistent with the requirements of due process.[75]

The Tennessee Valley Authority

Roosevelt's plans for the development of the hydroelectric potential of the Tennessee Valley were the closest that the New Deal came to socialism—government ownership of the means of production. Hughes, speaking for the Court in 1936, held construction of the Wilson Dam at Muscle Shoals, Alabama, an appropriate exercise of the war and commerce powers of the United States and the electricity generated by the dam was the property of the United States, which Congress had a right under

Article 4, section 3 to dispose of by means of sale to customers.[76] As a progressive Republican governor of New York, Hughes had advocated a state monopoly of all streams and reservoirs on public lands, state construction of hydroelectric plants, and the distribution of state-produced power.[77]

Substantive Due Process

Roosevelt opposed the use by the Supreme Court of the due process clauses of the Fifth and Fourteenth Amendments to strike down state and federal regulations of the economy which the justices disliked for moral or policy reasons. He argued that these clauses simply guaranteed certain procedural protections when the government attempted to deprive a defendant in a civil or criminal case of his life, liberty, or property. Between 1888 and 1905, the Supreme Court transformed the due process clauses of the Fifth and Fourteenth Amendments from a guarantee to accused persons of a fair trial into a prohibition on government regulation of the economy. Hughes, in his lectures on the Supreme Court delivered three years before his appointment as chief justice, defended this substantive reading of the phrase.[78]

As chief justice, however, Hughes did not support using the due process clause to strike down progressive legislation by the states and Congress. He dissented, for example, in *Morehead v. People ex rel. Tipaldo*, saying that, because the law met the rest of reasonableness, the due process clause did not prevent the state of New York from setting a minimum wage for women. In *West Coast Hotel Co. v. Parrish*, Hughes wrote the opinion of the Court sustaining the constitutionality of the Washington minimum wage for women, specifically overruling *Adkins v. Children's Hospital*.[79] The *Adkins* Court found the District of Columbia's minimum wage law for women to be a violation of due process. Hughes did not reject substantive due process—he simply used the criterion of reasonableness to determine if a particular policy was unfair. In *U.S. v. Darby Lumber Co.*,[80] Hughes joined Stone's opinion for the Court upholding minimum wages for men, above the subsistence level. Stone held that the Fair Labor Standards Act did not violate the ban on deprivation of liberty or property without due process of law on the grounds that it was a reasonable regulation of conditions affecting interstate commerce.

Liberty of Contract

In *Lochner v. New York*,[81] the Court invalidated a New York law limiting the number of hours that a baker could work on the grounds that it infringed on the "liberty of contract" enjoyed by employer and employee under the due process clause of the Fourteenth Amendment. The liberty-of-contract doctrine could be used by the Court to strike down any state or federal labor regulation. It presented a major potential threat to the New Deal. Hughes indicated his belief that the Constitution contained no such right as early as 1915, when he joined Justice Day's dissent in *Coppage v. Kansas*,[82] a case in which the majority prohibited legislatures from protecting the right of employees to join unions. In *West Coast Hotel*, Hughes concluded, "The Constitution does not speak of freedom of contract."[83] Reasonable regulation of freedom is due process and therefore constitutional, according to Hughes.[84]

The Double Standard

In *Near v. Minnesota*,[85] and *Stromberg v. California*,[86] Hughes strongly supported freedom of the press and freedom of speech. Robert Jackson commented on Hughes's retirement in 1948, "In the numerous cases dealing with civil liberties he has been a consistent and forthright champion of the American freedoms."[87] Both Roosevelt and Hughes established reputations as champions of the Negro, in the fight for civil rights for this abused minority.[88] In the *St. Joseph Stockyards* case, Hughes said there was no constitutional warrant for differentiating between personal liberty and property rights. He denied that greater latitude by courts in making independent determinations of fact in cases affecting personal liberty, as distinguished from those affecting property, was justified. All restrictions on liberty were subject to the same test—reasonableness. This was also Roosevelt's position. Unlike Justice Stone and subsequent Courts, however, Hughes did not subject infringements on personal liberties to a higher standard of scrutiny than limitations on property rights.

The Contracts Clause

In *Home Building and Loan Association v. Blaisdell*,[89] Hughes sustained the constitutionality of the Minnesota Mortgage Moratorium Act. He suggested "that limitations of the constitution may be put aside provided only that to enforce them would bring such a degree of violence and lawlessness as to place in jeopardy the authority of government to maintain peace and good order."[90] Hughes stated that "emergency may furnish the occasion for the exercise of power."[91] For Hughes, the contracts clause limitation came to equal the due process restriction, which meant reasonableness.

Although the contracts clause does not apply to Congress, the reasonableness standard was the one Roosevelt urged on the Court when judging the New Deal. Conservatives strongly criticized Hughes's opinion as a threat to property rights. The Court's decision in *Blaisdell* came soon after its decision in *Nebbia v. New York*[92] sustaining a New York statute that fixed maximum and minimum prices for the sale of milk. Chief Justice Hughes joined Justice Roberts's opinion for the Court. The four dissenters claimed that the sale of milk was not a business affected with a public interest and therefore lay outside the scope of the state's police power to protect the public welfare and health. James M. Beck, who had been

Republican president Warren Harding's solicitor general, called the *Nebbia* case "as unfortunate as the Dred Scott decision." The two decisions, *Blaisdell* and *Nebbia*, taken together meant, said Justice McReynolds, "the end of the Constitution as you and I regarded it."[93]

Tax Immunity of Governmental Instrumentalities

The first two acts of Congress declared unconstitutional by the Hughes Court were laws taxing states and their agencies. Hughes was with the majority in both cases.[94] The chief justice thus refused to disturb the precedent of *Collector v. Day*,[95] in which the Court exempted state instrumentalities from federal taxation. While governor of New York, Hughes had opposed the Sixteenth Amendment on the ground that it would nullify *Collector v. Day* and permit federal taxation of the states' employees. The immunity of state agencies from federal taxation, and the assumptions about state sovereignty on which the doctrine was based, were inconsistent with the principles of the New Deal.

Following the introduction of the president's plan for modifying the composition of the Supreme Court, Hughes in fact abandoned the view that the sovereignty of the states rendered them immune from federal taxation and concurred in Stone's opinions in *Helvering v. Gerhardt*[96] removing constitutional immunity of salaries of state employees from federal income taxation.

The Living Constitution

In *Home Building and Loan Association v. Blaisdell*, Hughes criticized the view that the Constitution's meaning was fixed when its words were drafted and ratified. He subordinated the original intention of the framers of the Constitution to judicial interpretation: "If by the statement that what the Constitution meant at the time of its adoption it means to-day, it is intended to say that the great clauses of the constitution must be confined to the interpretation which the framers, with the conditions and outlook of their time, would have placed upon them, the statement carries its own refutation." Hughes sharply dismissed the suggestion that the words of the Constitution had to mean to "the vision of our time" exactly what they meant to the founders.[97] Sutherland, Butler, McReynolds, and Van Devanter denied that the document's meaning changes with the times and insisted that judges are bound by the words' original meaning and their framers' intent.

Roosevelt likewise rejected the concept of the Constitution as a rigid document. In August 1935, Roosevelt dictated to George Creel an article that appeared under Creel's signature in *Collier's*. The essay, entitled "Looking Ahead with Roosevelt," stressed the president's "deep conviction" that the Constitution was not meant to be a "dead hand," chilling human aspiration and blocking humanity's advance, but rather "a living force for the expression of the national will with respect to national needs."[98] When he took the oath of office at the hands of Chief Justice Hughes in January 1937, Roosevelt said he wanted to cry out to Hughes, "I will support the Constitution as *I* understand it, flexible enough to meet any new problem of democracy—not the kind of Constitution your Court has raised up as a barrier to progress and democracy."[99] A good example of Roosevelt's flexible attitude toward constitutional exegesis is his approach to construing the commerce clause. During the Black Monday press conference, he said, "The country was in the horse-and-buggy age when [the interstate commerce] clause was written." In order for Congress to achieve the goals set out in the Constitution, it must have the ability to give phrases new meaning as conditions change, as FDR had argued since the beginning of his presidency. "The hope has been," intoned Roosevelt, "that we could, through a period of years, interpret the interstate clause of the Constitution in the light of these new things that have come to the country."[100]

The *Minnesota Mortgage* case revealed a similar liberal attitude on Hughes's part toward the task of constitutional construction. "The economic interests of the State may justify the excuse of its continuing and dominant protective power," Hughes stated in the opinion for the Court, "notwithstanding interference with contracts" as explicitly prohibited by Article 1, section 10.[101]

The Constitutional Legacy of the Hughes–Roosevelt Dialectic

Where FDR Prevailed

Roosevelt's constitutional understanding has been vindicated in a number of aspects, most importantly with regard to congressional power over the economy. His position has prevailed on the following issues.

The Powers of Congress

The doctrine of nondelegation of legislative power. No law since 1935 has been struck down on these grounds. Delegation without standards to guide executive discretion has become common in federal law, without judicial opposition.

Scope of the commerce, taxing, and general welfare powers. There are few limits on Congress's commerce power. The Supreme Court, however, in 1995 narrowed the scope of commerce somewhat in *United States v. Lopez*,[102] striking down a federal law banning handguns from the zone surrounding public schools. The majority thought the link between school safety and interstate commerce was too tenuous to justify federal regulation of firearms within school zones. The taxing power can be used for purposes of regulation, even in the area of legislating morality. Congress may tax, spend, and legislate in order to promote the general welfare.

The Reserved Powers of the States

The doctrine of dual federalism has been thoroughly discredited. It had a brief resurgence in *National League of Cities v. Usery*,[103] where the majority struck down the Fair Labor Standards Act to the extent it imposed minimum wage and maximum hour limitations on state and local governments, but it was again discarded in *Garcia v. San Antonio Metropolitan Transit Authority*.[104]

Where Hughes Prevailed

It is also the case that Hughes's positions on several constitutional questions have triumphed—most importantly his conception of the role of the courts in the American political system.

The Executive Power

Doctrine of emergency power. In *Schechter*, Hughes rejected the notion that emergencies enlarge the powers of the president. The Court reiterated this view when, in *Youngstown Sheet and Tube Co. v. Sawyer*,[105] it ordered President Harry Truman to return the nation's steel mills to their owners, mills that Truman had seized in order to prevent a strike that would disrupt the war effort in Korea.

Removal power of the president. According to Hughes's decision in *Humphrey's Executor v. U.S.*, the president cannot remove members of independent regulatory commissions except for cause. This view of the scope of the presidential removal power has stood.

The Judicial Power

The size of the Supreme Court. The Supreme Court's complement of justices has remained at nine since 1869.[106] This number has taken the form of a constitutional custom, accepted now by all parties. In Canada, Great Britain, and other countries patterned after British government, constitutional customs are as fixed as practices and institutions specifically delineated in the basic law. An example is the office of prime minister, which has no formal constitutional status but in practice heads the government. In a letter read to Congress in 1937, Hughes maintained that it was unconstitutional for the Supreme Court to work in panels. The entire Court must be involved with each case from the moment it is considered for review until the final judgment is rendered. The refusal to work in divisions is a key distinguishing mark of the U.S. Supreme Court as compared with analogous tribunals in other industrial democracies.

Mandatory retirement age for judges. Hughes's 1937 letter entered as testimony before the Congress in which he pointed out that the Court was not behind in its work and that the advanced age of many of the justices did not impede the institution's efficiency was effective in undermining the rationale for mandatory retirement of justices. The government can only encourage retirement through generous pensions and offers of reduced workload if a judge chooses senior status. This lack of a mandatory retirement age is another feature distinguishing the U.S. Supreme Court from its counterparts. The German Constitutional Court, for instance, sits in two permanent, specialized panels, called senates, of eight judges each. The justices serve for one twelve-year term, and there is a mandatory retirement age of sixty-eight.[107] The German justices must render decisions in those cases referred to them by lower court judges and the government. Commentators agree that these institutional differences render the German Court less capable of exercising judicial review than the U.S. Supreme Court. As a result of the Judges Act of 1925, strongly supported by Hughes, the Supreme Court acquired gradually complete discretion over its docket. It hears only those cases that the justices deem of great national significance. This discretion frees the Court from congestion and overload and, more importantly, maximizes the capability of the Court to have a major impact on the nation's policy agenda. Hughes, thus, played a central role in promoting and protecting the institutional foundation of a powerful high Court armed with the ability and the will to strike down important actions of the legislative and executive branches at the state and federal level.

Judicial review of administrative agency decisions. Chief Justice Hughes was ahead of his time in demanding that exercises of discretion by administrators be subject to judicial review and that administrative decision making processes resemble trials. In the 1970s a so-called "due process revolution" occurred, in which the Supreme Court greatly expanded the scope of judicial review of agency decisions and imposed stringent requirements of due process on administrative tribunals. Symbolic of this judicialization of the executive branch was the renaming of hearing officers as administrative judges. This process has developed to the point where for all practical purposes many federal administrative bodies, such as the Environmental Protection Agency, have been incorporated into the judicial branch of government.[108] There is now a very limited sphere of administrative discretion that is nonreviewable by the courts.

Supreme Court as final arbiter of the Constitution's meaning. Presidents and members of Congress rarely challenge the authority of the High Court to be the final word on the Constitution's meaning. The practice of attempting to overturn judicial decisions by means of constitutional amendment acknowledges the judiciary's supremacy in constitutional interpretation. President Ronald Reagan, for example, a vocal critic of judicial activism, asked Congress to propose to the states several amendments, including ones that would nullify *Roe v. Wade*,[109] *Engel v. Vitale*,[110] and *Abington School District v. Schempp*,[111] dealing with abortion, school prayer, and Bible reading, respectively. Roosevelt's Court-packing plan failed in large part because the American people had come, as Madison predicted they would in *Federalist* No. 49, to revere the

Constitution and to regard the Supreme Court as its guardian. The public is more likely to view the legislative and executive branches as enemies of the basic law than the judiciary, and this belief reinforces the tendency of the Court to view itself as the final arbiter of the document's meaning.

Conclusion

What emerged from the battle between Hughes and Roosevelt over the constitutionality of the New Deal in the period 1935-37 was a constitutional balance between the courts and the Congress that has persisted to the present. Hughes prevailed on issues of the independence of the Supreme Court and the role of the Court as the final arbiter of the Constitution. Hughes thus put himself at odds with Justice Felix Frankfurter, a close adviser to Roosevelt during his struggle with the Hughes Court, who declared in 1939, "The ultimate touchstone of constitutionality is the Constitution itself and not what we have said about it."[112] Unlike Jefferson and Lincoln, who also had battled chief justices over the meaning of the Constitution and the scope of legislative, executive, and judicial power, Roosevelt largely succeeded in persuading his judicial nemesis. He lost, however, the opportunity to subordinate the Court to the executive and Congress. The Madisonian view often expressed by FDR that constitutional conflicts would be resolved by reference to the people and that the greatest check against tyranny was in the country's political and economic structure did not prevail. Hughes, thus, laid the foundation for the judicial activism of the Warren and Burger Courts (1952-85)—an activism in favor not of property rights but of personal rights and equality for disadvantaged groups in American society.[113]

Roosevelt triumphed on the issue of the power of the federal and state governments to regulate the economy, making possible the modern welfare state, with its redistributive policies. Ironically, the New Deal represented the victory of an earlier chief justice, Roger Taney, who ruled for the Court in the *Charles River Bridge* case that, when in conflict, rights of private property must yield to the public interest.

ENDNOTES

1. Arthur M. Schlesinger Jr., *The Politics of Upheaval* (Boston: Houghton Mifflin, 1960), p. 484.

2. Martin Diamond restricts his list to liberty, majority rule, and competent government. See his *The Democratic Republic*, 2nd ed. (Chicago: Rand McNally, 1970), pp. 8–9. For Alexis de Tocqueville, however, "equality of condition" was what distinguished the United States from its European counterparts. See his *Democracy in America*, ed. Phillips Bradley, (New York: Alfred A. Knopf, 1945).

3. See James Madison, *The Federalist* No. 37 (New York: The New American Library, 1961), pp. 226–27.

4. Lief H. Carter, *Reason in Law*, 4th ed. (New York: HarperCollins, 1994), p. 3.

5. 31 U.S. 515 (1832).

6. Quoted in Charles Warren, *The Supreme Court in United States History*, rev. ed. (Boston: Little, Brown, 1926), vol. 1, p. 759.

7. *Ex parte Merryman*, 17 Fed. Cases 144 (1861).

8. See Kenneth M. Holland, "Abraham Lincoln and Roger Taney: President vs. Chief Justice," *Quarterly Journal of Ideology* 17 (June 1994): 5–33.

9. 1 Cranch (5 U.S.) 137 (1803).

10. 2 Black (67 U.S.) 635 (1863).

11. Schlesinger, *Politics of Upheaval*.

12. F.D.G. Ribble, "The Constitutional Doctrines of Chief Justice Hughes," *Columbia Law Review* 41 (1941): 1190, 1192–93.

13. *West Coast Hotel Co. v. Parrish* (1937).

14. Schlesinger, *The Politics of Upheaval*, p. 483.

15. *Panama Refining Co. v. Ryan*, 293 U.S. 389 (1935).

16. *Louisville Joint Stock Land Bank v. Radford*, 295 U.S. 555 (1935).

17. *Schechter Poultry Corporation v. United States*, 295 U.S. 495 (1935).

18. *Carter v. Carter Coal Co.*, 298 U.S. 238 (1936).

19. *United States v. Butler*, 297 U.S. 1 (1936).

20. *Humphrey's Executor v. United States*, 295 U.S. 602 (1935).

21. *Jones v. Securities and Exchange Commission*, 298 U.S. 1 (1936).

22. Quoted in Samuel Hendel, "Charles Evans Hughes," in *The Justices of the United States Supreme Court 1789-1969: Their Lives and Major Opinions*, vol. III, ed. Leon Friedman and Fred L. Israel (New York: R.R. Bowker Co., 1969), p. 1909.

23. 293 U.S. 388 (1935).

24. 295 U.S.495 (1935).

25. Ibid., p. 529.
26. Ibid., pp. 537–38.
27. Ibid., p. 542.
28. 298 U.S. 238 (1936).
29. 295 U.S. 495, 553–54 (1935).
30. 298 U.S. 238, 317 (1936).
31. Quoted in Hendel, "Charles Evans Hughes," p. 1909.
32. 234 U.S. 342 (1914).
33. 312 U.S. 100 (1941).
34. 297 U.S. 1 (1936).
35. Robert H. Jackson, *The Struggle for Judicial Supremacy* (New York: Alfred A. Knopf, 1941).
36. 301 U.S. 548 (1937).
37. Quoted in Samuel Hendel, *Charles Evans Hughes and the Supreme Court* (New York: Russell & Russell, 1951), p. 235.
38. Quoted in Michael Kammen, *A Machine That Would Go of Itself: The Constitution in American Culture* (New York: Alfred A. Knopf, 1987) p. 259.
39. Franklin D. Roosevelt, *Public Papers* (1933), pp. 14–15; (1935), p. 15.
40. 295 U.S. 602 (1935).
41. Charles Evans Hughes, *The Supreme Court of the United States* (Columbia University Lectures, 1927) (New York: 1928).
42. James MacGregor Burns, *Roosevelt: The Lion and the Fox* (New York: Harcourt, Brace & World, 1956), p. 232.
43. 299 U.S. 334 (1937).
44. 247 U.S. 251 (1918).
45. 301 U.S. 1 (1937).
46. *Houston, East and West Texas R.R. v. United States*, 234 U.S. 342 (1914).
47. 285 U.S. 22 (1932).
48. 298 U.S. 38 (1936).
49. 304 U.S. 1 (1938).
50. Ibid., p. 18.
51. *New York Times*, 13 May 1938.
52. Ribble, "Charles Evans Hughes," p. 1209.
53. 298 U.S. 38, 92 (1936).
54. Hendel, *Charles Evans Hughes*, pp. 111–13.
55. Burns, *Lion and the Fox*, p. 302.
56. Quoted in Schlesinger, *The Politics of Upheaval*, p. 484.
57. Ibid.
58. Ibid.
59. Ibid., p. 26.
60. Ibid., p. 485.
61. Quoted in Bernard Asbell, *The F.D.R. Memoirs* (Garden City, NY: Doubleday, 1973), p. 181.
62. Charles E. Hughes, *Addresses of Charles Evans Hughes* (New York: Putnam, 1916), pp. 185–86.
63. 297 U.S. 1, 29 (1936) (Stone, J., dissenting).

64. Hendel, "Charles Evans Hughes," p. 1896.

65. Burns, *Lion and the Fox*, p. 291.

66. Felix Frankfurter to Franklin D. Roosevelt, May 18, 1934, in *Roosevelt and Frankfurter: Their Correspondence 1928-1945,* ann. Max Freedman (Boston: Little, Brown, 1967), p. 217. Burns, *Lion and the Fox*, p. 46.

67. Irving Brant (1937), quoted in Schlesinger, *The Politics of Upheaval*, p. 467.

68. *Norman v. Baltimore & Ohio R. R.*, 294 U.S. 240 (1935).

69. *Perry v. United States*, 294 U.S. 330 (1935). Actually, Hughes and Roosevelt agreed that Congress could abrogate gold clause provisions in contracts issued by the states, such as municipal bonds, but disagreed on the question of whether the national government could renege on its own promises to redeem federal bonds in gold. Hughes held that the federal government had a moral obligation to honor its commitments and Congress had no power to override this obligation. Roosevelt won, in fact, however, because Hughes denied relief to the plaintiff on the grounds that he had failed to show damages as a result of the abrogation.

70. *Railroad Retirement Board v. Alton Railroad Co.*, 295 U.S. 330 (1935).

71. *Ashwander v. Tennessee Valley Authority*, 297 U.S. 288 (1936).

72. *Morehead v. People ex rel. Tipaldo*, 298 U.S. 587 (1936).

73. 294 U.S. 330 (1935).

74. 295 U.S. 330 (1935).

75. Ibid., pp. 375–92.

76. 297 U.S. 288 (1936).

77. Asbell, *F.D.R Memoirs*, p. 94.

78. Hendel, *Charles Evans Hughes*, p. 116.

79. 261 U.S. 525 (1923).

80. 312 U.S. 100 (1941).

81. 198 U.S. 45 (1905).

82. 236 U.S. 1 (1915).

83. 300 U.S. 379, 391 (1937).

84. Ibid.

85. 283 U.S. 697 (1931).

86. 283 U.S. 359 (1931).

87. Quoted in Hendel, "Charles Evans Hughes," p. 1906.

88. *The Nation*, June 14, 1941, p. 685.

89. 290 U.S. 398 (1934).

90. Quoted in Hendel, "Charles Evans Hughes," p. 1906.

91. Hughes in *Blaisdell*: "While emergency does not create power, emergency may furnish the occasion for the exercise of power." 290 U.S. 398, 426 (1934).

92. 291 U.S. 502 (1934).

93. Morton Keller, *In Defense of Yesterday: James M. Beck and the Politics of Conservatism* (New York, 1958), p. 254. Also see *Nebbia*, p. 555 (McReynolds, J., dissenting).

94. *Indian Motorcycle Co. v. United States*, 283 U.S. 5 70 (1931) and *Burnet v. Coronado Oil and Gas Co.*, 285 U.S. 393 (1932).

95. 11 Wall. (78 U.S.) 113 (1871).

96. 304 U.S. 405(1938).

97. *Home Building and Loan Association v. Blaisdell*, 290 U.S. 426, 437, 442 (1934).

98. George Creel, "Looking Ahead with Roosevelt," *Collier's*, September 7, 1935, p. 40.

99. Samuel I. Rosenman, *Working with Roosevelt* (New York: Harper & Brothers, 1952), p. 144.

100. Quoted in Asbell, *F. D. R. Memoirs*, p. 181.

101. 290 U.S. 398, 437 (1934).

102. 514 U.S. 549 (1995).

103. 426 U.S. 833 (1976).

104. 469 U.S. 528 (1985).

105. 343 U.S. 579 (1952).

106. Henry Abraham describes the ninth seat as a gift to President Ulysses Grant from the Reconstruction Congress, elated at the departure of the detested Andrew Johnson. *Justices & Presidents: A Political History of Appointments to the Supreme Court*, 2nd ed. (New York: Oxford University Press, 1985), p. 126.

107. Kenneth M. Holland, "The Courts in the Federal Republic of Germany," in *The Political Role of Law Courts in Modern Democracies*, ed. Jerold L. Waltman and Kenneth M. Holland (New York: St. Martin's Press, 1988), pp. 90–93.

108. Kenneth M. Holland, "The Role of the Courts in Environmental Policymaking in the United States," in *Federalism and the Environment: Environmental Policymaking in the United States, Canada, and Australia*, ed. Kenneth M. Holland, F.L. Morton, and Brian Galligan (Westport, CT: Greenwood Press, 1996), pp. 159–83.

109. 410 U.S. 113 (1973).

110. 370 U.S. 421 (1962).

111. 374 U.S. 203 (1963).

112. *Graves v. New York ex rel. O'Keefe*, 306 U.S. 466, 491–92 (1939).

113. Justice Stone announced the double standard, whereby regulations of economic rights would be subject to less stringent scrutiny than infringements on individual rights and the interests of racial and religious minorities, in *United States v. Carolene Products*, 304 U.S. 144 (1938).

5

The Nomination and Confirmation of Hugo L. Black to the U.S. Supreme Court

The Shreveport Reaction

Elaine T. King

In the dog days of 1937 as August humidity gripped the Ark-La-Tex like a sweaty hand, Shreveporters sipped iced tea and read in their local newspapers about the political heat wave engulfing New Dealers in Washington. President Franklin D. Roosevelt's surprise August 12 nomination of Senator Hugo Lafayette Black (D-AL) to the U.S. Supreme Court had rekindled tempers still smoldering from the firestorm ignited on February 5 by his impolitic Court-packing proposal. The political drama unfolded in the morning on the pages of the *Shreveport Times* and in the afternoon editions of its rival daily, the *Shreveport Journal*, from August 13 to October 12, 1937. "I know only what I have read in the newspapers," President Roosevelt told reporters regarding the controversy that erupted over Black's alleged membership in the Ku Klux Klan.[1] Local residents more so than the president knew only what they read in their newspapers, and a closer inspection of the two Shreveport dailies reveals that what readers knew was influenced by which paper served as their chief news source.

The Shreveport Papers React

With a population of approximately 82,000 in 1937, Shreveport was a two-newspaper town. The *Shreveport Times*, the staid morning daily owned by the Ewing family, boasted daily circulation of 40,721 and Sunday circulation of 49,805.[2] The afternoon *Shreveport Journal*, owned by the Attaway family, was a fierce competitor, but its circulation Mondays through Saturdays lagged at 31,470.[3] Even though both newspapers self-described their political perspective as "Democrat,"[4] in light of their keen competition it is not surprising that the two dailies approached their coverage from different perspectives or that both filled large portions of their news pages with stories devoted to the furor. The Black nomination received relatively little attention, however, in local editorials, syndicated columns, or photographs.

From its inception, the Hugo Black story was front-page news in Shreveport. Apart from the obvious national significance of the Supreme Court nomination in the wake of the recent bitter Court-packing battle, the senior senator from Alabama was a southerner, an added ingredient of local interest. The fifty-one-year-old Black was one of the president's staunchest New Deal lieutenants, having risen to national power from unlikely rural roots. Stories about Black contained almost no biographical information and only one story attempted to profile him at all. That story summarizes his early background: "A native of Clay County, Alabama, Black was born in 1886, and attended public school in the little town of Ashland. Later at the wish of his parents he attended Birmingham Medical College for a year, but switched to the law school at the University of Alabama."[5] The Associated Press report then touched on his professional life: "He started practice at Birmingham and held minor offices, including a police court judgeship, before his election to the senate as a 'dark horse' candidate in 1926."[6] The attention paid to Black's background seems particularly sketchy in light of the intense media scrutiny of today's Supreme Court nominees, but it was not unusual for its day.

The *Times* broke the nomination story locally on the morning of August 13, 1937, and played it for the major news that it was. Roosevelt had nominated Black to the Supreme Court allegedly as "payback" to southern congressmen who had taken the lead "in defeating or blunting a series of New Deal bills" in 1937. Black was "the most liberal southerner in the Senate, and [the conservatives] denied him the courtesy of automatic confirmation usually bestowed upon congressional colleagues."[7] The initial local story commanded a banner headline with four "decks," smaller headlines beneath the banner. A head and shoulders photograph of Senator Black appeared below the headline. It was one of only two photographs related to the story that the *Times* ran during the period. The page one layout underscored the significance of the story, displaying it down the left column of the front page before jumping the rest of the story to an inside page. The *Times*, which subscribed to both United Press (UP) and Associated Press (AP), selected a nonbylined UP story.

The *Journal* displayed the initial nomination story less prominently on its front page that same afternoon. "Subcommittee Favors Black" was the two-column headline above the fold, indicating by both layout and headline type that it was a significant story. The *Journal*, like the *Times*, used a layout technique common to the era and continued the story from the front page to an inside page.

Both the *Times* and *Journal* printed lengthy initial stories. As opposition to the nomination and appointment crescendoed, especially following accusations of Black's Ku Klux Klan membership, both newspapers continued to feed the public appetite for information about new developments in the political fight. In reviewing the coverage provided in the Shreveport dailies, the most obvious differences between the *Times* and *Journal* stories are stylistic. The *Journal* tended toward sensationalism in its stories, a direct reflection of what editors of an afternoon newspaper "felt they needed to do to get people to buy and subscribe. Afternoon papers were more flamboyant, more colorful than morning newspapers. It was a matter of style rather than political philosophy."[8] The *Times*, in the tradition of morning newspapers, selected stories that lacked much of the color found in the afternoon *Journal* stories, and also appear to be more objective. However, journalistic style is but one obvious measure. Equally significant but less apparent are other, more subtle factors such as possible editorial influence in news columns, number of stories used, sources of those stories, where editors allocated the stories within the paper, and column inches devoted to the stories over the eight-week period.[9] These constitute a framework against which the stories can be assessed.

Fundamental to any newspaper is its editorial position; it defines the character of the newspaper to the public. Its editorials provide a platform to espouse the newspaper's views, and its choice of editorial columnists contributes to the exchange of ideas on issues of public concern.

The *Journal* took an activist approach to the national debate when compared with the *Times*. *Journal* editors addressed the issue of Black's nomination and qualifications five times during August and September (see Figure 1). Initial editorial reaction to the president's nominee was negative. *Journal* criticism of FDR's choice was two-pronged: Black's lack of judicial experience and the appearance of political reward to a loyal New Dealer. "He does not seem to have the judicial temperament and experience . . . and his appointment, of course, will be generally regarded as the payment of a political debt due to his stalwart, unbroken support of the various New Deal proposals."[10]

As opponents of Black's nomination scrambled immediately to find defensible reasons to block his ascent to the high bench, *Journal* editorial writers noted apparent political overtones and chastised such efforts. "Those who oppose confirmation of Senator Hugo Black of Alabama as a member

Figure 1

Comparison of the newspaper coverages by the *Shreveport Times* and the *Shreveport Journal*, between August 13 and October 12, 1937, of Senator Hugo Black's nomination to the United States Supreme Court.

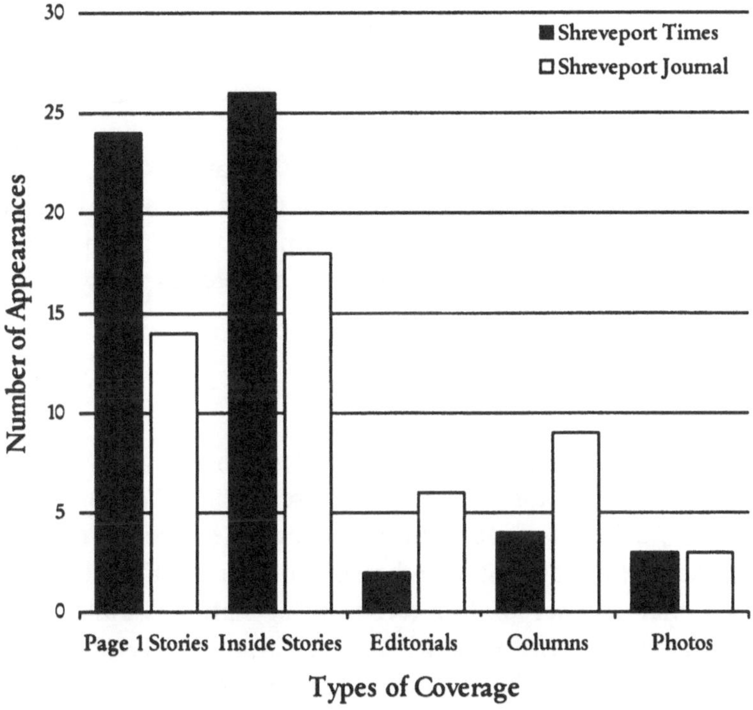

of the supreme court had plenty of arguments to support their contentions, without resorting to the sophomoric stuff of which some were guilty."[11] The *Journal* reaffirmed its argument that "the opposition to Senator Black should have been based on one thing—that his experience did not qualify him for the exalted position."[12] Four days later the *Journal* used its editorial page to direct criticism at Black's perceived lack of qualifications, this time reprinting a like-minded editorial from the Springfield, Massachusetts, *Union*.[13] The *Journal* and *Union* were but two editorial voices chanting warnings like the chorus in a Greek tragedy: "The press—no more a friend of the Senator's than of his President—roasted Black."[14] Attempts in the Senate by Roosevelt's foes to derail Black's nomination almost led to a fist fight among senators on August 16 before the Senate Judiciary Committee recommended approval of the nomination by a thirteen to four vote, sending the issue to the Senate floor.[15] On August 17, "after hours of bitter debate in which Black's foes pictured him as unfit for judicial robes because of Ku Klux Klan sympathies" the Senate confirmed Black as an associate justice of the Supreme Court by a vote of sixty-three to sixteen.[16]

The KKK Bombshell

Beginning September 13, after Black had sworn his oath privately but before he took his seat, the *Pittsburgh Post-Gazette*, a Hearst paper, ran an inflammatory series of articles that accused Black of membership in the KKK, bringing the emotional subject to the forefront of national attention and polarizing an entire nation.[17] Almost immediately, the *Journal* responded editorially, reminding readers that senators had been apprised of the charges of Klan membership against Black before they confirmed him on August 17: "The great majority of them saw nothing in that charge that should be sufficient to bar him from service."[18] Neither did the *Journal* find Klan membership a legitimate objection to Black serving on the high Court: "For that matter, what is there about membership in the klan to disqualify any man from holding any office?"[19] The editorial reflected the view of many white southerners of the period as well as that of administration supporters including the Order of Railway Conductors, representatives of organized labor.[20]

Complicating the issue of Black's appointment was President Roosevelt's public pronouncements of his continued interest in reorganizing the federal judiciary despite the decisive congressional defeat of his judicial reform measures in July. The indistinct line between FDR's court reorganization and Black's selection blurred further in the public eye. The *Journal* noted in an editorial in late September that opponents of the Court plan had been strengthened by the contest over Black's appointment: "They will be able to point to that selection and say if F.D.R. erred so grievously in his first selection, it would be extremely dangerous to give him authority to name five new members of the court at this or any other time." [21]

The final *Journal* editorial barb was thrown a few days later through commentary on the announcement from Washington that the Supreme Court had selected "a negro and a Catholic" for Black's messenger in keeping with then-standard practice. "Each justice is assigned a negro messenger, and we suspect Justice Black will not concern himself over the identity of the individual chosen. It remains to be seen what the Ku Kluxers have to say about it."[22]

By contrast, the *Times* exercised its editorial prerogative only once during the period to comment directly on the nomination, although it had editorially supported the judicial reorganization plan. The single editorial about Black appeared the day after the announcement story and justified the president's action as a response to his failed court reform effort. "We believe that the people—and the senate—understand the president's position and sense the rightness of his choice."[23] Black's southern heritage played at least some role in the *Times*' editorial support. "We express deep satisfaction over the fact that it would give the Deep South representation in the supreme court."[24]

Equally significant may be the editorial silence maintained by both papers after Black's unprecedented live radio speech on October 1, 1937. The twelve-minute address was broadcast "over three nation-wide chains to 285 stations."[25] As before in his political career, Black made skillful use of the radio to carry his own message unfiltered by reporters to the public. He answered his critics, set the record straight about his former association with the Klan, and affirmed his belief in and commitment to equality for all under the Constitution. The *Times'* extensive coverage the next morning included the complete text of Black's 1,066-word speech. Later that Saturday, the *Journal* printed a thorough summary story that wove sections of the historic address into the story but did not present the text in full. In his speech, heard by the second-largest radio audience at the time of the broadcast,[26] Black addressed the issue head on, citing his liberal record during his eleven years in the Senate to refute charges of religious and racial intolerance. When he spoke to the heart of the controversy it was simple and emphatic: "I did join the Klan. I later resigned. I never rejoined . . . and never expect to do so. . . When this statement is ended my discussion of the question is closed."[27] He assumed his seat on October 4, and he never discussed the issue again.[28] Later, in similar reaction to Black's radio address, the two Shreveport dailies apparently chose not to comment editorially about the Supreme Court's summary rejection of legal attempts by Black's opponents to remove him from his seat.

Although local editorials were limited, they offer some insight into the perspectives of the two papers on both court reform and Hugo Black as an associate justice of the Supreme Court. Those insights are helpful as other aspects of print coverage are examined.

Syndicated columns that appeared on both the news and editorial pages of both dailies gave local readers glimpses of others' perspectives on the issue and added tidbits of information. The *Journal* published eight columns that addressed some aspect of the controversy while the *Times* carried four columns during the same period, suggesting that *Journal* readers were exposed to more diverse views on the subject.

Photographs, that visual dimension of an otherwise print medium, are one indication of the prominence of a story, emphasizing the article by drawing the reader's eye. Four photographs of Black—two each in the *Times* and *Journal*—appeared over the course of the eight weeks. All were front-page photographs. It must be noted that in 1937 technology was still in its developmental stages, and photograph usage in that era cannot be compared to those in today's visually oriented newspaper layouts. Also worth noting is that both photos in the *Times* appear to have been file photographs but the *Journal* photographs represented Black in surroundings directly related to the Supreme Court issue.

A Comparative Evaluation

While all elements of coverage should be considered, the news columns themselves allow the most direct comparisons between the *Times* and *Journal*. Three variables are considered in the comparison of the news coverage: number of stories, source of story origin, and placement of stories within the newspaper.

From August 13, 1937, the day that the nomination was announced in both dailies, until October 12, when it was reported that the Supreme Court had rejected legal challenges to Black's appointment, the *Times* ran fifty-five articles, inclusive of news, editorials, and columns. During the same period, the *Journal* published forty-seven articles. This lesser number can be explained in part by the fact that the *Journal* published only six days a week, Monday through Saturday, while the *Times* published seven days a week. News stories predominated in both papers. The *Times* published fifty news stories; the *Journal* tally was thirty-three. Of the fifty news stories in the *Times*, twenty-four appeared on the front page of the paper. By comparison, the *Journal* placed only fourteen of its thirty-three stories on page one.

In addition to major stories, defined as those displayed on the front page, the *Times* and *Journal* devoted considerable inside news space to other stories about the events surrounding Black's nomination and appointment. Page one and inside stories were almost evenly divided in the *Times*, twenty-four to twenty-six. However, the *Journal* placed nineteen of its thirty-three stories inside. Based upon the number of stories and their placement, we can conclude that *Times* readers had access to more information than those who read only the *Journal*.

Source of origin comparisons show that the *Times* used an almost equal mix of stories from United Press and Associated Press. The *Journal* was affiliated only with Associated Press; twenty-eight of its thirty-three news stories were attributed to Associated Press. The source for the other four was not indicated. There were no local news stories written about Black and the ensuing political battle over his suitability to sit on the Supreme Court. Stories were national in focus; only one short Associated Press story that appeared in the late period had a direct Louisiana connection. That story quoted Senator Allen J. Ellender (D-LA) as supporting Justice Black, "I don't care if he was a member of the Ku Klux Klan. He is fitted [sic] to hold a supreme court justiceship and has taken the oath. So let's let him serve."[29]

The origins of stories published in the two papers are significant in terms of credibility of the articles. The Associated Press and United Press were respected national news services known for professional reporting standards. Therefore, both newspapers can be viewed as presenting generally accurate accounts of events as they transpired. However, even within the same wire service there is a menu of hard news and related "sidebar" stories were offered to subscriber papers, giving editors a choice of news stories from which to select.

Conclusion

It was the selection of stories coupled with editorial comment and editorial judgment of how to present the news that imprinted each paper's coverage with a particular style that, in retrospect, was perhaps as important in influencing Shreveporters about Hugo Black as the articles that appeared in their hometown papers. Those who depended entirely upon one or both of the two Democratic Shreveport papers were served a very different editorial menu from that provided to readers of the many vehemently anti-Roosevelt newspapers whose political policy was often Republican. Roosevelt and his administration had engaged regularly in skirmishes with his anti-New Deal editorial foes since his first election: "Anti-Roosevelt publishers used to complain that FDR had hypnotized their Washington reporters with his charm and misled them with his propaganda, as Leo Rosten put it in his 1937 book on the Washington Correspondents."[30] The furor over Black predictably juxtaposed Roosevelt Democrats against Republicans, a battle played out in national headlines and editorial columns, including local ones.

What none of the newspapers locally or nationally were able to foresee was Black's potential as a justice, although the optimistic predictions of a few seem prophetic in retrospect: "Out in St. Louis, Irving Brant . . . wrote an editorial predicting that the new Justice would become the Court's foremost champion of civil rights, only to see it suppressed in favor of one attacking Black as a Klansman."[31] The *Montgomery Advertiser* wrote: "What a joke it would be on Hugo's impassioned detractors if he should now turn out to be a very great justice of the Supreme Court."[32]

The ex-Ku Klux Klan member would go on to develop his own jurisprudence and become one of the most vigorous defenders of the First Amendment in the history of the Supreme Court. Moreover, the crudely educated Southerner had the audacity to challenge Felix Frankfurter, Roosevelt's third and most intellectual appointee to the Court, convincing his brethren to "nationalize" the Bill of Rights. For these accomplishments, scholars have selected Hugo L. Black from the 108 justices, at the time of this survey, to sit on the nation's highest bench as one of its dozen best.[33]

ENDNOTES

1. "F.D.R. Silent on Possible Court Action," *The Shreveport Times*, September 15, 1937, p. 1. FDR's widely quoted comment to reporters is contradicted by sources including Black himself. A statement dictated by Black thirty years later unequivocally asserts that FDR knew about his Klan membership prior to the nomination and assured Black that there was no reason to worry about it. However, no other evidence supports Black's assertion and FDR stated to others privately that he had no such knowledge beforehand. See Roger K. Newman, *Hugo Black: A Biography* (New York: Pantheon Books, 1994), pp. 243–44, 250–51. See also Henry J. Abraham, "Hugo Black as a Great Justice," in *Great Justices of the U. S. Supreme Court*, ed. William D. Pederson and Norman W. Provizer (New York: Peter Lang Publishing, Inc., 1993), p. 253.

2. *International Yearbook, Editor and Publisher* (New York: Editor and Publisher, 1937), p. 48.

3. Ibid.

4. Ibid.

5. "Nomination Means Home to Justice," *The Shreveport Times*, August 14, 1937, p. 6.

6. Ibid.

7. Roger Biles, *The South and the New Deal* (Lexington: University Press of Kentucky, 1994), p. 144.

8. James Montgomery, *Shreveport Journal* page editor, interview with the author, June 1994, in Shreveport.

9. The microfilm format made it impossible to measure column inches for comparison.

10. "Senator Black's Appointment," *Shreveport Journal*, August 13, 1937, p. 8.

11. "Straining a Point," *Shreveport Journal*, August 24, 1937, p. 8.

12. Ibid.

13. "Views from Other Newspapers," *Shreveport Journal*, August 28, 1937, p. 8.

14. Henry J. Abraham, *Justices and Presidents: A Political History of Appointments to the Supreme Court* (New York: Oxford University Press, 1974), p. 201.

15. "Fist Fight Threatened Over Black Nomination," *The Shreveport Times*, August 17, 1937, p. 1.

16. "Black Nomination Confirmed," *The Shreveport Times*, August 18, 1937, p. 1.

17. Publisher William R. Hearst felt aggrieved over Senator Black's aggressive lobbying investigation. See Gerald T. Dunne, *Hugo Black and the Judicial Revolution* (New York: Simon and Schuster, 1977), pp. 64, 159, 234.

18. "Attacking Justice Black," *Shreveport Journal*, September 15, 1937, p. 2.

19. Ibid.

20. Virginia Van Der Veer Hamilton, *Hugo Black;The Alabama Years* (Baton Rouge: Louisiana State University Press, 1972), p. 280.

21. "Renewing the Court Fight," *Shreveport Journal*, September 23, 1937, p. 6.

22. "What'll the Ku Klux Say?" *Shreveport Journal*, September 27, 1937, p. 8.

23. "The Nomination of Senator Black," *The Shreveport Times*, August 14, 1937, p. 4.

24. Ibid.

25. John Hightower, "Black Denies Present KKK Ties," *Shreveport Journal*, October 2, 1937, p. 1. The number of stations that broadcast Black's radio address was placed at 318 by Newman, *Hugo Black*, p. 257.

26. Abraham, *Great Justices of the U.S. Supreme Court*, p. 254.

27. "Text of Address by Justice Black," *The Shreveport Times*, October 2, 1937, p. 18.

28. Abraham, *Great Justices of the U.S. Supreme Court*, p. 254. See also Newman, *Hugo Black*, pp. 96–100, which documents Black's discussion of the Klan controversy on other occasions in various settings although not in public statements.

29. "Ellender for Justice Black," *The Shreveport Times*, September 30, 1937, p. 18.

30. Kenneth Thompson, ed., *Ten Presidents and the Press* (Lanham, MD: University Press of America, 1983), p. 26.

31. Dunne, *Hugo Black and the Judicial Revolution*, p. 80.

32. During Black's campaign for reelection in 1932, the *Montgomery Advertiser* printed on its front page a copy of the Klan's Grand Passport that was given to Black in 1926. Ironically, Grover Hall, the editor who won a Pulitizer Prize in 1928 for his editorials against the Klan, overcame his initial reservations about Black to become his friend and staunch supporter. Newman, *Hugo Black*, pp. 148, 206–7. See also Abraham, *Justices and Presidents*, p. 202.

33. Abraham, *Great Justices of the U.S. Supreme Court*, p. 250.

6

Felix Frankfurter's Transition to the Judicial Role

William D. Bader

> Without strict adherence to reason, and a refraining from permitting personal biases to enter adjudication, judges become covert little Hitlers.[1]
>
> ~Justice Felix Frankfurter

Felix Frankfurter was appointed by Franklin Roosevelt to the U.S. Supreme Court in 1939 with a reputation as a liberal activist professor and attorney. He had made a name for himself representing progressive legal causes, particularly those related to the labor movement, and informally advising the Roosevelt administration on a range of issues.[2] Thus when Frankfurter quickly revealed himself to be a "conservative" justice who exemplified a consistent judicial restraint, some commentators commenced speculation about his apparent legal inconsistency. In reality, these critics have merely been disappointed and frustrated liberals.[3] They certainly have applied a different standard to Earl Warren, who went from a pre-Court conservative to a Court liberal; Warren's change, they maintain, does not indicate inconsistency, but, rather, growth.[4]

The real explanation for Felix Frankfurter's so-called change was his high regard for legal principle. Specifically, Frankfurter respected the fact that the role of a judge calls for a much different methodology than the role of a professor, attorney, or politician. Some of the other FDR Supreme Court appointees, who remained staunchly oriented toward liberal political results in their judicial opinions, never realized this, or never cared to realize this. Hugo Black, for instance, remained Senator Black, and Frank Murphy remained Governor Murphy, in their politically active modes of operation as justices. Felix Frankfurter, however, respected the special institutional constraints of the judiciary and the concomitant legal method of the judge.[5]

Frankfurter's somewhat unique stance among New Deal justices can be better understood through an examination of his early background. He was born in the Jewish ghetto of Vienna in 1892. He spent his first twelve years there, under the emperor's all powerful and arbitrary rule. Thus Frankfurter was sensitized at an early age to the dangers of arbitrary procedures that aimed for particular results, and the dangers of poorly checked concentrations of governmental power. Frankfurter wrote, "I do take law very seriously, deeply seriously, because fragile as reason is and limited as law is as the expression of the institutionalized medium of reason, that's all we have standing between us and the tyranny of mere will and the cruelty of unbridled, undisciplined feeling."[6] These early lessons are similar to those learned by the framers of the Constitution in their conflict with British rule.[7] Virtually identical concerns animate our Constitution, and Felix Frankfurter was extremely sensitive to them.

The second major influence on Felix Frankfurter's judicial approach came from Professor James Bradley Thayer, whose judicial philosophy, if not his earthly being, pervaded the Harvard Law School when Felix Frankfurter was a student.

Thayer advocated a principled judiciary that deferred to the democratically elected branches whenever their actions were rational. Thayer's approach tended to maximize our democracy, consistent with constitutional intent. His corollary to judicial restraint was the necessity of a very responsible citizenry, which was extremely active in democratic politics.[8] True to Thayer's philosophy, Felix Frankfurter was a politically active citizen-attorney-professor on the one hand, but a restrained and legally principled judge on the other. Frankfurter, in fact, remarked that an 1893 Thayer law review article was the very best piece of scholarship ever written on American constitutional law.[9] Frankfurter's words and deeds certainly reveal the profundity of Thayer's influence.

In 1939, when Felix Frankfurter was appointed to the Court, he was immediately looked upon as a leader by the other FDR justices, Black, Douglas, Reed, and Murphy.[10] The ensuing rift was inevitable, however. President Roosevelt arguably had no understanding of judicial philosophy, and probably no interest in trying to understand it. As a high powered politician he chose justices primarily for one political reason: They would not strike down New Deal economic reform legislation as unconstitutional. FDR did not foresee the issues of individual rights and liberties that were on the legal horizon.[11] Predictably, his nominees were not to agree on these individual liberties questions with the near unanimity that they manifested when resolving the economic ones.

Until 1937, the Court often offered rather formalistic interpretations to congressional powers and broad substantive interpretations to the due process clauses of the Fifth and Fourteenth Amendments to strike down economic reform legislation.[12] All FDR's appointees agreed that such judicial activism was constitutionally flawed.[13] Nevertheless, when legislation involving individual liberties started to reach the Court for review, Justices Black, Douglas, and Murphy began to espouse a double standard. This standard would require the Court to actively strike down legislation impinging on so-called individual liberties, while permitting it to give continued deference to politically desirable economic legislation.[14] Justice Frankfurter, however, continued to uphold the Constitution in the tradition of James Bradley Thayer, and he therefore advocated a consistent judicial restraint. He struck down clearly irrational legislation as unconstitutional, and deferred to the people and their democratically elected representatives in all other cases, whether economic or individual liberty was at stake.[15]

Justice Frankfurter also realized that the distinction between economic liberty and so-called individual liberty was illusory. After all, if the government seizes the entirety of your property, without due process of law, it would obviously violate your economic liberty as well as your individual liberty; these liberties are really indistinguishable. Furthermore, as a true judicial methodologist, Frankfurter attached great importance to the constitutional text, which treats both kinds of deprivations in the same manner.[16]

Thus, in 1940, Justice Frankfurter in *Minersville School District v. Gobitis* upheld the right of a local school board to require all students to recite the Pledge of Allegiance, despite a claim of First Amendment exemption by the Jehovah's Witnesses. It was not unreasonable, Frankfurter maintained, for a local political entity to require such simple patriotic socialization of children in a public educational context. Interestingly, the vote was eight to one, with Justices Black, Douglas, and Murphy joining Justice Frankfurter's majority opinion.[17] Three years later, the same issue came up again in *West Virginia Board of Education v. Barnette*, and Justice Frankfurter was now in the minority.[18] Justices Black, Douglas, and Murphy, who were very sensitive to political and journalistic criticism, vacillated, using their new double standard, and voted to overrule *Gobitis*.[19] Theirs was a constitutional law du jour, and certainly not Felix Frankfurter's constitutional law. The latter was specifically judicial with its respect for text and precedent.

Similarly, even though Felix Frankfurter was a legal activist on behalf of labor in his pre-Court days, in 1949 he upheld Arizona's "right to work law" as a not unreasonable exercise of state legislative power.[20] A perusal of Frankfurter's opinions reveals his deep understanding of the fact that what might be good, progressive policy was not necessarily constitutional, and what might be bad, reactionary policy was not necessarily unconstitutional.

Justice Frankfurter spent his final years on the Warren Court. The activist Warren majority involved itself in the most rampant legislating in Supreme Court history. In 1962, *Baker v. Carr*, which mandated the reapportionment of every state legislature, represented a high water mark of these political decisions.[21] Felix Frankfurter, with his longstanding respect for the judiciary's institutional constraints, took a different approach, a judicial one. He predicted the ensuing mess of reapportionment, and warned about the attendant dangers when the Court usurped political power.[22] At nearly age eighty, he displayed the influence of his early upbringing and Thayerism, and he wrote in dissent:

> There is not under our constitution a judicial remedy for every political mischief, for every undesirable exercise of legislative power. The Framers carefully, and with deliberate forethought, refused to enthrone the judiciary. Appeal must be to an informed civically militant electorate. In a democratic society like ours, relief must come through an aroused popular conscience that sears the conscience of the peoples' representatives.[23]

Thus Felix Frankfurter exemplifies a most successful transition from the results-oriented political role to the method-oriented judicial perspective. Justice Stanley Reed, who was also appointed by FDR, put Felix Frankfurter the judge versus Felix Frankfurter the private citizen, in simple and accurate perspective; in a 1956 note to Justice Frankfurter, he wrote:

One thing you always do, better than most of us, vote your view of the law without direction from your own wishes.[24]

ENDNOTES

1. William T. Coleman Jr., "Mr. Justice Felix Frankfurter: Civil Libertarian as Lawyer and as Justice" in *Six Justices on Civil Rights*, ed. Ronald D. Rotunda, (New York: Oceana, 1983), p. 90, n. 22.

2. Liva Baker, *Felix Frankfurter* (New York: Coward-McCann, Inc., 1969), pp. 87–210.

3. Ibid., pp. 222–23.

4. Bernard Schwartz, *Super Chief: Earl Warren and His Supreme Court: A Judicial Biography* (New York: Columbia University, 1983); David Halberstam, "Earl Warren and His America" in *The Warren Court: A Retrospective*, ed. Bernard Schwartz, (New York: Oxford University Press, 1996), pp. 12–17.

5. Wallace Mendelson, "Hugo Black and Judicial Discretion," *Political Science Quarterly* 85 (1970): 17; Melvin Urofsky, *Felix Frankfurter: Judicial Restraint and Individual Liberties* (Boston: Twayne Publishers, 1991), p. 48.

6. Baker, *Felix Frankfurter*, p. 16.

7. Daniel J. Boorstin, *The Genius of American Politics* (Chicago: The University of Chicago Press, 1953) pp. 66–76.

8. James B. Thayer, "The Origin and Scope of the American Doctrine of Constitutional Law," *Harvard Law Review* 7 (1893):129.

9. Harlan Phillips, *Felix Frankfurter Reminisces* (New York: Reynal & Co., 1960), pp. 299–300.

10. Robert A. Burt, *Two Jewish Justices* (Berkeley: The University of California Press, 1988), pp. 48–49.

11. Robert G. McCloskey, *The American Supreme Court* (Chicago: University of Chicago Press, 1960), pp. 168–9.

12. Ibid., pp. 136–79.

13. Gerald Gunther, *Learned Hand* (New York: Alfred A. Knopf, 1994), p. 656.

14. Ibid.

15. *West Virginia State Board of Education v. Barnette*, 319 U.S. 624, 646, 650 (1943) (Frankfurter, J., dissenting); *American Federation of Labor v. American Sash & Door Co.*, 335 U.S. 538, 555 (Frankfurter, J., concurring); *Rochin v. California*, 342 U.S. 165, 172, 173 (1952).

16. Ibid.

17. *Minersville School Dist. v. Gobitis*, 310 U.S. 586 (1940).

18. 319 U.S. 624 (1943).

19. Ibid.

20. 335 U.S. 538 (1949) (Frankfurter, J., concurring).

21. *Baker v. Carr*, 369 U.S. 186 (1962).

22. Ibid.

23. Ibid., p. 270.

24. Wallace Mendelson, *Supreme Court Statecraft* (Ames: The Iowa State University Press, 1985).

7

"An Interesting Game of Poker"
Franklin D. Roosevelt, William O. Douglas, and the 1944 Vice Presidential Nomination

James L. Moses

Supreme Court Justice William O. Douglas began the third volume of his autobiography by stating that he had "barely reached the Court when people were trying to get me off."[1] Friends and admirers, such as Interior Secretary Harold Ickes and Navy Secretary James Forrestal, promoted Douglas for a variety of political offices throughout the 1940s, including the presidency and vice presidency. During the final two terms of Franklin D. Roosevelt's presidency, Douglas's name figured prominently as a possible successor to FDR and, more frequently, as his running mate. The most serious move to put Douglas on the ticket with "the Boss" occurred in 1944, when Roosevelt himself made known his preference for Bill Douglas as his vice president. A Douglas vice presidency, however, provoked a less-than-enthusiastic response from the Democratic party leadership, which viewed Douglas as a potential liability, a political neophyte with no campaign experience, and set out to convince Roosevelt to look elsewhere for a vice president in 1944.[2] Likewise, Justice Douglas himself had no desire for the office. Like his colleague and nemesis Felix Frankfurter, Douglas liked to play his politics behind the scenes and from the security of his lifetime-tenured position on the bench. Judicial propriety and ethics forbad his participation in electoral politics. In addition, he often expressed to friends and colleagues his desire to remain on the Supreme Court and his disinterest in holding any political office. A large body of such evidence supports the notion that Douglas did not seek the vice presidency in 1944, and harbored no presidential ambitions.

Historians in general have discounted Douglas's statements about his possible political ambitions, and have viewed him as politically ambitious throughout the 1940s, including aspirations for the White House. This is the view put forth by Douglas's principal biographer James Simon, as well as constitutional historian and Douglas scholar Melvin Urofsky, and can be safely said to represent the generally-held view.[3] Simon researched his 1980 biography of Douglas, *Independent Journey*, prior to the opening of the Douglas papers in Washington. The book rests primarily on personal interviews with many of the people treated here, including Douglas himself. These interviews, some conducted more than thirty-five years after the events of 1944, elicited some suspect memories. Eliot Janeway is perhaps the best example. Simon hangs much of his thesis concerning Douglas's presidential ambitions on Janeway's 1979 statement to him that "Douglas thought he had the vice-presidential nomination [in 1944] and he wanted it."[4] Yet the historical record reflects a different reality. In 1944, on at least three separate occasions, Janeway acknowledged that Douglas had *no* ambition for the White House and did not seek political office. He even published this opinion in *Fortune* magazine that September.[5] Why he told Simon that Douglas wanted the job is a mystery. Perhaps it is as simple as a failed memory, or perhaps it is due to Janeway's own intense desire that Douglas accept a draft for the vice presidency in 1944. There is no question that Janeway wanted Douglas to be president. That does not mean that Douglas himself wanted it. Unfortunately, Simon put a great deal of weight on Janeway's statement, and it has been repeated in other historical works.

Not only historians, but many of Douglas's colleagues and contemporaries believed he sought the Oval Office. It is certainly no exaggeration to state that Justice Felix Frankfurter obsessed over the idea of Douglas and the presidency. His diary and correspondence is replete with venom directed at Douglas and his supposed quest for the White House. Likewise, Douglas friend Clark Clifford believed the Justice sought the presidency.[6]

It is my thesis that Justice William O. Douglas indeed did *not* have such presidential aspirations. By examining the historical record regarding Douglas and the 1944 vice presidential nomination, a clear picture emerges. Though actively supported by such political insiders as Harold Ickes, Joseph P. Kennedy, Tom Corcoran, and James Forrestal, and by such influential journalists as Edward R. Murrow, Eric Sevareid, Henry Luce, and Eliot Janeway, Justice William O. Douglas did not seek the White House, neither overtly nor covertly, nor did he desire the presidency or the vice presidency. As he later recorded in his memoirs, "I never had the Potomac Fever and could not be excited about catching it."[7]

Had Douglas truly harbored such presidential ambitions, he could not have planned a better opportunity to achieve the White House than the 1944 contest for the Democratic vice presidential nomination. Well aware of Roosevelt's failing health, Douglas and other Washington insiders knew with certainty that the man chosen for the second spot in 1944 would be the next president of the United States, either through FDR's death or resignation due to illness. This scenario served as one impetus for dumping Vice President Henry Wallace from the ticket. Yet Douglas did nothing to advance his candidacy; indeed, he took all reasonable measures to discourage those who politically promoted him, even though he knew that Roosevelt was considering him for the second spot on the ticket. In letter after letter, Justice Douglas repeatedly asked his admirers to cease their political activity on his behalf. Douglas even took the remarkable step of physically closeting himself prior to and during the Chicago convention—should he be drafted by the convention against his will, he would be inaccessible.

Many Roosevelt insiders admired William O. Douglas, and saw him as the heir apparent to the president. An attractive "self-made" man, a rugged outdoorsman, and an experienced New Deal administrator as member and chairman of the Securities and Exchange Commission (SEC), Douglas had many factors in his favor to be an excellent candidate for president; his friends and admirers recognized these qualities in him as well. They pressured him to run for president, imploring him to recognize the inevitability of the "situation" by accepting a draft as his duty. He refused, and in fact continually refused any and all offers and opportunities for political office made to him through the 1940s. Such opportunities included a possible Douglas vice presidency in 1940, Roosevelt's offer to make him head of the War Manpower Board in 1942, FDR's desire for him as a running mate in 1944, President Truman's two separate offers to appoint Douglas secretary of the interior, and Truman's request that Justice Douglas step down and run with him in 1948. Clearly, if Douglas had sought to enter electoral politics at the highest levels, he had many opportunities from which to choose. He chose to remain on the Court.

This is not to say that the vice presidency in 1944 was Douglas's for the asking. But had he wanted the second spot in 1944, he had only in some fashion to make his wishes known to Roosevelt, whom he saw on a regular basis. The president favored him, and had Douglas made known to Roosevelt any ambition for the vice presidency, FDR may have asked him to join the ticket. In such an event, the party leadership would have had little choice but to go along. The party bosses were powerful, but not so powerful as to deny a sitting President his choice of running mate.[8]

This is also not to say that Justice William O. Douglas remained above political activity while on the bench. The record is quite the reverse: Douglas remained a prominent behind-the-scenes political player throughout his career. He served as confidant and adviser to FDR, and the occasional speechwriter. He advised presidents from Roosevelt to Johnson, suggested names for government vacancies, offered foreign policy advice, and spoke out publicly on a host of national and international issues, often to the displeasure of the occupant of the Oval Office.

These instances, though, have more to do with Douglas's judicial activist philosophy and his unique vision of appropriate judicial behavior than with presidential or vice presidential ambitions. Douglas, schooled at Columbia Law School in the jurisprudence of legal realism, saw "legal doctrines not as autonomous but as devices that could be manipulated for social good or ill."[9] He viewed the Court as the institution that kept the law in stride with the times, advancing the common good in the process. Additionally, during his first term on the Court Douglas joined a seven-to-two majority in the case of *O'Malley v. Woodrough* sustaining the constitutionality of a statute subjecting the salaries of federal judges to federal income tax.[10] With that vote, Douglas decided, "I voted myself first class citizenship. The tradition had been that Justices never even voted in public elections." Douglas resolved to take "a different course. Since I would be paying as heavy an income tax as my neighbor, I decided to participate in local, state, and national affairs." Douglas would register and vote. He would speak out on issues such as conservation and would travel widely and "speak out on foreign affairs. Many people assume that a Supreme Court Justice should be remote and aloof from life," Douglas wrote, "but if Justices are to enjoy First Amendment rights, they should not be relegated to the promotion of innocuous ideas."[11] Involvement in political affairs is not the same thing as ambition for political office, and while Douglas never shied away from political involvement, neither did he pine for the Oval Office.

"You Could Help the Boss a Lot, Bill": Drafting Douglas

Talk of William Douglas running with FDR in 1944 began immediately after Roosevelt's defeat of Wendell Willkie in November 1940. Only days after that victory, President Roosevelt and Interior Secretary Harold Ickes discussed who should be "built-up" as the presidential successor. Ickes brought up Bill Douglas as a possibility. Roosevelt turned a critical eye: "No one knows whether he can make a campaign or not. He has never been tried out."[12] FDR threw out several other names for discussion; however, the President would soon change his mind and come to prefer Douglas as his 1944 running mate. But the selection of a future vice president or the anointing of a successor simply was not very important to Roosevelt, who immensely enjoyed the presidency, its power, and ceremony, and believed he would continue in office for years and terms to come.[13] FDR did not really care either about who would run with him or succeed him in the White House—not at this time nor subsequently. In fact, after the 1944 Chicago convention he told his son James Roosevelt that he "didn't give a damn whether the convention chose Douglas or Byrnes or Truman; the important thing was to get on with the war."[14] But FDR had a genuine personal affection for Douglas, admired his poker skills and his raconteur's way with a story, and would have been just as pleased to run with the justice as with anyone. Perhaps if Roosevelt had felt stronger about personally selecting a running mate, he would have called on Douglas to serve; instead, he allowed the party machinery to make the selection.

Douglas's supposed run for the White House in 1944 became a source of increasing gossip in Washington after Roosevelt's third term election. Felix Frankfurter certainly thought Douglas was "making a 'build-up' for the White

House," and Judge Learned Hand rued "what a 'build-up' it is getting to be!"[15] Frankfurter wrote Chief Justice Harlan Stone acknowledging that "there have been Presidential hopefuls on the Court since 1789—too many of them—but never before has any Justice sought a Vice-Presidential nomination!"[16] Vice President Henry Wallace worried about a potential Douglas candidacy as well. He believed that political gadfly Thomas "Tommy the Cork" Corcoran had been constantly arranging for Justice Douglas "to meet a great variety of people," presumably to increase Douglas's chances in a future political bid. Wallace thought Corcoran planned to "bring out Douglas as a breath of fresh air from the Far West" for the upcoming election.[17] Justice Robert Jackson told Wallace that Chief Justice Stone "was deeply concerned about the way in which Bill Douglas was running for President or Vice President." Also, Justice Frank Murphy told Wallace he had witnessed Tom Corcoran visiting Douglas's office "very frequently."[18] Wallace also worried with his knowledge that Joseph P. Kennedy "was strong for Bill Douglas for Vice President."[19]

Henry Wallace had no cause to fear a Douglas candidacy, however; Douglas wanted to remain on the Supreme Court. Initially, perhaps Justice Douglas believed that he was "too young to go on the Court."[20] But in early February 1943, Douglas told Harold Ickes that he "wouldn't be interested in political appointments," since he had "come to like [his] job, and doubtless appreciat[ed] its security."[21] Concerns about economic security had always played a role in Douglas's life. Raised in poverty, he had worked since childhood to help support his widowed mother and two siblings, and to put himself through Whitman College and Columbia Law School. There was never enough money. When he completed his tenure as chairman of the Securities and Exchange Commission, he planned to return to a tenured position on the law faculty of Yale University, which prompted this question from journalist Arthur Krock: "What is it about this law faculty at Yale that has drawn you back to it despite all your promise of advancement in public life and political affairs?" Douglas responded with one word: "security."[22] Doubtless "security" played a role in Justice Douglas's decision to remain out of politics in 1944 as well.

Speculation about Douglas's political ambitions continued to grow throughout the early 1940s. Douglas and Harold Ickes reminisced over lunch late in 1943 about the 1940 election, in which Douglas had been cited as a possible vice presidential candidate and had "called off" an Oregon movement to get him on the ticket. "He did not want to be mixed up in the Vice Presidency," Ickes recalled. Douglas further "said that he had never been ambitious politically, and was not now."[23] Douglas and politics also fueled the dinner conversation between Palmer Hoyt, publisher of *The [Portland] Oregonian*, and SEC official Jerome Frank, both close friends of Douglas. They agreed that even though the justice's "modesty forbad any discussion of the topic," Douglas should run for president.[24] Such gossip caught up with Douglas early in 1944 when he attended a small dinner party that he believed to be "a purely social affair." In fact, it served as an occasion to propose that Justice Douglas begin a drive for the presidency or vice presidency. Douglas, caught off-guard and shocked that the talk of his "political ambition" had come to this, told his admirers that "I would not give my approval, that I had no political ambitions, that I wanted to stay on the Court for the rest of my life, that I would not authorize any such undertaking." Having forcefully conveyed his disinterest to the group, Douglas left feeling "quite confident that that will be the end of the matter." He related this event to his friend Senator Frank Maloney of Connecticut. Should anyone approach Maloney about a Douglas candidacy, the justice wanted the senator to "have the facts and to know that I am not a candidate for any office, that my sole desire is to remain on the Court until I reach retirement, that any proposal to launch openly or silently any campaign for me is wholly without my authority and contrary to my desire, and that I do not think it would comport with judicial standards for one on the Court to nurture political ambitions."[25] Maloney assured Douglas that he would keep the Justice's wishes in mind. "I know that you do not aspire to either of these places—*because you have so many times told me that you were happy in your present position.*" Maloney recalled Douglas's "intense desire" to avoid the 1940 vice presidential nomination and promised, should anyone approach him on the matter, to "remember that you want to stay where you are."[26]

In the months following this exchange with Douglas, Maloney—nudged along by Eliot Janeway—came to believe that Douglas had a duty to serve if called upon, regardless of his personal wishes in the matter: "I am unhappy," he wrote Douglas, "at my ability to come completely in line with your intense feeling. I have tried but I can't do it." Knowing it would "aggravate" Douglas, Maloney tried to convince his friend that "if you are called upon to be a candidate, you cannot 'easily' decline. I see the situation as one calling for a great sacrifice—and cannot see how you can refuse."[27] Douglas's friends continued to apply pressure on the justice to be a candidate. Expressing his desire to remain out of politics did little to deter his admirers.

Douglas often had told Harold Ickes of his desire to stay on the Court, yet in late spring 1944, Ickes busily floated Douglas trial balloons wherever he could, as did FDR adviser and speechwriter Judge Sam Rosenman, who told Douglas that he had suggested his name to the president. Rosenman and Ickes were "in hearty concurrence" as to a Douglas candidacy.[28] Justice Douglas, though, still tried to call them off. He had lunch with Ickes on June 2 and discussed the vice presidency. Both agreed that Wallace should be dropped, and Douglas once again "disclaimed any interest in the place himself"—a statement Ickes said he "sincerely believed." Yet Ickes plowed ahead with his various Douglas vice presidential scenarios, trying to persuade others that Douglas "would be a great strength to the ticket" and would assure the Democrats of carrying Washington and California in 1944. Having failed miserably to dissuade Ickes from promoting him for political office, Douglas finally told him that "before the convention went into session [Douglas] would be in a canoe going up a certain river from Idaho into Oregon where he could not be reached by telephone, messenger or even by airplane."[29] Justice Douglas surely must have believed that he was making his wishes clearly known. He did not want to be in the vice presidential picture, and as a last resort would hide in the mountains from the would-be drafters who might nominate him despite his clear and expressed wishes.

Thomas Dewey may have been one reason many people felt so strongly about a Douglas candidacy. Ickes and Forrestal agreed that Douglas matched up very favorably against the Republican nominee for president, and in many respects Douglas would have been an ideal candidate for the Democrats to run against Dewey. His youth (Douglas was 45) would act as a deterrent to the so-called age issue which confronted FDR in 1944.[30] Douglas and Dewey graduated from Columbia Law School together, and while Douglas finished second in his class, Dewey ranked in the bottom third. Dewey had earlier proposed to Douglas a law partnership, but Douglas had declined. Dewey made his name busting racketeers as New York's tough district attorney, while Douglas cleaned up Wall Street as chairman of the SEC. Tom Corcoran, particularly taken with the comparisons between the two, thought "Dewey had a particularly strong inferiority complex" with respect to Douglas: "Dewey would not take a moot court case [at Columbia] when Douglas was on the other side." Corcoran believed a Douglas candidacy would have a "bad psychological effect upon Dewey."[31]

In the spring of 1944, Edward R. Murrow and Eric Sevareid approached Douglas looking for "the word" on the vice presidential situation. As personal friends of the justice, both men assured Douglas that they "would treat the news discreetly." Douglas just "shook his head," unwilling to make a public statement of any kind.[32] Douglas's lack of public statements disavowing his candidacy have troubled many historians. Why did not Douglas simply tell Murrow and Sevareid—or any other reporters, for that matter—in unequivocal terms that he was not nor would be a candidate for the vice presidency? The answer lies in Douglas's unique sense of judicial propriety. Douglas believed that any statement by him, even a stern denial of candidacy, could be misread as a political maneuver. Additionally, Douglas felt that the issuance of such a statement went beyond the bounds of his definition of proper judicial behavior. Better to answer with silence, Douglas believed, than risk being misinterpreted and in the process damage the image and reputation of the institution he greatly respected. He told Frank Maloney just that: "Public denial of political aspirations has too often in our history been actual public assertion of the very ambitions which are denied. Aside from that, it is conduct unbecoming a judge of a high court."[33] And, as one Douglas scholar has noted, the very fact that Douglas accepted appointment to the Supreme Court implicitly carried the understanding that he had withdrawn from electoral politics, therefore obviating the need for any public statement removing himself from vice presidential consideration.[34]

By early summer 1944 talk of the justice as a vice presidential candidate approached its peak. Harold Ickes talked to FDR about the vice presidency in mid-June, mentioning Douglas as a possibility. Unlike the critical assessment he gave a Douglas candidacy immediately after the 1940 election, this time Roosevelt's "reaction was pleasant." While waiting to see the boss, Ickes ran Douglas's name past FDR's appointments secretary Edwin "Pa" Watson, who "felt all right about Douglas" as well.[35] A friend wrote Douglas: "You could help the boss a lot, Bill, even though you yourself might not like the idea."[36] This became the common refrain in the early summer of 1944. The Ickes-Corcoran strategy involved getting as many influential people as possible talking about Douglas. In addition to the suggestions made personally to the president, Douglas supporters hoped the gossip would catch the president's attention.

FDR, however, played a different game, telling various vice presidential hopefuls that they had his personal support. At various times, Roosevelt made assurances or wrote letters supporting Henry Wallace, James F. Byrnes, William O. Douglas, and Harry Truman as his running mate. Indeed, only an hour after FDR told Henry Wallace that he favored him for a second term as vice president, Roosevelt "clearly" indicated to both Sam Rosenman and Harold Ickes that he believed Douglas would be the strongest candidate.[37] Roosevelt never wanted to be the bearer of bad news, especially to his friends. His "unwillingness to be unpleasantly frank was notorious among those who knew him well," and he demonstrated that trait in his handling of the vice presidential selection.[38] Everything about the selection of a running mate, historian Robert Ferrell noted, was "reduced to indirection."[39] Thus the vitally important choice of a vice president became a battle of influence; who could sway FDR to their candidate, and who stood in the best position to make up the president's mind for him, since Roosevelt did not think it a significant decision and was content to let the contenders fight it out in Chicago. Party leaders, though, certain that FDR would not survive his fourth term, knew they had the responsibility of selecting the next president. They did not want to leave it up to chance.

"No One Wanted Douglas": The July 11 Meeting

By early July 1944, Roosevelt had decided on William Douglas as his personal favorite for a running mate. Douglas's supporters were still hard at work promoting their candidate, who with as little fanfare and publicity as possible continued to call them off. National party chairman Robert Hannegan had been as equally hard at work trying to move fellow Missourian Harry Truman into vice presidential contention. By the second week of July he had not yet succeeded in convincing FDR. It "was still not clear" in Hannegan's mind "just who the

President wanted for Vice President," but Hannegan thought "Douglas was still first on the list."[40] Harold Ickes had the same impression. He spoke to Roosevelt in early July 1944: "More clearly than ever the President indicated that he believed that Bill Douglas would be the strongest candidate."[41] Harry Hopkins agreed with Hannegan and Ickes that Roosevelt "would have preferred Bill Douglas [for the vice presidency], because he knew him better [than Truman] and he always liked Bill's toughness."[42] By the morning of July 11, only eight days before the convention, neither Ickes nor Hannegan knew "anything definite about the Vice Presidency," but hoped a White House meeting scheduled for that evening would "clear it up."[43] That history-making meeting became Hannegan's chance to convince FDR that Truman, and not Douglas, should be his running mate.

Dining with the president on that Tuesday evening were party chairman Bob Hannegan, Chicago mayor Edward J. Kelly, Democratic National Committee (DNC) officials Edwin Pauley and George Allen, postmaster general and former DNC chairman Frank Walker, "Bronx boss" Edward Flynn, DNC vicechair Oscar Ewing, and FDR's son-in-law John Boettiger. Ed Pauley told Tom Corcoran that the group (minus Boettiger) met in his room at the Mayflower Hotel before leaving for the meeting, and afterward "had all gone to the White House prepared to hear the President declare for Douglas and equally prepared to accept the suggestion."[44] There is much room to doubt this statement. It could not have been true for Hannegan, who, "all hot and bothered about getting the nomination for Senator Truman,"[45] had already invested "several weeks" trying to convince Roosevelt that "Douglas was not enough of a party man to have a following."[46] Of this group probably only Mayor Ed Kelly enthusiastically supported Douglas. Boettiger, who met the group at the White House, may have been influenced by his wife, the president's daughter Anna, who had been inquiring as to Douglas's drinking habits. She reportedly had seen Douglas intoxicated out West on "two or three occasions."[47]

After martinis and dinner, the group adjourned to the president's "sweltering" second-floor study and began their dissection of prospective vice presidents.[48] The group discussed a wide range of possibilities, including James Byrnes, House Speaker Sam Rayburn, and Senator Alben Barkley; Vice President Wallace was hardly mentioned. Throughout the meeting FDR said little, instead allowing the other participants to carry the discussion of various candidates. They disposed of Rayburn, then Barkley, and then Byrnes.

No one brought up Douglas, so the president himself raised his name, much to the surprise of Truman advocate Robert Hannegan, who doubtless believed he already had talked the President out of Douglas. FDR, however, had been steadily warming to the idea of running with the justice, and he told his dinner guests about it. The president pointed out that Douglas, like Wallace, had a following in the party's left wing. He was young and dynamic; also, Douglas "looked and acted on occasions like a Boy Scout," and would have, in his opinion, "appeal at the polls—and, besides, played an interesting game of poker."[49] FDR's obviously favorable attitude toward Douglas did nothing to sway anyone but Ed Kelly, and the justice's name "fell flat. No one wanted Douglas any more than Wallace."[50] The discussion turned to Truman, who found general acceptance among the group. Knowing that these men would run the campaign, Roosevelt bowed to their wishes. "I know this makes you boys happy," Roosevelt told Hannegan, "and you are the ones I am counting on to win this election. But I still think Douglas would have the greater public appeal."[51] While Roosevelt would have been pleased to run with his friend Douglas, he did not feel so strongly about it as to press his case with the party men. A run with Douglas would have been enjoyable, but in the end it did not really matter to the president with whom he ran.

For Douglas supporters, however, the question was critical. Unaware of the outcome of the July 11 meeting, they continued to push Justice Douglas toward accepting a draft.

Eliot Janeway, a zealous Douglas campaigner as well as personal friend, tried to convince the justice that "this is not a campaign or a draft—it's a situation. We can't order situations." He recognized that Douglas was "honestly anxious to stay on the Court," and tried to convince the Justice that his judicial image as well as the image of the Court would not be harmed with a Douglas draft for office. Janeway suggested a strategy: "It's a sacrifice on your part," he said, implying that Douglas could accept a draft by playing up the theme of "sacrificing" his Court position to serve the country in a greater capacity. Sensing his inability to make any headway with Douglas, Janeway also chastised Douglas for being unwilling to acknowledge the present "state of affairs."[52]

In the days following the July 11 meeting, the Douglas campaign—run wholly without the consent of the candidate—hit its stride. Supporters turned up the heat on FDR, sending him telegrams and letters that seemed to support the president's belief that Douglas had public appeal, at least in the West. The chairmen of the California and Oregon delegations to the upcoming convention wired both the White House and party chairman Hannegan expressing their support of Douglas for vice president.[53] They did not know that Hannegan had been trying to torpedo Douglas for months, and were probably unaware that FDR, though he personally preferred Douglas, had already allowed the party men to select Truman. FDR could also see support for Douglas in the editorial pages of newspapers around the country. At least one newspaper thought Douglas had a "firmness and down-to-earth interest in the details that make the clock tick which would command a very considerable respect on Capitol Hill."[54]

During the midsummer of 1944, while admirers furiously promoted Justice Douglas for office, the reluctant candidate vacationed at his remote cabin in the mountains of Washington. He had no telephone, and had to ride into the nearest small town to receive his mail from the local post office. Douglas and his fishing companions were "pretty well isolated" and got "news of national affairs only infrequently." On July 12 he wrote from his retreat to Chief Justice Harlan F. Stone about his startling discovery that, despite his best efforts to quietly remove himself from the vice presidential name game, he continued to be "rather actively promoted as [a] vice-presidential candidate." He told Stone, his former professor at Columbia, that there had been "some such effort made before I left Washington and I did all I possibly could to put an end to it." Certain delegates to the convention from western states had approached Douglas prior to his vacation, asking if they could with authority promote him as a vice presidential candidate. His answer, as he related it to Stone, was first, that he was not a candidate, had not been a candidate, and would not be a candidate; secondly, that no one was authorized to promote his nomination, and he would give no such authority; and thirdly, that if nominated, he would not accept. "I hope this puts an end to the matter," he told Stone. "I think political ambitions are incompatible with [the] performance of our judicial functions. I do not think the Court should be used as a stepping stone to any political office."[55]

He sent a very similar letter to Connecticut Senator Frank Maloney, his close friend in whom he had earlier confided his plans to remain on the bench and out of politics. Douglas thought Maloney knew better than anyone else his "personal feelings and desires on the matter," so he asked him to make these feelings known to the convention, and if need be to act in Douglas's name to keep him out of consideration for the vice presidency.[56] As Eliot Janeway wrote in a *Fortune* article on the convention, Douglas gave Maloney effective "power of attorney to take him out of any convention floor cat-and-dog fight into which overzealous supporters [like Janeway] might thrust him."[57]

Douglas's letter to Maloney is very revealing. Marked "Personal and Confidential," the letter spells out Douglas's feelings as to the vice presidency and to his "candidacy." As he had told Stone, Douglas thought he had "done all that is possible to discourage the use of my name. I now want to add," he continued, "that if by chance the nomination were tendered me, I would not accept it." Isolated at his mountain retreat, Douglas admitted to Maloney that he did not "know very much about the political situation." He acknowledged, as he had to Stone, that before he left "there had already been some small talk about various persons, including me, as a possible candidate for vice president. I for the most part ignored this, treating it merely as gossip." When personally confronted with questions or supporters, as in the dinner party ambush, Douglas had always "indicated my displeasure and lack of interest as forcefully and as diplomatically as I could under the circumstances."[58] He told Maloney that he did not want the job because of any disdain for the office: He thought the vice presidency was "a great office in itself and even greater as its occupant is great." But, he added, "I am a member of the Supreme Court and a lawyer. As a lawyer and as a judge, I have some deep convictions not only about the responsibilities of the office I hold but of the limitations such a position imposes on the incumbent. One of those responsibilities is scrupulously to refrain from such conduct as might be considered as political. One of the limitations is to refrain from public political utterances, since public denial has too often in our history been actual public assertion of the very ambitions which are denied." For those reasons, Douglas did not feel it wise at that point to do anything but speak to Maloney in order to make his true intentions known to the convention and to "those who are interested and affected."[59]

Having unburdened himself by arming Frank Maloney with the statement of disinterest, Douglas left his cabin retreat for a ten day trek into the mountains, feeling the problem had been solved and confident that he no longer figured into the vice presidential sweepstakes. While Douglas lost himself amid the splendor of the Wallowa Mountains, the Democrats met in Chicago to select a vice president, and in the process anoint a successor to Franklin Roosevelt.

"What Do We Do Now?": The Convention

Prior to the 1944 Democratic Convention, it seemed that President Roosevelt had given everyone running for vice president his personal assurance that he was Roosevelt's choice for a running mate. Roosevelt told James Byrnes that he "was devoted to him and regarded him better qualified than any other one proposed."[60] Robert Hannegan carried a letter to the convention from FDR stating he would be "very glad to run" with Harry Truman or Bill Douglas. The president also provided a letter for Henry Wallace stating that were he a delegate, he "personally would vote for [Wallace's] renomination."[61] And yet Roosevelt wrote just prior to the convention, "I am honestly trying to keep out of the Vice Presidential contest which includes a score of active candidates and another score who have their lightning rods up and would like to be struck."[62] Roosevelt seemed to provide at least a touch of "lightning" for all of the prominent candidates, arming each with evidence that the president *really* preferred him. However, with the convention delegates Roosevelt affected an air of detachment. He would leave it up to them to select his running mate. Oscar Chapman, assistant secretary of the Interior, stopped by the White House on his way to the convention to ask the president for directions on the vice presidential question: "Do you have any word that you want to leave with me?" FDR replied, "As far as a candidate is concerned, I would not try to dictate to individual delegates in any form."[63]

With Roosevelt thus taking a stance against "dictating" a running mate, delegates to the 1944 Democratic National Convention met in Chicago in late July knowing that while FDR again would head the Democratic ticket, the choice of running mate was theirs. William O. Douglas's supporters hoped for a scenario whereby a first or second ballot logjam among such front-runners as Wallace, Byrnes, Truman, and Alben Barkley—as well as a surfeit of favorite sons—would pave the way for Douglas as the best compromise vice presidential candidate. Tom Corcoran envisioned just such a deadlock, "with Barkley and Byrnes ready to throw to Douglas to defeat Wallace." Ickes, too, believed that Byrnes—who did not want to see Wallace, Barkley, or Truman get the nomination—"would rather throw to Douglas."[64] But for any Douglas scenario to be successful, Wallace would have to drop out, since the vice president appealed to the same constituency as Douglas. There could be no Douglas movement with Wallace still in the picture.[65]

For his part, Harold Ickes initially did not plan to attend the convention. "In the end," he wrote Roosevelt, "I went hoping that I might be able to be of some help, if there were any chance to nominate Bill Douglas."[66] With that goal in mind, Ickes, Eliot Janeway, and the other Douglas supporters hoped that a particular series of events would unfold in Chicago, and accordingly, armed themselves with a plan of action to get the justice nominated as a compromise candidate. The Douglas people—Maloney, Ickes, Janeway, Corcoran, Attorney General Francis Biddle, delegation chairmen Bob Kenny and Henry Hess, and Chicago mayor Ed Kelly, among others—were counting on first and second ballot deadlocks. If no candidate could break from the pack after the second ballot, they planned to call for a recess to work the floor for a Douglas "landslide compromise," which would be jump-started by a pledge of support from the California and Oregon delegations.[67]

On the first ballot, Wallace received 429½ votes to Truman's 319½, with 589 votes needed to carry the nomination. Fourteen others received votes as well, creating exactly the situation for which the Douglas supporters had hoped: a first ballot deadlock. After the voting, Maloney sought out Ed Kelly and they agreed to move for a recess after the second ballot to begin the Douglas drive. Douglas supporters had agreed before the convention that Bob Kenny, chairman of the California delegation, would nominate Douglas, and that Frank Maloney—despite his first-hand knowledge of the Justice's wishes to remain out of contention—would second the nomination. In order to protect Douglas, this would be done "only as ratification of an accomplished fact, when, as and if Wallace and Truman got into a stalemate."[68] Everyone clearly understood that "nothing would be done except to carry out a certainty," thus insulating Douglas from everything save a *fait accompli*. However, maneuvers by Hannegan and the party regulars to get Truman nominated prevented any chance of a Douglas "landslide compromise." Additionally, the justice's admirers found it difficult to promote Douglas as a candidate when, as Ickes later wrote, "the suggestion of his name was always met with the statement that 'I understand that Douglas doesn't want to be nominated and would not accept.'"[69]

On the second ballot, Truman showed early substantial gains and delegates hopped aboard the Truman bandwagon, many primarily as a means to stop Wallace, who, to the horror of Hannegan and the party officials, had been very warmly received by the convention and had been the subject of an extended floor demonstration. The second ballot showed Truman with 1,031 votes to Wallace's 105. During the second round of voting, Henry Hess grabbed Maloney's shoulders, tears in his eyes, and cried, "What do we do now?"[70] Douglas received four votes from the Oregon delegation. There would be no Douglas compromise candidacy.

Ed Kelly was furious. He and others believed that Hannegan and the "party bosses" had forced Truman—the product of Missouri machine politics—on the convention. Red faced, Kelly cursed Hannegan, Flynn, and Pauley, "calling them sons-of-bitches in one breath and sons-of-bitching lunatics in the next, swearing that they would never steam-roller Truman through or everybody would go to jail."[71] This convention "bossism" especially bothered Ickes, who during the convention dashed off a telegram to the president: "No one here is deceived as to the impetus behind the Truman candidacy," he wrote. He thought "the ghost of Pendergast" presided over the convention. "Here is an issue made to order for Dewey whose whole reputation and whose nomination today is based upon his apparently fearless onslaught on the kind of machine and corrupt politics represented" by Hannegan.[72] Ickes, so bothered by the possibility that Dewey would make campaign hay over Truman's background, became a Wallace promoter as a means to block Truman. He remained unaware that the president had sanctioned the drafting of Truman for the vice presidency until he discovered that FDR had armed Hannegan with a controversial letter naming Truman and Douglas as acceptable running mates. That letter and Hannegan's handling of it proved to be a source of discord at the convention as well.

During the convention, Hannegan carried a postdated letter from Roosevelt citing Truman and Douglas by name as the vice presidential candidates of choice:

> July 19, 1944
>
> Dear Bob,
> You have written me about Harry Truman and Bill Douglas. I should, of course, be very glad to run with either of them and believe that either one of them would bring real strength to the ticket.
>
> Always sincerely,
> Franklin D. Roosevelt[73]

The controversy revolved around the ordering of the names in the letter. Douglas among others maintained that originally the letter read "Bill Douglas and Harry Truman."[74] Roosevelt dictated the letter to his secretary Grace Tully, who also stated that the original letter FDR gave to Hannegan on July 11 named "Douglas and Truman in that order." Shortly thereafter the president and his staff left by train for the West Coast with a stopover in Chicago. Hannegan requested the stopover. While the president's train sat in a Chicago rail yard, Hannegan came aboard to talk political strategy with the president. "Hannegan had a lengthy palaver with the Boss," wrote Tully, "and when he came out of the President's sitting room he was carrying in his hand the letter naming Douglas or Truman as an acceptable running mate." He approached Tully with the letter. "Grace," said Hannegan, "the President wants you to retype this letter and to switch these names so it will read 'Harry Truman or Bill Douglas.'"[75]

The reason was clear: With Truman listed first, it would appear as though the president preferred him as a first choice, and Douglas as a second choice. Hannegan later denied reversing the names, but Tully, not known for dishonesty, had no reason to fabricate such a story. Additionally, Tully's assistant Dorothy Brady, who retyped the letter aboard the train, corroborated the story of the juxtaposition. Missouri's state Democratic party chairman, Sam Wear, stated as well that he personally knew Hannegan switched the names to put Truman's ahead of Douglas.[76]

Hannegan initially concealed the letter from the convention, primarily because Roosevelt had listed Douglas along with Truman as an acceptable running mate. Ed Kelly gave a dinner the evening of July 18 in honor of Hannegan. At this dinner, Hannegan, already in possession of the Truman-Douglas letter, "worked the table saying the president was for Truman but not saying a word about Douglas." When word leaked that Hannegan had the letter listing two names, a controversy developed and Hannegan had to divulge before the press the letter and its contents. "The effect," noted Henry Wallace, "was damaging to Hannegan's reputation."[77] Ickes noted that "some of the delegates were very indignant about this deception," and there were calls for "Chairman Shenanigan's" resignation.[78] Hannegan's handling of the letter helped both to promote Truman's stock at the convention and to downplay Douglas, but it did not play a crucial role either in the nomination of Truman or in the grounding of the Douglas supporters' efforts.

"I Had no Political Ambitions": Aftermath and Conclusions

When Justice Douglas returned to Washington from his combined vacation and hiding place, he expressed to Chief Justice Stone relief that the convention had ended, and tried to convince Stone that the whole affair concerning Douglas and the vice presidency had been overblown. "For a while I feared that pressure might be put on me to go on the ticket. It was not," Douglas lied. "Every one of my friends knew I had no political ambitions," but just in case, Douglas added, he vacationed "where not even the Lone Ranger could find me."[79] In fact, tremendous pressure had been put on Douglas to accept the vice presidency. In being less than truthful about this with Harlan Stone, Douglas perhaps tried to downplay the episode in order to reassure Stone, who had been concerned about the possibility of a member of his Court being politically ambitious.

Some months after the convention, Douglas made the following admission to Harold Ickes: "[Douglas] told me that if the President had sent for him and asked him to run for Vice President he would have done so although he did not want to make the race."[80] This is not surprising: Douglas had a profound affection for FDR and had the president specifically sent for him and asked him to run on the ticket, the justice would have been hard pressed to refuse. "An FDR 'draft' would have been difficult to resist," Douglas wrote in his memoirs. "I am glad I never had to face up to it in 1944."[81]

While Douglas did not want his friends to make a campaign for the vice presidency on his behalf, he nevertheless thanked them for their sentiments toward him. Genuinely touched by the display of affection his admirers expressed in their attempt to draft him, Douglas nevertheless did not waver in his belief that his "place was on the Court. But the fact," he told Ickes, "that we had a difference of opinion does not make me less grateful for the great confidence you expressed in me."[82] Douglas reiterated that though flattered, he had "thoroughly frowned upon any effort to make him the Vice

Presidential nominee."[83] Even Felix Frankfurter came to believe Douglas did not seek the 1944 nomination. "What a pity that those who actively promoted Douglas for V.P. not only before but at the convention," Frankfurter wrote Stone, "did not realize that Douglas, like General Sherman for the Presidency, was unalterably unavailable."[84]

After the convention others wrote Douglas of their difficulties in not bringing his name into the contest. Oregon chairman Henry Hess told the justice "it was a terrible struggle with the inner self, not only for me, but for many of your other friends and admirers, to obey your wishes and not present you before the convention."[85] Douglas supporters still believed that had they been allowed to introduce the justice's name early in the convention, the results may have been different.

After the 1944 convention and FDR's reelection, Douglas's core of supporters felt that he would be well positioned for the 1948 presidential nomination. "Destiny," Hess told Douglas, "is saving you for the Presidency at a later date."[86] Janeway, Ickes, Forrestal, and Corcoran all believed Douglas should carry FDR's banner in 1948. "To your role as a Justice," wrote Janeway, perhaps the most adamant of Douglas's supporters as well as the most disappointed in his failure to accept a draft, "has been added that of a leader. You have an organization. You did not build it. You did not ask for it. You have implored those of its leaders and members who have come to you to go elsewhere." Nevertheless, Janeway told Douglas, unalterable political momentum had been created for a "Douglas movement" for political office and political leadership. "Nothing you do can stop it."[87]

Janeway was correct both about the future and the past. Douglas did not seek political office and would not seek it, but no amount of graceful deterrence or forceful denial of political ambition dissuaded his admirers from attempting to draft their hero for office. Douglas biographer James Simon is inaccurate when he writes that the justice "did not exert pressure on his friends to drop their campaign on his behalf."[88] Bill Douglas made all reasonable efforts to stop his friends from promoting him for political office. His personal papers are replete with such evidence. Douglas did not harbor the presidential ambitions historians have traditionally ascribed to him. Though Roosevelt wanted him, and though he had an active and able core of supporters, Douglas chose to remain on the Court and eschewed any and all opportunities for political office.

ENDNOTES

1. William O. Douglas, *The Court Years, 1939-1975: The Autobiography of William O. Douglas* (New York: Random House, 1980), p. 3. Douglas's other autobiographical works are *Of Men and Mountains* (New York: Harper and Brothers, 1950), and *Go East, Young Man: The Early Years* (New York: Random House, 1974).

2. Polling data reveal that William O. Douglas was not exactly a household name prior to the 1944 election. In November 1942, 75 percent of Democrats polled either had "no opinion" of Douglas or said he was "unfamiliar." In February 1943, 79 percent of polled Democrats said "no opinion" or "unfavorable" when asked about Douglas. In a May 1943 poll, only 2 percent of polled Democrats favored Douglas for president, and by November 1943, only 1 percent. It is clear that Douglas had little name recognition among rank-and-file Democrats. See George H. Gallup, *The Gallup Poll: Public Opinion, 1935-1971*, vol. 1: 1935-1948 (New York: Random House, 1972), pp. 358, 375, 385, 423.

3. James F. Simon, *Independent Journey: The Life of William O. Douglas* (New York: Harper and Row, 1980), pp. 257–75; Melvin I. Urofsky, ed., *The Douglas Letters: Selections from the Private Papers of Justice William O. Douglas* (Bethesda, MD: Adler and Adler, 1987), pp. 213–14. Simon's work in general is quite excellent—my only qualm lies with what I believe to be his misinterpretation of Douglas's "political ambitions," which have been recounted in other works of political history and biography of the Roosevelt era, as well as in works of judicial history, including such volumes as Frank Freidel, *Franklin D. Roosevelt: A Rendezvous with Destiny* (Boston: Little Brown, 1990), p. 535; and G. Edward White, *The American Judicial Tradition*, 2nd ed., (New York: Oxford University Press, 1988), pp. 399–400.

4. Janeway, interview with James F. Simon, May 28, 1979, in Simon, *Independent Journey*, p. 265.

5. Janeway, "Birth of the Tickets," *Fortune* 30 (September 1944), pp. 127–32, 260. Janeway wrote, "Douglas did not want the job. To each White House confidant who brought him word that he was the man, his answer was the same" (p. 132). The other instances of Janeway's awareness that Douglas had no presidential ambitions are cited.

6. See Joseph Lash, ed., *From the Diaries of Felix Frankfurter* (New York: W.W. Norton, 1975), especially pp. 309–38; Clifford, *Counsel to the*

President: A Memoir (New York: Random House, 1991), p. 216: "Douglas wanted to be President, of that I had no doubt." Oscar Chapman, Truman's secretary of the Interior (after Douglas had twice refused the position) also believed that "Bill Douglas wanted to be President of the United States very much." See the Oscar L. Chapman Oral History transcript, pp. 72–73, Harry S. Truman Presidential Library, Independence, Missouri.

7. Douglas, *Court Years,* p. 283.

8. See Robert H. Ferrell, *Choosing Truman: The Democratic Convention of 1944* (Columbia: University of Missouri Press, 1994), p. 10: "Roosevelt could choose any running mate he wanted. The party needed him against Governor Dewey. The leaders were not powerful enough to dictate a running mate." Ferrell also believed that Douglas sought the presidency, but "had no judgment about how to advance his candidacy" (p. 84).

9. Dennis J. Hutchinson, "William O. Douglas," in *The Oxford Companion to the Supreme Court of the United States*, ed. Kermit Hall (New York: Oxford University Press, 1992), p. 233.

10. 307 U.S. 277(1939).

11. Douglas, *Go East Young Man,* pp. 466–68; Melvin Urofsky, "William O. Douglas as Common Law Judge," in *The Warren Court in Historical and Political Perspective*, ed. Mark Tushnet (Charlottesville: University of Virginia Press, 1993), p. 69.

12. The Harold Ickes Manuscript Diary, Library of Congress, Manuscript Division, Washington, DC, Container 6, p. 5020 (December 1, 1940), hereafter cited as Ickes Diary. The date of a diary entry is not necessarily the date on which described actions occurred. It was Ickes's practice to record the week's events on the weekend.

13. Ferrell, *Choosing Truman,* pp. ix, 3.

14. Quoted in James MacGregor Burns, *Roosevelt: The Soldier of Freedom, 1940-1945* (New York: Harcourt Brace Jovanovich, 1970), p. 509.

15. Learned Hand to Felix Frankfurter, September 7, 1942, Felix Frankfurter Papers, Box 64, Library of Congress, Manuscript Division, Washington, DC.

16. Frankfurter to Stone, August 22, 1944, Harlan F. Stone Papers, Box 74, Library of Congress, Manuscript Division, Washington, DC (hereafter HFSP).

17. Henry A. Wallace, *The Price of Vision: The Diary of Henry A. Wallace, 1942-1946*, ed. by John Morton Blum (Boston: Houghton Mifflin, 1973), p. 139. Diary entry is dated November 30, 1942.

18. Ibid., p. 250 (diary entry of September 15, 1943).

19. Ibid., p. 213 (diary entry of May 31, 1943); see also Michael R. Beschloss, *Kennedy and Roosevelt: The Uneasy Alliance* (New York: W.W. Norton, 1980), p. 254: "Kennedy had hoped for months that the Democrats would nominate William O. Douglas."

20. Douglas allegedly said this to his SEC assistant Gerhard Gesell after hearing of his nomination to the high Court. See Simon, *Independent Journey*, p. 259.

21. Ickes Diary, Container 10, p. 7430 (February 7, 1943).

22. Arthur Krock, *Memoirs: Sixty Years on the Firing Line* (New York: Funk & Wagnall, 1968), pp. 176–7.

23. Ickes Diary, Container 11, p. 8490 (December 26, 1943).

24. E. Palmer Hoyt to Douglas, February 27, 1943, William O. Douglas Papers, Box 340, Library of Congress, Manuscript Division, Washington, DC, (hereafter WODP).

25. Douglas to Francis T. Maloney, January 14, 1944, WODP, Box 353.

26. Maloney to Douglas, January 17, 1944, WODP, Box 353, emphasis added. See also Douglas, *Court Years*, pp. 281–2.

27. Maloney to Douglas, July 10, 1944, WODP, Box 537.

28. Ickes Diary, Container 11, p. 8922 (June 27, 1944): "During the last few days I have tried Bill Douglas out on several people and I have found a good response." Ickes Diary, Container 12, pp. 8948–49 (June 2, 1944).

29. Ickes Diary, Container 12, pp. 8957–58 (June 4, 1944).

30. Ibid., p. 8966 (June 4, 1944).

31. Ibid., p. 9083 (July 16, 1944).

32. Douglas, *Court Years*, pp. 281–2.

33. Douglas to Maloney, July 14, 1944, WODP, Box 357.

34. Melvin I. Urofsky, "Conflict Among the Brethren: Felix Frankfurter, William O. Douglas, and the Clash of Personalities and Philosophies on the United States Supreme Court," *Duke Law Journal* 71 (February 1988): p. 104.

35. Ickes Diary, Container 12, p. 9012 (June 18, 1944).

36. Richard Neuberger to Douglas, July 8, 1944, WODP, Box 359.

37. Quoted in Freidel, *Franklin D. Roosevelt*, p. 533.

38. Samuel I. Rosenman, *Working with Roosevelt* (New York: Harper & Brothers, 1952), p. 440.

39. Ferrell, *Choosing Truman*, p. 3.

40. Ickes Diary, Container 12, p. 9080 (July 16, 1944). Hannegan and Ickes spoke "earlier in the week," presumably prior to the July 11 meeting in which FDR finally decided upon Truman as his running mate.

41. Ibid., pp. 9082–83. Ickes noted that FDR had already ruled out James Byrnes and Henry Wallace as potential running mates, and "did not say much about Truman." Abe Fortas later corroborated this story in a postconvention letter to Douglas, writing "the President told Ickes that he would very much like to have you as the Vice Presidential nominee," but—importantly—"Ickes never construed this as an absolute commitment. The general impression among the 'insiders,'" Fortas added, "was that you were the President's first choice." (Fortas to Douglas, July 25, 1944, WODP, Box 537).

42. Quoted in Robert E. Sherwood, *Roosevelt and Hopkins: An Intimate History* (New York: Harper & Brothers, 1948), p. 881.

43. Ickes Diary, Container 12, p. 9086 (July 16, 1944).

44. Ibid., also see Ferrell, *Choosing Truman*, p. 11: "Pauley was flying in from Chicago and did not have a chance to converse at the Mayflower."

45. Oscar R. Ewing, Oral History transcript, p. 105, Truman Library.

46. Ferrell, *Choosing Truman,* p. 10.

47. Ickes Diary, Container 13, p. 10125 (November 14, 1945).

48. The meeting is discussed in Burns, *Soldier of Freedom*, pp. 504–5 (source of quote); Freidel, *Franklin D. Roosevelt*, pp. 533–4; Ferrell, *Choosing Truman*, pp. 11–14; Rosenman, *Working with Roosevelt*, pp. 444–5; David McCullough, *Truman* (New York: Simon and Schuster, 1992), pp. 300–1; George

E. Allen, *Presidents Who Have Known Me* (New York: Simon and Schuster, 1950), pp. 128–9; Matthew J. Connelly Oral History transcript, p. 92, Truman Library. Doubtless there are other sources.

49. Quoted in Ferrell, *Choosing Truman*, p. 13, among many other places.

50. McCullough, *Truman*, p. 300; Burns, *Soldier of Freedom*, p. 504. In his discussion of the meeting, McCullough misstates Douglas's age as fifty-three. Douglas, born in October 1898, was forty-five years old.

51. Edwin Pauley overheard FDR tell this to Hannegan. Quoted in Ferrell, *Choosing Truman*, p. 14.

52. Janeway to Douglas, July 11, 1944, WODP, Box 537.

53. For example, Bob Kenny to Franklin Roosevelt, July 12, 1944, Harold Ickes Papers, Box 237, Library of Congress, Manuscript Division, Washington, DC, hereafter cited as HIP (Kenny chaired the California delegation); Henry L. Hess to Robert Hannegan, July 13, 1944, WODP, Box 537 (Hess cochaired the Oregon delegation).

54. "For Vice-President: Why Not Douglas?" *St. Louis Star-Times*, July 14, 1944, p. 12. Copy in HIP, Box 237.

55. Douglas to Harlan F. Stone, July 12, 1944, HFSP, Box 74.

56. Douglas to Maloney, July 14, 1944, WODP, Box 537.

57. Janeway, "Birth of the Tickets," *Fortune*, September 1944, p. 132. Janeway's statements about Douglas and Maloney in the article corroborate statements Douglas made to Maloney in his letter.

58. Douglas to Maloney, July 14, 1944, WODP, Box 537.

59. Ibid.

60. See Ickes Diary, Container 12, p. 9092 (July 16, 1944).

61. See Rosenman, *Working with Roosevelt*, pp. 446, 449.

62. Roosevelt to George W. Norris, July 17, 1944, in Elliott Roosevelt, ed., *F.D.R.: His Personal Letters, 1928-1945* (New York: Duell, Sloan and Pearce, 1950), vol. 2, p. 1523.

63. Oscar Chapman Oral History transcript, Truman Library, pp. 21–22.

64. Ickes Diary, Container 12, p. 9092 (July 16, 1944).

65. See Ferrell, *Choosing Truman*, p. 83.

66. Ickes to Roosevelt, July 24, 1944, HIP, Box 237. See also T.H. Watkins, *Righteous Pilgrim: The Life and Times of Harold L. Ickes, 1874-1952* (New York: Henry Holt, 1990), p. 812.

67. After the convention, Eliot Janeway apprised Douglas of the convention's events, what transpired and about the specific plan to draft him should a ballot deadlock occur. Janeway to Douglas, August 4, 1944, WODP, Box 537. See also George Killion to Douglas, August 1, 1944, WODP, Box 537, about Maloney's desire to nominate Douglas; but also see Maloney's own brief explanation in Maloney to Douglas, July 27, 1944, WODP, Box 537: "I fought like hell to keep some of [your admirers] from nominating you."

68. Abe Fortas to Douglas, July 25, 1944, WODP, Box 537.

69. Ickes Diary, Container 12, p. 9705 (May 6, 1945).

70. Janeway to Douglas, August 4, 1944, WODP, Box 537.

71. Ibid.

72. Ickes, telegram to Roosevelt, July 19, 1944, HIP, Box 237.

73. Letter reprinted in Ferrell, *Choosing Truman*, p. 81; Rosenman, *Working with Roosevelt*, p. 446; McCullough, *Truman*, p. 306; Freidel, *Franklin D. Roosevelt*, p. 534.

74. See Douglas, interview with Eric Sevareid, CBS, "CBS Reports," September 1972, "Mr. Justice Douglas." The transcript of this televised interview is in Robert H. Keller Jr., ed., *In Honor of Justice Douglas: A Symposium on Individual Freedom and the Government* (Westport, CT: Greenwood Press, 1979), pp. 148–69; see p. 152. See also Douglas, *Court Years*, p. 283.

75. Grace Tully, *F.D.R.: My Boss* (New York: Charles Scribner's Sons, 1949), p. 276.

76. See Ferrell, *Choosing Truman*, pp. 83, 120.

77. Wallace, *Price of Vision*, p. 368. Wallace described these events in a section of his diary he called a "summary of the political maneuvering at the 1944 Democratic convention."

78. Ickes Diary, Container 12, p. 9113 (July 23, 1944).

79. Douglas to Stone, August 12, 1944, HFSP, Box 74.

80. Ickes Diary, Container 12, p. 9279 (October 7, 1944).

81. Douglas, *Court Years*, pp. 283–84.

82. Douglas to Ickes, August 21, 1944, HIP, Box 237.

83. Ickes Diary, Container 13, p. 9775 (June 2, 1945).

84. Frankfurter to Stone, August 22, 1944, HFSP, Box 74.

85. Henry L. Hess to Douglas, August 5, 1944, WODP, Box 537.

86. Ibid.

87. Janeway to Douglas, August 4, 1944, WODP, Box 537.

88. Simon, *The Antagonists: Hugo Black, Felix Frankfurter and Civil Liberties in Modern America* (New York: Simon and Schuster, 1989), p. 190.

III

Constitutional Law as Applied to Politics: The Roosevelt Legacy

8

Federalism, the Roosevelt Coalition, and Civil Rights
FDR's Political Leadership

Donald W. Jackson and James W. Riddlesperger Jr.

Most presidential scholars agree that during his entire tenure Franklin D. Roosevelt exhibited great restraint—if not deep-seated reluctance—against fully embracing and aggressively pursuing a civil rights agenda on behalf of African Americans. Was his reluctance the product of constitutionally prescribed federalism (that is, states' rights, according to the South), of political realities, of his leadership style, or of some combination of these? We are particularly interested in evaluating the claim that presidential reluctance to intervene in civil rights conflicts then, and some twenty years later during the Kennedy Administration, were founded *primarily* on the absence of constitutional or statutory federal power.

We will explore three interesting parallels between the political positions and civil rights policies of Franklin D. Roosevelt and John F. Kennedy. First, we can focus on FDR in 1941 and on Kennedy in 1963, for both presidents then confronted the prospect of a "March on Washington" by civil rights protesters, led by A. Philip Randolph.[1] In both instances the protesters sought more aggressive federal civil rights enforcement.

FDR was evidently apprehensive about "his march" which was planned for July 1, 1941, while the nation was then—still relatively quietly—preparing for war. To forestall the march, after meeting with the leaders of the March on Washington Committee, he issued Executive Order 8802 on June 25, 1941. That order established the Committee on Fair Employment Practice and stated a policy of nondiscrimination in federal and defense industry employment practices.[2]

The Kennedy administration was unable to dissuade civil rights leaders from the march on Washington of August 27, 1963, though various administration leaders tried, including the president himself, who met with the march leaders on June 22.[3] His June 19, 1963 civil rights message to Congress, which called for broad civil rights legislation, had already solicited restraint by leaders of the civil rights movement. The 1963 march, which included the magnificent "I Have a Dream" address of Dr. Martin Luther King Jr., probably contributed to the eventual enactment of the Civil Rights Act of 1964 (during the Johnson administration), despite the fears of the Kennedy administration that it might have the opposite effect.

Second, we can focus on the status of the Democratic coalition during the two administrations. Stephen Skowronek[4] has pointed out that political coalitions go through several stages in their life cycle—including reconstruction, regime articulation, and regime disjunction. The Roosevelt and Kennedy administrations can be seen as illustrative of two of those coalition stages—reconstruction and articulation. Roosevelt's coalition was built over the issue of the revival of the American economy. To accomplish that task, he was able to enlist the support of not only northern liberals but also southern "Bourbons" and big business.[5] He was, in fact, dependent on southern leaders in Congress to accomplish economic reform, but such dependence precluded major action in civil rights policy. While he had to manage conflict among those groups to pursue his economic policies, the preoccupation with economic (and later war) policy allowed him largely to finesse the issue of civil rights. When Kennedy came to power, he too had priorities other than civil rights, most notably "the New Frontier" and international concerns. Kennedy was in many ways heir to the Roosevelt coalition. Unlike during the Roosevelt years, however, Kennedy took power at a time when African American migration into the North had occurred and when "an ever more aggressive civil rights movement in the South had made it increasingly difficult for a Democratic president to resist a more definitive commitment."[6] In other words, Roosevelt, because of the time in which he served and his agenda, soft pedaled civil rights, while Kennedy eventually was forced to confront them.

A third comparison can be drawn from Burke Marshall's *Federalism and Civil Rights*.[7] First delivered as a lecture series at Columbia University in the spring of 1964, Marshall's book argued that federal civil rights intervention was made difficult, and sometimes impossible, by the lack of federal authority.

Robert Kennedy's introduction to Marshall's book specifically concludes that federal authority sustained military intervention in Oxford in September 1962 (to enforce the federal court-ordered admission of James Meredith to the University of Mississippi) and the use of federal marshals in May 1961 in Montgomery (to protect the Freedom Riders in their interstate travel), but that *no* federal authority existed to support federal intervention in Birmingham in May 1963 (to protect peaceful protestors), or in the Mississippi summer of 1964 (to protect voting rights volunteers).[8]

Marshall himself first reviewed voting rights enforcement and concluded, fairly enough, that case-by-case voting rights enforcement, even by the Department of Justice, was unlikely to produce significant inroads against massive voting discrimination by county officials intent on resistance. The Voting Rights Act of 1965 eventually brought an effective solution to this problem through its 50 percent "triggering device," which suspended state restrictions on voting and provided for federal voting registrars.

Marshall's chapter on "The Administration of Justice" is more problematic. He argued that when local law enforcement authorities engage in discriminatory law enforcement, chiefly against "Negroes" and in aid of Jim Crow traditions, the only options open to the federal Justice Department were to bring criminal charges against local officials for violating federal constitutional rights, or to complain to local authorities about their conduct. He then proceeds to review a series of examples of discrimination by local officials in the South between 1961 and 1963, each of which seems to involve a violation of federally protected rights. He concludes, that while some of these instances are clear violations, "In many cases, however, the constitutional limits on police action were sufficiently vague, or so much in flux at the time that no implication of deliberate double standard is provable."[9] Marshall adds two additional principles that constrain the federal government: (1) the premise that rights must be asserted by individuals, and (2) the presumption that "federal courts will not interfere while the system is at work—that is, they will not enjoin a *pending* or *future* state criminal proceeding." Of course, neither of these principles would be involved in a federal criminal prosecution of local officials, though he did not mention that in presenting his two principles.

Marshall noted that the department of Justice had already proposed two basic amendments to federal civil rights law. The first would have allowed the Department to seek federal injunctions against state deprivation of federally protected rights, and the second would have provided for removal to federal courts of any criminal prosecution that might infringe "constitutional guarantees." But while thus allowing for the possibility of statutory change he revealed a large measure of skepticism. He admits that, "There is no constitutional or doctrinal difficulty involved. But the consequences would be to destroy the means by which Mississippi maintained order."[10] Thus, he expressed concern about the "practical consequences of federal intervention." His concluding paragraph in his lecture on the administration of justice sums this up:

> Those who say that civil rights issues cut into the fabric of federalism are correct. They cut most deeply where police power is involved, for the police as well as for those in conflict with the police. There would be vast problems in any attempts at federal control of the administration of justice, even through the moderate method of federal court injunctions. Yet vast problems have been created already by police indifference to Negro rights in the South, and they will grow if the trend is not turned. The loss of faith in law—the usefulness of federal law and the fairness of local law—is gaining very rapidly among Negro and white civil rights workers. The consequences for the future cannot be foreseen.[11]

To be sure, we must be conscious of the potential error of anachronism in reviewing Marshall's words. The fact that federal intervention, following the Civil Rights Act of 1964 and the Voting Rights Act of 1965 (and subsequent civil rights legislation) did not destroy local authority in the South, is not a fair argument against Marshall's prior concerns expressed in 1964. Nor should we discount the fact that before his words were spoken the Kennedy administration had already chosen to introduce and work for the strong civil rights legislation that eventually would become the Civil Rights Act of 1964, (through the efforts of the Johnson administration). Probably the best way to avoid anachronistic analysis is to examine the precedents of *prior administrations*, and that is why we choose to examine civil rights during FDR's administration. Nonetheless, we ought to recognize that the key concerns Marshall expressed are *practical or political* rather than strictly constitutional. Was this also the case during Franklin

Roosevelt's presidency? Was federalism the real culprit, or was it the presidential politics or the "racial politics" of the time? To answer such questions we can examine the efforts to pass antilynching legislation during the 1930s, as well as the new understanding of federalism that followed the "switch in time that saved nine" in 1937.[12] Indeed, we will find that these two seemingly disparate issues are related.

Antilynching Bills During the New Deal

Harvard Sitkoff[13] has suggested that the idea that the federal government had the "right and duty to intervene on behalf of the economic well-being of its citizens led to the corollary that the federal government had the obligation to protect the lives and constitutional rights of African-Americans."[14] The Costigan-Wagner antilynching bill was a manifestation of that idea. The NAACP, which had launched its antilynching campaign in 1933, began pushing the Costigan-Wagner Act in 1935.[15] But in the early days of the Roosevelt Administration, leaders of the antilynching fight found it difficult even to meet with the president.[16] Given their difficulty even in seeing FDR, the president's December 1933 address to the Federal Council of Churches, in which he acknowledged that lynching was "murder, and a deliberate and definite disobedience of the Commandment, 'Thou shalt not kill,'" was rightly regarded as a symbolic step forward.[17] While Roosevelt had condemned lynching in his 1934 State of the Union Address,[18] he also told newsmen gathered at a May 1934 press conference that there were doubts about the bill's constitutionality.[19] However, newspaper accounts, and First Lady Eleanor Roosevelt herself, suggested that it was the president's concern about offending key southern congressmen that kept him from giving antilynching legislation his full support. For whatever reason, the farthest the president was prepared to go was on June 8, 1934,[20] when Mrs. Roosevelt, in a conference with National Association for the Advancement of Colored People (NAACP)

Executive Secretary Walter White, directed White to give Costigan and Wagner the following message:

> If the sponsors of the bill will go at once to Senator Robinson and say to him that, if, in a lull, the anti-lynching bill can be brought to a vote, the President authorizes the sponsors to say that the President will be glad to see the bill pass and wishes it passed.[21]

Perhaps it is not surprising that the bill did not come to a vote in the Senate in 1934, and the bill failed again in the Senate in 1935.

More than sixty antilynching measures were introduced for the 1937 session. In that same year the American Civil Liberties Union (ACLU) also made antilynching legislation its top priority. One of the key proposals was written by the NAACP itself, and that bill was the subject of a revealing appraisal by the Department of Justice.

On January 29, 1937, Attorney General Homer Cummings had asked his staff to study the NAACP bill (the Wagner-Van Nuys bill), and on February 8 they sent him an eighteen-page memorandum response.[22] He in turn sent the memorandum to the president on February 11. The memo found this antilynching bill to be strongly based on Section 5 of the Fourteenth Amendment, which gives Congress specific authority to enforce that amendment by appropriate legislation. The memo also reviewed case authorities that previously had upheld the power of Congress, under Section 5, for example, under 18 U.S.C.A. sec. 51, which had made it a federal crime to conspire to injure persons in the exercise of their civil liberties. The memo distinguished the Wagner-Van Nuys bill from the 1935 Costigan-Wagner bill. The Costigan-Wagner bill sought, under certain circumstances, to impose criminal liability on private citizens who were members of a lynch mob, while the 1937 NAACP-drafted version proposed to punish only state or local governmental officials who, while acting on behalf of the state, actually denied a citizen equal protection or due process of law by failure to perform a duty imposed by state law. The memorandum unambiguously endorsed the constitutionality of that approach and rejected the objection that such federal criminal liability would invade the powers of states reserved by the Tenth Amendment.

To the objection that the states already had sufficient and effective laws against lynching, the memorandum reported that only nine states had made lynching a crime, and that in a thirty-year period only "8/10 of one per cent of reported lynchings were followed by convictions."[23]

The only serious substantive changes suggested by the Department of Justice memo were to the provision which would have amended the federal kidnapping statute[24] to include the transporting in interstate or foreign commerce of any person "unlawfully abducted and held for purposes of punishment, coercion or intimidation." Even those changes were for clarification rather than substance.

Remember that it was on January 29, 1935, that Homer Cummings had asked his staff to review the NAACP-drafted bill. In his diary entry of January 30, 1937, Secretary of Commerce Harold Ickes reports a conversation with Vice President Garner, who expressed his support for antilynching legislation, although the vice president noted the difficulty of enacting a bill that would be effective and withstand constitutional challenge. Garner specifically mentioned amending the Lindberg Act and also founding the bill on the Equal Protection Clause.[25] If even a conservative Texan like Garner was prepared to support antilynching legislation, it seems quite clear that by early 1937, President Roosevelt was well aware that antilynching legislation might be enacted that would pass constitutional muster. The states' rights arguments of southern congressmen therefore were tactical and political rather than constitutional. It will be instructive, however, to put this reality in perspective by examining what was happening in other political arenas in February 1937.

The Court-Packing Plan and New Federalism

On February 5, 1937, President Roosevelt disclosed his "Court-packing" plan to his cabinet. Remember that Cummings sent the president the Department of Justice memorandum on the antilynching bill on February 11. Probably it could not have arrived at the White House at a more inopportune time, for the president and his senior staff were preoccupied with the intense reaction the Court-packing plan had produced.[26]

According to most accounts the only senior officials who were involved in formulating the Court-packing plan were Attorney General Homer Cummings and Solicitor General Stanley Reed. At the final drafting stage Judge Sam Rosenman and Donald Richberg were added to the team,[27] although Raymond Moley[28] suspected the encouragement of Thomas Corcoran and Benjamin Cohen.[29]

Conflict between President Roosevelt and the Supreme Court had been building, especially since the *Schechter* case[30] was decided in May 1935. There a unanimous Supreme Court struck down the National Industrial Recovery Act of 1933, and not only did the Court reject the delegation of legislative power, it went on to declare the act to be beyond the powers of Congress under the interstate commerce clause. In a carefully staged meeting with 200 reporters on May 31, 1935, Roosevelt spoke for ninety minutes and castigated the Court's "horse and buggy definition of interstate commerce."[31] The Supreme Court's result was reached despite the government's brief, which, relying on the 1824 decision in *Gibbons v. Ogden*,[32] had argued that, "business in the United States has become a single integrated whole." The principal author of the brief pondered that since virtually every business in America had come, through the national market, to affect businesses in other states, Congress could regulate all aspects of commerce (Irons, 1982: 92).[33]

A year later the Court also held coal mining (*Carter v.*

Carter Coal Co.[34]) and agriculture (*U.S. v. Butler*[35]) to be local activities and therefore intrastate rather than interstate commerce. Alsop and Catledge[36] wrote that the Court had labeled industrial, agricultural, and social problems as, "Local do not touch." Attorney general (and later associate justice) Robert H. Jackson wrote in 1941:

> The Court conducted a dual campaign against the powers which the Congress thought had been granted it by the Constitution. On the one hand, it *narrowed* the scope of the great clauses of the Constitution granting powers to Congress. It seriously contracted the interstate commerce clause and it read startling exemptions into the taxing power. Simultaneously, it *expanded* the scope of the clauses that limited the power of Congress, such as the "due process clause" and the clauses withholding power from the federation. At the same time, it used the "due process" concept to cut down the effective power of the states."[37]

Two days after the *Schechter* case was decided, Felix Frankfurter, then still a professor at Harvard Law School, wrote the president privately outlining the conflict with the Supreme Court. Frankfurter counseled caution, urging the president to let the Court continue to strike down New Deal legislation, and when they had prejudiced themselves to the country at large to "propose a Constitutional amendment that would give the national Government adequate power to cope with national economic and industrial problems."[38] The idea of a constitutional amendment continued through the next year when Cummings wrote the president suggesting that the 1936 Democratic platform ought to include a proposed amendment.[39] But in the actual event, Roosevelt rejected the amendment option, arguing that with sufficient resources and organization it would be easy to postpone ratification of such an amendment until after the 1940 election.[40] Instead he proposed his Court-packing plan on February 5, 1937.

The story of the Court-packing plan is an oft-told tale that need not be repeated here. Our purpose instead is to suggest that while the Court-packing plan itself failed, the constitutional turnabout that began with the "switch in time that saved nine" on April 12, 1937, produced, for most practical purposes a new Constitution, at least with respect to the powers of Congress and the president over domestic affairs. In a memorandum said to be dictated by Roosevelt himself in May or June 1937,[41] five cases decided before the Court-packing bill were contrasted with three cases decided after the bill, and the president traced by hand the decisional connections between the two sets. The memorandum cites the "Wagner Act Case" (*NLRB v. Jones and Laughlin*[42]) and the "Social Security Case" (*Steward Machine Co. v. Davis*[43]) for having provided "new interpretations" for the federal commerce power and of the federal spending and taxing power. At the bottom of the page Roosevelt[44] concluded that, "The President has attained the most difficulty [sic] of his *objectives*, i.e., the liberalization of the interpretation of the Constitution. He has yet to obtain: [hand written insertion: these two *objectives*] (a) insurance of the continuity of that liberalism and (b) a more perfect judicial mechanism for giving a maximum of justice in a minimum of time."[45] Raymond Moley who eventually split with the president and embraced the opposition to the post-1936 New Deal, even argued that as a consequence of the Court's turnabout, the Roosevelt Court had "stretched not only the general welfare clause, but the interstate commerce provisions of the Constitution to an altogether dangerous degree."[46]

Whether dangerous or not, after 1937 Congress and the president had the keys to whatever power was necessary to achieve a national solution to national emergencies. The state of the economy was seen as such an emergency, but lynching and the rights of "Negroes" in general were not. The principal difficulties for civil rights were neither in "the stars" nor in the Constitution, but in American politics—in general—and in presidential leadership in particular.

A simple example of what could be done, when an administration chose to—in January 1942 an African American man named Cleo Wright was lynched in a small Missouri town. Attorney General Francis Biddle authorized an investigation of the lynching:

> Though Biddle's efforts were fruitless, they signaled a policy change in Washington. Federal officials had traditionally maintained that such incidents were local matters. Since southern blacks could hardly expect local law-enforcement personnel (some of whom may have been involved in, or at least knowledgeable of the attack) to undertake an inquiry, let alone to redress a denial of due process, the intervention of federal authorities established an important precedent.[47]

While an unproductive investigation seems at best a tiny step forward, if it was indeed an important precedent for 1942, it seems to represent a lesson largely overlooked in Marshall's 1964 lectures on federalism and civil rights.

The Politics of the Possible

There are many illustrations of Franklin Roosevelt's policy priorities and of his concern about the intrusion of civil rights issues that might defeat the "main chance." The following examples are presented in chronological order.

1933-34

From the beginning, Roosevelt and his key advisers knew that the Democratic coalition required that southern congressmen be placated on racial issues, something that could be done because of the time in which he served.[48] This required the administration to concede that the federal government ought not to meddle with southern racial segregation.[49] Economic recovery was the top priority, and Roosevelt insisted that "First things come first," and that "I can't alienate certain votes I need for measures that are more important at the moment by pushing any measures that would entail a fight."[50]

From 1933, but especially in 1934 and 1935, as we have seen, it was Roosevelt's fear of offending southern congressmen that kept him from giving his full support to antilynching legislation, and Roosevelt remarked that he "did not choose the tools with which I must work.":

> Had I been permitted to choose them I would have selected quite different ones. But I've got to get legislation passed by Congress to save America. The Southerners by reason of the seniority rule in Congress are chairman or occupy strategic places on most of the Senate and House committees. If I come out for the anti-lynching bill now, they will block every bill I ask Congress to pass to keep America from collapsing. I just can't take that risk.[51]

1935

Norman Thomas visited Roosevelt to express his grave concern about the plight of southern sharecroppers, in this instance tenant farmers in Arkansas. Most of the agricultural support provided by the New Deal reached landowners, but rarely their tenants. In response Roosevelt agreed that the tenancy situation bothered him as well, but made clear his agreement with his advisers (Rexford Tugwell among others) who were concerned about offending southern congressmen, thereby crippling the New Deal coalition. Arthur Schlesinger Jr.'s massive history of the Roosevelt administration contains the following quote:

> "Norman, I'm a damned sight better politician than you are." "Well certainly, Mr. President," Thomas replied. "You are on that side of the table and I'm on this." Roosevelt added: "I know the South and there is arising a new generation of leaders in the South and we've got to be patient. [52]

1936

Schlesinger also reports that Mary McLeod Bethune, who

served as the director of the Office of Negro Affairs of the National Youth Administration from 1936 through 1944, said that Roosevelt always was cautious on racial issues:

> Mrs. Bethune reports that, when she proposed drastic steps to him, he usually demurred, saying that a New Reconstruction in the South would have to keep pace with democratic progress on a national scale. "Mrs. Bethune, if we do that now, we'll hurt our program over there. We must do this thing stride by stride, but leaving no stone unturned." Yet he communicated a genuine sense of commitment in the midst of his recognition of complexity. "People like you and me are fighting and must continue to fight for the day when a man will be regarded as a man regardless of his race or faith or country," he once said to Mrs. Bethune. "That day will come, but we must pass through perilous times before we realize it."[53]

1937

Even Harold Ickes, self identified as the strongest advocate for "Negroes" in the Roosevelt cabinet, wrote in his diary on April 9, 1937 that:

> As a matter of fact, I think it is up to the states to work out their own social problems if possible, and while I have also been interested in seeing that the Negro has a square deal, I have never dissipated my strength against the particular stone wall of segregation. I believe that wall will crumble when the Negro has brought himself to a higher educational and economic status. After all, we can't force people on each other who do not like each other, even when no question of color is involved.[54]

From the perspective of our time, Ickes's words seem to concede far too much, but Steven Lawson and Harvard Sitkoff both concluded that Roosevelt held a similarly condescending view toward racial affairs, believing that the "Negro" was "an unfortunate ward of the nation to be treated kindly and with charity as a reward for good behavior."[55]

1940

Lawson reported that when African American leaders pressed Roosevelt to integrate the military in the fall of 1940, the president refused, citing practices that had "been proved satisfactory over a long period of years." "To do otherwise . . . would risk upsetting white soldiers and would lower their morale, thereby jeopardizing the war effort."[56] "Dr. 'in-the-War' insisted that the war must be won first."[57]

1941

At the beginning of this chapter we reported that President Roosevelt had issued Executive Order 8802 on June 24, 1941 only when confronted with the prospect of 100,000 "Negroes" marching on Washington. According to Harvard Sitkoff, Roosevelt feared the possibility of violence, wanted to avoid the embarrassment of a protest march in Washington, and was concerned that the march might split the Democratic coalition in Congress.[58] In Roosevelt's meeting with Walter White and A. Philip Randolph, White reported that:

> The President turned to me and asked, "Walter, many people will *really* march?" I told him no less than one hundred thousand. The President looked me full in the eye for a long time in an obvious effort to find out if I were bluffing or exaggerating. Eventually he appeared to believe that I meant what I said. "What do you want me to do?" he asked.[59]

Sitkoff's conclusion was that Roosevelt "capitulated as a last resort," but only partially. Apart from the issuance of the Executive Order 8802, he was trying to balance the forces of reaction on one side against the demands of civil rights activists on the other.[60]

These examples represent the contemporaneous appraisals of the political situation by President Roosevelt and his key advisers. Whether they were correct is not the issue. Neither is our retrospective judgment relevant. The examples serve instead to illustrate the point that President Roosevelt's reluctance to act on racial issues was political, rather than constitutional, and that even then he was capable of action, albeit mostly symbolic, when forced by circumstances. Such conduct was also characteristic of his leadership style.

FDR's Leadership Style

Alsop and Catledge recount a fascinating anecdote about Roosevelt. The "hottest bloods" amongst the New Dealers wanted a more radical, more progressive program. In response to their urgings, Roosevelt told the following parable about a missionary to the totem-worshiping Indians of the Pacific Northwest:

> One man, he said, sought to woo the Indians from their superstitions by main force. He and his fellow zealots marched into the villages and cast down the poles, and told the tribes to worship totems no longer. Instead they killed the missionary and adhered more fervently to their ancient beliefs. The advocate of force was followed by a wiser fellow, who went to live among the Indians as a friend. Once they had lost their suspicion of him he began going out every night in the darkness, to scrape away a few handfuls of earth from around the bases of the totems. Eventually the poles fell of their own weight, and the Indians complaisantly accepted the wise missionary's substitute for the totem worship. A man who wishes to guide the government in new directions, added the President, must imitate the wise missionary.[61]

There can be little doubt that this parable sums up Roosevelt's approach to policy making during his first two terms, except when overtaken by hubris in his Court-packing plan, following his reelection in 1936. Scholars generally agree that the conspicuous successes of the first hundred days were not produced by Roosevelt's philosophy, nor by his zealotry, but by the force of emergency and by his ability to improvise during rapidly changing circumstances.

James MacGregor Burns, Roosevelt's first political biographer, found that FDR was indeed a consummate pragmatist, rather than a theorist. The president's method, especially during the first term, was to mediate between contending interest groups. Policy emerged, "shaped only roughly by his underlying concept of the public good, from the day-to-day projects and improvisations of his regime." Burns concluded that this:

> meant that he took the more passive method of responding to major political and economic pressures, rather than the more positive one of deliberately building up some voting alignment of the left or right that would recast the basic pattern of political power. It meant that he ignored the possibilities for the future of a voting alignment of great strength—one composed of less privileged farm groups, masses of unorganized or ill-organized industrial workers, consumers, Negroes, and other minority groups. It meant that . . . he was hazy and cool on the subject of the pending antilynching bill.[62]

Burns was probably right about the first term, but perhaps not about the second, for it was during the 1936 campaign that Roosevelt began to embrace the prospect of the sort of future voting alignment that Burns described.[63] But if that alignment ever embraced African Americans during the 1936 campaign, it was more often by virtue of their economic condition than by their race.[64]

Raymond Moley, who by the time he wrote *The First New Deal* in 1966 was certainly no longer a loyal friend of FDR, nonetheless wrote a fascinating passage about the virtues of political leadership:

> Sincerity, as a quality known to the generality of people, is not fairly applicable to a politician. Or to put it another way, in a

> category of virtues appropriate to a politician, sincerity occupies a less exalted place than it does among the qualities of a novelist, a teacher or a scientist. And that is no way damning the politician, for he may exalt virtues such as kindness, understanding, and public service far beyond those who sniff at his lack of sincerity.[65]

Moley's remarks represent a level of subtlety rarely achieved by political analysts, but they suggest an important injunction: that we ought to judge a leader by the values he achieves, rather than the ones he represents with his own life.

John Roche has referred to Roosevelt as a "master of the politician's trade," a "champion broker," and a "superb manipulator;" "[h]e could also be sly, dishonest, disingenuous, disloyal and ruthless—a very tough customer to deal with."[66] This was the leader that Justice Oliver Wendell Holmes once described as having a "second-class intellect, but a first-class temperament."[67] His temperament, according to Roche, was that "of a superb mediator and conciliator, who unhindered by intellectual commitments to precision and efficiency, untroubled by the 'logical consequences of his actions,' rushed from one problem to another with an endless supply of ad hoc remedies."[68] On a more Machiavellian note, Rexford Tugwell added that, "Sometimes it was quite true that he did not know his own mind. He had not fully decided; but oftener he was simply determined not to let others know it until the time to act had come."[69] But whether by design or inadvertence, if Franklin Roosevelt was the embodiment of the politics of the possible, what did he actually achieve with respect to civil rights, given the political realities he confronted?

Symbolic Victories (and Some Quiet Tangible Ones)

Some achievements were quietly accomplished by subordinates like Harold Ickes, who in 1933 ended segregation in the Commerce Department's Washington, D.C. cafeterias and restrooms.[70] Ickes also persuaded Roosevelt to authorize an interdepartmental committee on Negro affairs in 1933, which eventually became known as the Black Cabinet, although it had no real power.[71]

Writing in 1973, Ralph Bunche said of the National Youth Administration (NYA) (which provided educational and work programs for the disadvantaged) that from its beginning it had included "Negroes" into every phase of its program, noting particularly the appointment of Dr. Mordecai Johnson, president of Howard University, and of Mary McLeod Bethune, founder of Bethune-Cookman College, to the NYA's National Advisory Committee.[72] Credit is often given to Roosevelt for appointing to office men and women who were well-disposed to move forward on racial justice, even though Roosevelt himself was not a crusader for civil rights.[73] Many have seen the hidden hand of Eleanor Roosevelt in such appointments.

On a more tangible level, Roosevelt issued Executive Order 7046, mandating that the Works Progress Administration hire people based on qualifications rather than practicing discrimination.[74] As another example, the NYA program in Texas in 1935-36 under State Director Lyndon B. Johnson had quietly helped African Americans, hispanics, and whites on a relatively equal, though segregated, basis.[75]

But not all New Deal programs served African Americans so well. The general idea was that the economic recovery programs were expected to help everyone, and that African Americans would benefit from them along with everyone else. However, payments to landowners for keeping acres out of production were not likely to benefit either agricultural laborers or tenant farmers, at least not without substantial federal regulatory protection. Meanwhile, if labor policy proved successful in raising wages and reducing hours, certain jobs that previously had been attractive only to African Americans, might begin to attract whites. African Americans did better from direct relief programs, like the jobs or education provided by the NYA or through federally subsidized housing.[76]

African Americans benefited from these programs because of their poverty, not their race, and in the South benefits routinely were administered and delivered through segregated programs.[77]

Many of the appraisals of New Deal programs report a paradox, either directly or implicitly. For example, several studies of the President's Committee on Fair Employment Practices (FEPC) (created by FDR only when faced with the prospect of the 1941 march on Washington) agree that World War II—and eventual scarcity in the labor market—had far more to do with "Negro" employment opportunity than did the work of the FEPC.[78] Yet the studies which report such conclusions often themselves contain paeans of praise for the symbolic victory the creation of the president's committee represented, suggesting, for example that the FEPC had brought "a point of focus which changed the climate of race relations and the vision of Negro leadership," or that the federal government had performed "a decisive act on behalf of the Negro citizen."[79]

Sometimes the symbolic victory was seen as that of "Negro" leadership and political action, rather than flowing from the New Deal itself:

> The FEPC's activity was unique. Never before had an agency of the federal government cooperated in such a way with minority groups and their organizations. Nevertheless its stance by no means reflected the sentiments of the Roosevelt Administration, which opposed its creation, gave it lip service instead of support, used it callously to defuse black protest, and blocked it when political expediency so dictated.[80]

More often, however, we find statements like the following:

> The inexorable fact cannot be avoided: under the Presidency of Franklin D. Roosevelt, the United States left the paths of tribalism for the high road of due process of law and substantive justice and equality. When he died in 1945, he left a nation far

> different from the one he inherited in 1933, a nation which had fought the greatest war in history without chauvinism or xenophobia, and in which even the most downtrodden minority, the Negroes, were sensing the light that heralds the dawn.[81]

Conclusion: "The Weasel" or "The Light That Heralds the Dawn"?

Arthur Spingarn worked in the Truman White House on civil rights issues. In his oral history interview he referred to James MacGregor Burns' description of Roosevelt's personality as containing the qualities of both the lion and the fox. Spingarn added that Roosevelt was more the fox than the lion, but that on civil rights issues, "he was pretty much of a weasel."[82] Yet others see the Roosevelt Administration as representing the "light that heralds the dawn." Which is the better metaphor?

The answer depends, in large measure, on what criteria one uses in evaluating a president, and the proper choice of criteria itself represents an important and enduring perplexity. Ought we to evaluate a president primarily for the personal qualities and values that he embodies, or for the results he obtains? Should we evaluate a president strictly by the standards, possibilities, and values of the times in which he lived? Or should we allow the standards, possibilities, and values of our own time to intrude, or even prevail? Obviously, no one can give final answers to such questions, but they nonetheless are important. In this conclusion, we choose to evaluate Franklin D. Roosevelt for what he was able to achieve and to judge him by the values, standards, and possibilities of the times in which he lived.

We believe that the historical record provides clear answers to the questions we raised at the beginning of this chapter. Especially after the constitutional revolution of 1937, Roosevelt's reluctance to take bold initiatives on civil rights was not the product of federalism—of his concession to constitutionally protected states' rights—but rather was his response to the combination of the political realities he confronted with his own leadership style. To draw comparisons with Kennedy's leadership is appropriate. Like Roosevelt, Kennedy sought to build a coalition including the leaders of the South. And like Roosevelt, Kennedy's commitment to civil rights, at least at first, was mostly abstract. The changing of the Democratic coalition led Kennedy to make civil rights a higher priority than did Roosevelt,[83] and made circumstances such that even had he wished to take a "go slow" approach to the issue, he would have been unable to, as the case of the march on Washington illustrates. Neustadt makes the same point in another way, writing that "he sought to steer a course toward integration that could hold inside our social order both impatient blacks and reactive whites—as tough a task of politics as we have known, and one faced no sooner than he had to."[84] But Kennedy's interpretation of the limits that federalism placed on civil rights action, as evidenced by Burke Marshall's book, seemed to ignore the lessons of the Roosevelt administration.[85]

While it seems evident that Roosevelt personally had little zeal for racial issues, he was not opposed to the rights that "Negro" leaders sought. As opportunities presented themselves and as political pressures dictated, he was able to respond with steps forward that represented—*relative to what had gone before*—a national change of direction. That change of direction was clearly perceptible to Negro leaders and to potential Negro voters, certainly both seen and feared by the traditional southern leadership in the Congress, but probably not very much recognized by the average white voter, especially in the North. In brief, most of the accomplishments during the Roosevelt years were symbolic, rather than tangible, and whenever tangible benefits were achieved they were due to programs directed at economic problems in general, rather than being strictly designed for African Americans or other minorities. Whether more could have been done by President Roosevelt, given both his political resources and the obstacles he confronted, is the most difficult question of all, and our attempts to answer it are most susceptible to twenty-twenty hindsight. Perhaps we can suggest, rather than answer, with the following two illustrations:

1. In a letter to an FDR presidential assistant, shortly after Roosevelt's death, a Negro voter wrote:

> You know what Mr. Roosevelt meant to Negroes. the think I am riting you for is will you try to make clear to Mr. Trueman what the Negroes want. and that is first class citizenship. we kno Mr. Roosevelt would have give us that. . . . Most Negroes believe Mr. Trueman is a Negro Hater. the town he came from is very unfair to Negroes. I feail you can explain to him that God created all men equal.[86]

2. In 1948, after the Democratic Convention had adopted a strong civil rights plank, which led to the Dixiecrat revolt, then governor Strom Thurmond of South Carolina was asked why southerners were leaving the party when Roosevelt had also endorsed equal rights for "Negroes?" Thurmond replied, "I agree, but Truman really means it."[87]

What better illustration could be offered for the proposition that political reality exists largely (perhaps only) in the minds of its varied observers? So probably both metaphors about President Roosevelt are true. "Weasel" to some, the "light that heralds the dawn to others"—not to mention the "lion" and the "fox." In all, Franklin Roosevelt was an unusually complex person, with a multifaceted political style, who, like all presidents, was not allowed to choose the tools with which he had to work.

ENDNOTES

1. A. Philip Randolph, founder (in 1925) and longtime president of the Brotherhood of Sleeping Car Porters, was the first to call for a march on Washington in January 1941. Herbert Garfunkel, *When Negroes March: The March on Washington Movement in the Organizational Politics for FEPC*

(Glencoe, IL: The Free Press, 1959), p. 7. Although Bayard Rustin first suggested the 1963 march, Randolph was the senior and "spiritual leader" of the 1963 march on Washington, which for him was the consummation of a lifelong dream. Louis Ruchames, *Race, Jobs, & Politics: The Story of the FEPC* (New York: Columbia University Press, 1953) p. 9; Mark Stern, *Calculating Visions* (New Brunswick, NJ: Rutgers University Press, 1992) p. 93.

2. Ruth P. Morgan, *The President and Civil Rights* (New York: St. Martin's Press, 1970), p. 38.

3. Bruce Miroff, *Pragmatic Illusions: The Presidential Politics of John F. Kennedy* (New York: David McKay Co., 1976), pp. 260–65.

4. Stephen Skowronek, *The Politics Presidents Make: Leadership from John Adams to George Bush* (Cambridge: Belknap Press of Harvard University Press, 1993), pp. 34–35.

5. Stephen Skowronek, "Presidential Leadership in Political Time," in *The Presidency and the Political System*, ed. Michael Nelson (Washington, DC: Congressional Quarterly Press, 1990), p. 127.

6. Ibid., p. 139.

7. Burke Marshall, *Federalism and Civil Rights* (New York: Columbia University Press, 1964).

8. Ibid., pp. vii–viii.

9. Ibid., pp. 49–51.

10. Ibid., p. 72.

11. Ibid., p. 81.

12. This phrase apparently was first used by Joseph Alsop and Turner Catledge to describe the Supreme Court's decision in *NLRB v. Jones & Laughlin Steel Corp.* on April 12, 1937 to uphold the constitutionality of the Wagner Act. The "conversions" of Chief Justice Hughes and of Justice Roberts were the "switch in time" that helped save the Court from the prospect of FDR's Court-packing plan. *168 Days* (New York: Doubleday and Company, Inc., 1938), 135 *et seq*.

13. Harvard Sitkoff, *A New Deal for Blacks: The Emergence of Civil Rights as a National Issue, Vol I: The Depression Decade* (New York: Oxford University Press, 1978), p. 272.

14. Chapter 11 of the Sitkoff book is devoted to the effort to secure antilynching legislation. The background of the antilynching campaign presented here is drawn in part from that chapter.

15. The Costigan-Wagner antilynching bill was introduced early in January 1934. A similar bill had been passed by the House in the 1920s, but a Senate filibuster had defeated it. Joseph J. Huthmacher, *Senator Robert F. Wagner and the Rise of Urban Liberalism* (New York: Athenum, 1968), pp. 171–75.

16. Correspondence between Charles H. Houston and Stephen Early (assistant secretary to the president) of August 16, 17, and 23, 1933 (Franklin D. Roosevelt Library, Official File 93a, Box 7). It is interesting to note that in Houston's letter of August 23 he complained about a White House staff member having received them by asking, "What do you *boys* want?" Houston responded by suggesting that such language, "when addressing grown men, albeit Negroes,"

was a discourtesy which, "should be beneath the dignity of the central administration for its own sake."

17. Address of the President before the Federal Council of Churches of Christ in America, December 6, 1933. *The Public Papers and Addresses of Franklin D. Roosevelt*, compiled by Samuel I. Rosenman (New York: Random House, 1934, vol. 2).

18. Annual Message to the Congress, January 3, 1934. *The Public Papers and Addresses of Franklin D. Roosevelt*, compiled by Samuel I. Rosenman (New York: Random House. vol. 3, 1934), pp. 12–13.

19. Press conference remarks of May 25, 1934. *The Press Conferences of Franklin D. Roosevelt, 1933-45*, (Microfilm) (Hyde Park, NY: Franklin D. Roosevelt Library).

20. Sitkoff reports an hour and a half meeting between FDR and Walter White in which: "The President listened attentively, expressed his desire to see lynching banished from the land, and then explained why his need for recovery and relief legislation precluded his being able to challenge the Southern leadership of the party." Sitkoff also says that the message to Costigan and Wagner about his willingness to see the bill passed occurred at a meeting between FDR and the bill's sponsors on May 24, 1934. Sitkoff, *A New Deal for Blacks*, p. 283.

21. Robinson was the Senate Majority Leader and U.S. Senator from Arkansas. Huthmacher, p. 173.

22. The memorandum reviewed here is from the Franklin D. Roosevelt Library, PSF (Justice), Box 55.

23. The memo made extensive use of the Southern Commission on the Study of Lynching's 1931 Report, which reported 715 lynching between 1914 and 1932 and 704 attempted lynchings which had been prevented during that same period. The memo also cited a Tuskeegee Institute report which revealed that lynching was a national, rather than a southern problem.

24. The "Lindberg Act," 18 U.S.C.A, Sec. 408 (as it was then).

25. Harold Ickes, *The Secret Diary of Harold L. Ickes* (New York: Simon and Schuster, 1954), p. 61. Ickes also reports in his diary entry for December 20, 1936 that Garner had expressed his support for antilynching legislation at a Cabinet meeting on December 18. Garner insisted, "that some measure of justice ought to be accorded to the Negroes." "Of course, my [Ickes] stand on the Negro question is well known. I have been in advance of every other member of the cabinet, and the Negroes recognize this." Ibid., p. 20.

26. For example, it was reported that Congressman Hatton Sumners of Texas, chairman of the House Judiciary Committee, after hearing the president's announcement of the Court-packing plan said, "Boys, here's where I cash in." James M. Burns, *Roosevelt: The Lion and the Fox* (New York: Harcout, Brace, and World, 1956), p. 294.

27. Alsop and Catledge, *168 Days*, pp. 36–45.

28. Raymond Moley, *After Seven Years* (New York: Harper and Brothers, 1939), pp. 357–59.

29. Ibid. Thomas G. Corcoran and Benjamin V. Cohen were protégés of Brandeis and Frankfurter. Among other accomplishments they drafted New Deal legislation regulating the securities market. Both were White House insiders and

Corcoran particularly was the consummate political wheeler and dealer. Moley suggests that Corcoran and Cohen were responsible for the Second New Deal, which began in 1935 after the demise of the NRA.

30. *Schechter Poultry Corp. v. U.S.*, 295 U.S. 495 (1935).

31. Burns, *Roosevelt: The Lion and the Fox*, p. 222; Peter H. Irons, *The New Deal Lawyers* (Princeton, NJ: Princeton University Press, 1982), p. 106.

32. *Gibbons v. Ogden*, 22 U.S. (9 Wheat.), 1 (1824).

33. Irons notes that Robert Stern, the author of the brief, could think only of barbershops as exceptions. Irons, *The New Deal Lawyers*, p. 92.

34. *Carter v. Carter Coal Company*, 298 U.S. 238 (1936).

35. *U.S. v. Butler*, 297 U.S. 1 (1936).

36. Alsop and Catledge, *168 Days*, p. 9.

37. Robert H. Jackson, *The Struggle for Judicial Supremacy: A Study of a Crisis in American Power Politics* (New York: Vintage Books, 1941), p. xii.

38. Frankfurter to the president, May 29, 1935. Franklin D. Roosevelt Library, PSF (Felix Frankfurter), Box 135.

39. Cummings to the president, June 20, 1936, Franklin D. Roosevelt Library, PSF (Justice), Box 55.

40. Roosevelt to Frankfurter, February 9, 1937, Franklin D. Roosevelt Library, PSF (Frankfurter), Box 135. See also Roosevelt to Charles C. Burlingham, February 23, 1937, Franklin D. Roosevelt Library, PSF (Supreme Court), Box 165.

41. Elliott Roosevelt, ed., *F.D.R.: His Personal Letters, 1928-1945*, (New York: Duell, Sloan and Pearce, 1950), p. 685.

42. *NLRB v. Jones and Laughlin Steel Corp.*, 301 U.S. 1 (1937).

43. *Steward Machine Co. v. Davis*, 301 U.S. 548 (1937).

44. Elliott Roosevelt, *F.D.R.: His Personal Letters*, p. 685.

45. Franklin D. Roosevelt Library, PSF (Supreme Court, 1935-36), Box 165.

46. Raymond Moley, *The First New Deal* (New York: Harcourt, Brace & World, 1966), p. 263.

47. David R. Goldfield, *Black, White, and Southern: Race Relations and Southern Culture, 1940 to the Present* (Baton Rouge: Louisiana State University Press, 1990), p. 33.

48. Skowronek.

49. Sitkoff, *A New Deal for Blacks*, p. 42.

50. Ibid., p. 44.

51. Ibid., p. 46; Walter White, *A Man Called White* (New York: Viking Press, 1948), pp. 169–70.

52. Arthur M. Schlesinger Jr., *The Age of Roosevelt, Vol. II: The Coming of the New Deal* (Boston: Houghton Mifflin, 1959), p. 378.

53. Arthur M. Schlesinger Jr., *The Politics of Upheaval* (Boston: Houghton Mifflin, 1960), p. 434–35.

54. Ickes, *The Secret Diary of Harold L. Ickes*, p. 115.

55. Steven F. Lawson, *Running for Freedom: Civil Rights and Black Politics in America Since 1941*, (Philadelphia: Temple University Press, 1991), p. 11.

56. Ibid., p. 5.

57. Ibid., p. 12.

58. Sitkoff, *A New Deal for Blacks*, p. 317.

59. Garfunkel, p. 54.

60. Sitkoff, *A New Deal for Blacks*, p. 322.

61. Alsop and Catledge, *168 Days*, p. 19.

62. Burns, *Roosevelt: The Lion and the Fox*, p. 198.

63. Moley distinguished between the first New Deal, which was designed to engagé business with government in a cooperative effort to save capitalism, and the Second New Deal, which appealed more to the relatively deprived urban masses, who, joined with others in the Democratic coalition, would insure the reelection of the president. Moley, *The First New Deal*, pp. 527–30.

64. Steven Lawson has argued that Blacks profited from New Deal programs for the ill-housed, the ill-clothed, and the ill-fed. These, of course, include poor whites as well as blacks. Lawson, *Running for Freedom*, p. 3. On the other hand, "Negro" delegates were seated as delegates for the first time at the 1936 Democratic National Convention. Sitkoff, *A New Deal for Blacks*, p. 93.

65. Moley, *The First New Deal*, p. 7.

66. John P. Roche, *The Quest for the Dream: The Development of Civil Rights and Human Relations in Modern America* (New York: The Macmillan Company, 1963), p. 138.

67. Burns, *Roosevelt: The Lion and the Fox*, p. 157.

68. Roche, *The Quest for the Dream*, p. 141.

69. Rexford Tugwell, *Roosevelt's Revolution: The First Year—A Personal Perspective* (New York: Macmillan, 1977), p. 102.

70. Sitkoff, *A New Deal for Blacks*, p. 66.

71. Ibid., p. 47.

72. Ralph Bunche, *The Political Status of the Negro in the Age of FDR* (Chicago: University of Chicago Press, 1973), p. 623.

73. Roche, *The Quest for the Dream*, p. 178.

74. Sitkoff, *A New Deal for Blacks*, p. 69; Doris Kearns Goodwin, *No Ordinary Time: Franklin and Eleanor Roosevelt: The Home Front in World War II* (New York: Simon and Schuster, 1994), p. 163.

75. Lyndon B. Johnson Library, Oral History Interview of Richard R. Brown, former deputy director of the National Youth Administration, pp. 19–24. When Johnson was elected to Congress in 1937, Mrs. Bethune wrote him the following congratulatory letter:

> We feel certain that the same energy and vigorous imagination that characterized the outstanding success of your program with the National Youth Administration will write your name high in the annals of the House of Representatives.
>
> We are indeed happy that one who has proven himself so conscious of and sympathetic with the needs of all the people should take his place in a Congress that is indelibly writing a more human and more Christian concept of American democracy (Mary McLeod Bethune to L.B.J, May 5, 1937, on public display in the Lyndon B. Johnson Library).

On the other hand, in a five-page, single-space typescript letter of September 22, 1935, from Johnson to NYA Assistant Director John J. Corson, Johnson explains how and why local traditions prevent him from appointing blacks to an integrated Texas state advisory committee. A separate "Colored Advisory Committee" was created (Lyndon B. Johnson Library, LBJA Subject Files [NYA. Appointments and Other Correspondence] Box 73).

76. Goldfield, *Black, White, and Southern*, p. 27.

77. Lawson, *Running for Freedom*, p. 3.

78. Ruchames, *Race, Jobs, & Politics*, p. 157; Merl R. Reed, *Seedtime for the Modern Civil Rights Movement: The President's Committee of Fair Employment Practice, 1941-46* (Baton Rouge: Louisiana State University Press, 1991), p. 6.

79. Lerone Bennett Jr., *Confrontation: Black and White* (Chicago: Johnson Publishing Co., 1965), p. 179.

80. Reed, *Seedtime for the Modern Civil Rights Movement*, p. 345.

81. Roche, *The Quest for the Dream*, p. 134.

82. Harry S. Truman Library, Oral History Interview of Arthur Spingarn, p. 472.

83. Martin Luther King Jr. suggests that the critical turning point for Kennedy was the Birmingham riots of 1963. Before the riots, King remembered that Kennedy was "long [on] intellectual commitment but that he didn't quite have the emotional commitment." After Birmingham "you see a new Kennedy who had come to see the moral issues involved in the civil rights struggle and who not only came to see them but was now willing to stand up in a courageous manner for them" (Oral History, John F. Kennedy Library, 1964: 3, 17).

84. Richard E. Neustadt, *Presidential Power and the Modern Presidents* (New York: Free Press, 1990), pp. 170–71.

85. Marshall, *Federalism and Civil Rights*.

86. William E. Leuchtenburg, *In the Shadow of FDR: From Harry Truman to Ronald Regan* (Ithaca, NY: Cornell University Press, 1983), p. 26.

87. This quote appears in the Andrew J. Biemiller Oral History, Harry S. Truman Library, p. 53. It is also quoted in Steinberg (1962); David McCullough, *Truman* (New York: Simon and Schuster, 1992), pp. 300–1; and Leuchtenburg, p. 26.

9

Present at the Creation
The Roosevelt Court, Religion, and the First Amendment

Stephen K. Shaw

> Prior to 1940 the Supreme Court of the United States had never upheld a claim of free exercise of religion, had never found any governmental practice to be an establishment of religion, and had never applied the religion clause of the First Amendment to the states. The religion clauses were part of the American vision; they were not at work in the judicial process. . . . Their force and power were yet to be realized. Beginning in 1940 the Court changed all that. . . . With the sonorous simplicity of John Marshall laying out the foundations, the Court set out basic principles in the new area of law it was creating. The course of development . . . has been vigorous. No area of modern law . . . has been so marked by sectarian struggle, so strained by fundamental fissures, so reflective of deep American doubts and aspirations.[1]

In 1940 the Supreme Court of the United States delivered a decision that "was monumental in its effects."[2] The case of *Cantwell v. Connecticut,*[3] in which the Court unanimously struck down a permit requirement for soliciting funds on public streets and reversed a conviction for committing a breach of the peace, "was the first freedom of religion case involving the Jehovah's Witnesses to be decided by the U.S. Supreme Court."[4] Citing the statutory requirement that a permit to solicit funds in public would be granted only upon the finding by a public official that the cause or group involved was religious, Justice Owen Roberts declared, "Such a censorship of religion as the means of determining its right to survive is a denial of liberty protected by the First Amendment and included in the liberty which is within the protection of the Fourteenth."[5] He then concluded simply, "The Fourteenth Amendment has rendered the legislatures of the states as incompetent as Congress to enact such laws."[6]

For the first time the Supreme Court in the *Cantwell* decision ruled that the free exercise clause was binding on the states as well as the federal government. The Court's decision incorporating the free exercise clause into the Fourteenth Amendment was not, as Justice William Brennan later would demonstrate in the 1963 Bible reading case,[7] a completely unexpected event. Rather, *Cantwell* was the culmination of a process begun nearly two decades earlier,[8] and served to "usher in a new era of Supreme Court jurisdiction over religion in America."[9] The "reborn court,"[10] therefore, heralded a revolution "not in the political but in the religious arena."[11]

According to Michael Smith, "Religion had no special constitutional place until after the constitutional revolution of 1937."[12] From the late eighteenth century to nearly the mid-twentieth century, the Court heard only a handful of religion-clause cases, most of which are forgettable, such as *Davis v. Beason*,[13] which according to one analysis of the Court's jurisprudence, "now seems more like gross religious bigotry further tainted by bad anthropology"[14] However, before the end of the 1940s, "the Court was to decide more religion cases than during the entire one hundred fifty preceding years."[15] In these cases, almost all of which involved the Jehovah's Witnesses,[16] not only would the Court declare that religion occupied "a preferred position";[17] the Court would begin to issue decisions and develop principles still reverberating today.[18]

In his classic study of the Roosevelt Court, C. Herman Pritchett concluded, "The Roosevelt Court is clearly a Bill of Rights Court."[19] Writing in the late 1940s, Pritchett argued, "Civil liberties problems have given the Roosevelt Court one of its most controversial groups of cases."[20] At that time one of the key provisions of the Bill of Rights, the establishment clause of the First Amendment, "was a very nearly forgotten and untested clause."[21] However, that soon would change, and the case of *Everson v. Board of Education of Ewing Township, New Jersey*[22] would become "the controversial fountainhead of contemporary establishment clause doctrine."[23]

Writing for the Court in *Everson*, in which the Court ruled five to four that a state program of reimbursing parents for the bus fare of children attending private religious schools did not violate the establishment clause, Justice Hugo Black, the first member of the Court nominated by President Franklin Roosevelt, asserted, "In the words of Jefferson, the clause against establishment of religion by law was intended to erect a 'wall of separation between Church and State.'"[24] According to Justice Black, "That wall must be kept high and impregnable. We could not approve the slightest breach. New Jersey has not breached it here."[25]

Today, *Everson* "is chiefly remembered not for its holding that the transportation reimbursement program at issue was constitutionally valid, but for its wholehearted espousal of a particular view of the essential purpose of the Constitution's religion language."[26] In large measure, Justice Black enunciated this view in what has to be one of the most frequently quoted and frequently assailed paragraphs in the Court's history:

> The "establishment of religion" clause of the First Amendment means at least this: Neither a state nor the Federal Government can set up a church. Neither can pass laws which aid one

> religion, aid all religions, or prefer one religion over another. Neither can force nor influence a person to go to or to remain away from church against his will or force him to profess a belief or disbelief in any religion. No person can be punished for entertaining or professing religious beliefs or disbeliefs, for church attendance or non-attendance. No tax in any amount, large or small, can be levied to support any religious activities or institutions, whatever they may be called, or whatever form they may adopt to teach or practice religion. Neither a state nor the Federal Government can, openly or secretly, participate in the affairs of any religious organizations or groups and vice versa. In the words of Jefferson, the clause against establishment of religion by law was intended to erect "a wall of separation between Church and State."[27]

In the words of James Reichley, "The bomb planted by Chief Justice Waite six decades before in *Reynolds* had gone off."[28]

Justice Black, who went through six drafts in developing his majority opinion for the Court, was influenced by Justice Felix Frankfurter and Wiley Rutledge in producing his separationist dicta.[29] He was affected even more directly, however, by his reading of history. In his historical excursion Justice Black discovered political unrest, religious censorship, and enslaved minds whenever church and state acted in unison.

> The centuries immediately before and contemporaneous with the colonization of America had been filled with turmoil, civil strife, and persecutions, generated in large part by established sects determined to maintain their absolute political and religious supremacy. With the power of government supporting them, at various times and places, Catholics had persecuted Protestants, Protestants had persecuted Catholics, Protestant sects had persecuted other Protestant sects, Catholics of one shade of belief had persecuted Catholics of another shade of belief, and all of these had from time to time persecuted Jews. In efforts to force loyalty to whatever religious group happened to be on top and in league with the government of a particular time and place, men and women had been fined, cast in jail, cruelly tortured and killed. . . . These practices of the old world were transplanted to

> and began to thrive in the soil of the new America. . . . These practices became so commonplace as to shock the freedom-loving colonials into a feeling of abhorrence. The imposition of taxes to pay ministers' salaries and to build and maintain churches and church property aroused their indignation. It was these feelings which found expression in the First Amendment.[30]

It was, according to Laurence Tribe, a reading of history that later courts accepted "with remarkable consensus . . . as historical truth."[31] In spite of recent efforts to imagine (or recreate) the alleged halcyon days on the *Everson* Court,[32] there was a marked degree of division within the Court with respect to translating "historical truth" into legal fact and political reality.

Justice Robert H. Jackson, President Roosevelt's eighth appointee to the Court, who is remembered as the Court's "most gifted wielder of words,"[33] dissented, along with Justices Frankfurter, Rutledge, and Harold Burton. Referring to "the religious freedom Amendment" to the Constitution, Jackson maintained that "it was set forth in absolute terms, and its strength is its rigidity."[34] According to Jackson, the purpose served by the "religious freedom Amendment" was "not only to keep the states' hands out of religion, but to keep religion's hands off the state, and above all, to keep bitter religious controversy out of public life by denying to every denomination any advantage from getting control of public policy or the public purse."[35]

Justice Jackson concluded his dissent with both a frank acknowledgement and sage counsel:

> The policy of our Federal Constitution has never been wholly pleasing to most religious groups. They all are quick to invoke its protections; they all are irked when they feel its restraints. . . . But we cannot have it both ways. Religious teaching cannot be a private affair when the state seeks to impose regulations which infringe on it indirectly, and a public affair when it comes to

> taxing citizens of one faith to aid another, or those of no faith to aid all.[36]

For Jackson, who later would complain, erroneously, that the battle to separate church and state had been lost,[37] the initial assault on establishment clause principles, namely separationism, had been successfully conducted in *Everson*.

Justice Wiley Rutledge, the final Roosevelt nominee, wrote a lengthy dissent in *Everson* that is noted for its inclusion, in full, of James Madison's 1785 "Memorial and Remonstrance Against Religious Assessments," and for its role in constructing, along with Justice Black's opinion for the Court, "what has become the orthodox judicial history of the religion clauses."[38] Insisting that *Everson* was not "just a little case over bus fares"[39] Rutledge argued that the religion language of the First Amendment "was broadly but not loosely phrased."[40] Its purpose, according to Rutledge, "was broader than separating church and state in [a] narrow sense. It was to create a complete and permanent separation of the spheres of religious activity and civil authority by comprehensively forbidding every form of public aid or support for religion."[41]

Justice Rutledge, as did Justice Black before him and virtually every other member of the Court who has followed him, purported to find the meaning of the establishment clause in history.[42] He relied more heavily on Madison than Black did on Jefferson, focusing directly and at length on the former's classic 1785 missive during the assessment battle in Virginia.[43] What Rutledge found in his analysis of history was that the establishment clause embodied Madison's views, "formed during his long struggle for religious freedom. . . . For Madison," argued Rutledge, "as also for Jefferson, religious freedom was the crux of the struggle for freedom in general."[44]

Moreover, Rutledge found that, based on his reading of Madison and the "Memorial," the word "religion" in the First Amendment "does not have two meanings, one narrow to forbid 'an establishment' and another, much broader, for securing 'the free exercise there of.' . . . 'Establishment' and 'free exercise' were correlative and coextensive ideas, representing only different facets of the single great and fundamental freedom."[45] Because of their experience with and fear of coerced religious belief and conduct, and the concomitant violation of the fundamental right of conscience, Madison and Jefferson sought, claimed Rutledge, "to tear out" the institution of an establishment of religion "not partially but root and branch, and to bar its return forever."[46] Thus, in order to ensure the maximum play for religious freedom, the Court should recognize and heed what for Rutledge was the unequivocal command of the First Amendment: "the complete division of religion and civil authority which our forefathers made."[47]

The year following *Everson* the Court handed down its initial decision on religion in the public schools, the arena in which so many disputes would arise in the future. In *McCollum v. Board of Education*,[48] which involved a "released-time" program of religious instruction for public school students on school premises, the Court, again speaking through Justice Black, struck down the program for violating the First and Fourteenth Amendments. Reiterating the separationist dicta he relied on in *Everson*, Black, writing for a nearly unanimous Court,[49] contended that the released-time program was "beyond all question a utilization of the tax-established and tax-supported public school system to aid religious groups to spread their faith."[50] In an admirably pithy statement, Black concluded, "This is not separation of Church and State."[51]

Justice Black also addressed an issue (over the years it would become mantra-like) that would resurface continually in cases to come—the Court's alleged hostility to religion.

> To hold that a state cannot consistently with the First and Fourteenth Amendments utilize its public school system to aid any or all religious faiths or sects in the dissemination of their doctrines and ideals does not . . . manifest a governmental

> hostility to religion or religious teachings. A manifestation of such hostility would be at war with our national tradition as embodied in the First Amendment's guaranty of the free exercise of religion.[52]

Stressing the spherical separationism he employed (in principle) in *Everson*, and to which he would return later,[53] Justice Black asserted that "the First Amendment rests upon the premise that both religion and government can best work to achieve their lofty aims if each is left free from the other within its respective sphere."[54]

As in *Everson*, there was deep division within the Court in *McCollum*, especially between Justices Black and Frankfurter concerning the precedential role and value of the holding in *Everson*.[55] Justice Frankfurter, appointed after Stanley Reed and before William O. Douglas, "saw the Jeffersonian metaphor of the wall of separation as epitomizing the entire constitutional doctrine."[56] He objected strongly to Black's reliance in *McCollum* on *Everson*, which Frankfurter considered "mischief-breeding,"[57] and demanded that Black remove all references to *Everson* as the cost of Frankfurter joining the Court's opinion, a price Black refused to pay.[58] As a result, Frankfurter wrote his own concurring opinion, one that "violated nearly every assumption upon which his system of judicial belief supposedly rested."[59] Justices Black and Frankfurter, who "towered over a Court replete with probably more talent than any other in the tribunal's history, left a legacy for American constitutional law and jurisprudence that was not only profound but seminal."[60] They shared an unmistakable, profound commitment to the rule of law and the Constitution, yet they parted company decisively with respect to interpreting the Constitution and the degree of judicial deference to show to other political actors.[61] In *McCollum*, however, these battling brethren were in closer accord than a cursory read would indicate.

While Justice Black returned in *McCollum* to his

opinion in *Everson*, the Court, with the exception of Justice Reed, essentially adopted the strong separationist stance stipulated by Justice Rutledge in his *Everson* dissent. Justice Frankfurter proffered his own separationist argument, doing so as comprehensively as he did in any written opinion, with the exception perhaps of *McGowan v. Maryland*,[62] where he penned an eighty-four-page concurrence. In the released-time program at issue in *McCollum*, Frankfurter found a clear violation of "the basic Constitutional principle of absolute separation."[63] Providing his own pithy phrase, he argued, "Separation means separation, not something less."[64] According to Frankfurter, separation of church and state "is one of the vital reliances of our Constitutional system for assuring unities among our people stronger than our diversities. It is the Court's duty," he declared, "to enforce this principle in its full integrity."[65]

Justice Frankfurter advanced his interpretation of the history and purpose surrounding the First and Fourteenth Amendments and their respective roles in the development of establishment clause jurisprudence, particularly concerning the transition in education in the United States from religious, sectarian education to public, secular education.

> The evolution of colonial education, largely in the service of religion, into the public school system of today is the story of changing conceptions regarding the American democratic society, of the functions of State-maintained education in such a society, and of the role therein of the free exercise of religion by the people. The modern public school derived from a philosophy of freedom reflected in the First Amendment. It is appropriate to recall that the Remonstrance of James Madison, an event basic in the history of religious liberty, was called forth by a proposal which involved support to religious education.[66]

Echoing his opinions in *Gobitis*[67] and *Barnette*,[68] Frankfurter argued, "The public school is at once the symbol of our democracy and the most pervasive means for promoting our common destiny. In no activity of the State is it more vital to keep out divisive forces than in its schools, to avoid confusing, not to say fusing, what the Constitution sought to keep strictly apart."[69]

Moreover, citing the move toward public education in states like Virginia, New York, and Massachusetts, Frankfurter wrote that, given "often long and fierce" controversies over saving the public school from potential destruction caused by sectarian strife, "long before the Fourteenth Amendment subjected the States to new limitations, the prohibition of furtherance by the State of religious instruction became the guiding principle, in law and feeling, of the American people."[70] The Fourteenth Amendment, for Frankfurter, "merely reflected a principle then dominant in our national life. To the extent that the Constitution thus made it binding upon the States, the basis of the restriction is the whole experience of our people."[71] Quoting from Justice Rutledge's dissent in *Everson*, Frankfurter concluded, "We renew our conviction that, 'we have staked the very existence of our country on the faith that complete separation between the state and religion is best for the state and best for religion.'"[72]

Concurring in the Court's interpretation and implementation of separationist principles in *McCollum*, and joining Justice Frankfurter's strong separationist-centered opinion, Justice Jackson nonetheless "was critical of the majority's abstract, broad language, and of the regulatory character of its ruling."[73] Justice Jackson's opinion contained a caveat addressed to the Court concerning that which might (or did) appear to some eyes as the expulsion of religion from the public schools. "One can hardly respect a system of education," Jackson argued, "that would leave the student wholly ignorant of the currents of religious thought that move the world society for a part in which he is being prepared."[74]

Justice Jackson admitted that "[t]he task of separating the secular from the religious in education is one of magnitude, intricacy and delicacy."[75] Moreover, he conceded that "[i]t is idle to pretend that this task is one for which we can find in the Constitution one word to help us as judges to decide where the secular ends and the sectarian begins in education. . . . It is," he frankly acknowledged, "a matter on which we can find no law but our own prepossessions."[76]

Finally, Justice Jackson expressed doubts, not so much about the ability of the Court's attempting to declare "a sweeping constitutional doctrine"[77] that would apply to diverse, local conditions in public schools throughout the country but about the wisdom of doing so. Ever the wordsmith (and not too mean a prophet as well), Jackson concluded his concurrence by predicting that the Court, given the nature of the task as he saw it, was "likely to make the legal 'wall of separation between church and state' as winding as the famous serpentine wall designed by Mr. Jefferson for the University he founded."[78]

The solitary dissenter in *McCollum* was Justice Stanley Reed, who was President Roosevelt's second appointee, joining the Court in 1938. Described by one scholar as "the least glamorous and least mercurial of the Roosevelt Justices"[79] his dissent in *McCollum* is perhaps most well known for the warning it contained for his colleagues: "A rule of law should not be drawn from a figure of speech."[80] Already beginning to distance himself from the Court's reading of history, and in particular its interpretation of the respective roles of Madison and Jefferson,[81] Reed maintained that the majority's emphasis on "absolute separation" as the core principle entailed in the establishment clause misconstrued the salient fact that the clause does not, in Reed's words, "bar every friendly gesture between church and state."[82] According to one of the few works on Reed's jurisprudence,[83] he essentially urged upon the Court an accommodationist argument that would, ironically, be at the center of Justice Douglas's opinion for the Court in the 1952 New York released-time case of *Zorach v. Clauson*.[84]

The general reaction to the Court's decisions in *Everson* and *McCollum* was swift and predictable. The more scholarly response focused on the Court's allegedly erroneous interpretation of history,[85] while public commentary accused the Court of being hostile to religion in general and God in particular.[86] This criticism (at times rather vitriolic), however, would prove to be at best a cheap imitation of the reaction that would occur immediately following the Court's ruling in "what quickly became one of the most contentious and most misunderstood opinions of our time, the *New York Prayer Case*."[87]

Faced with a twenty-two-word, nondenominational prayer written by the New York State Board of Regents,[88] the Court, through the majority opinion of Justice Black, held that "the State of New York has adopted a practice wholly inconsistent with the Establishment Clause."[89] With *Everson* and *McCollum* as controlling precedents, and armed with his dissent in *Zorach*[90] as well as *The Book of Common Prayer* and John Bunyan,[91] Black declared "that the constitutional prohibition against laws respecting an establishment of religion must at least mean that in this country it is no part of the business of government to compose official prayers for any group of the American people to recite as a part of a religious program carried on by government."[92]

As he did in *Everson* and *McCollum*, Justice Black leaned heavily on his understanding of history and its accompanying lessons of political unrest and religious persecution in order to divine the essential purpose served by the establishment clause.[93] He also made a critical distinction between the establishment clause and the free exercise clause concerning the issue of coercion, rebutting the argument that there was no constitutional violation since observance of the prayer by students was voluntary.

> The Establishment Clause, unlike the Free Exercise Clause, does not depend upon any showing of direct governmental compulsion and is violated by the enactment of laws which establish an official religion whether those laws operate directly to coerce nonobserving individuals or not. This is not to say, of

> course, that laws officially prescribing a particular form of religious worship do not involve coercion of such individuals. When the power, prestige and financial support of government is placed behind a particular religious belief, the indirect coercive pressure upon religious minorities to conform to the prevailing officially approved religion is plain. But the purposes underlying the Establishment Clause go much further than that. Its first and most immediate purpose rested on the belief that a union of government and religion tends to destroy government and to degrade religion. . . . The Establishment Clause thus stands as an expression of principle on the part of the Founders of our Constitution that religion is too personal, too sacred, too holy to permit its "unhallowed perversion" by a civil magistrate.[94]

Given the evidence of history, governmental neutrality toward religion was a fundamental prerequisite for a civil polity, since governmental involvement with or sponsorship of religion only bred divisiveness and partiality among religious groups.

As in *McCollum*, Justice Black took pains to defend himself and the Court against the now constant refrain that the Court was hostile to religion. "The history of man," wrote Black, "is inseparable from the history of religion."[95] According to Black, who ended his *Engel* opinion with a lengthy quote from Madison's "Memorial and Remonstrance against Religious Assessments,"[96] "It is neither sacrilegious nor antireligious to say that each separate government in this country should stay out of the business of writing or sanctioning official prayers and leave that purely religious function to the people themselves and to those the people choose to look to for religious guidance."[97] "To do otherwise," Black argued, "would sanction not only a mistaken reading of history but also allow for a clearly impermissible application of the Establishment Clause."[98]

Justice Douglas, with whom Black had broken ranks in *Zorach v. Clauson*, concurred in *Engel* in an opinion that is notable for two reasons: One, it evidences Douglas's uncertainties about the Court's ruling itself, and two, Douglas announces he now considers *Everson* to have been decided incorrectly.

Justice Douglas, who penned one of the most famous declarations in the Court's establishment clause jurisprudential history,[99] could not (or did not) rely on either *Everson* or *McCollum*. Rather, for him, the narrow question in the case was "whether New York oversteps the bounds when it finances a religious exercise."[100] According to Douglas, the government, through the use of school facilities and the teaching staff, was essentially financing a religious exercise. Such involvement constituted impermissible aid in Douglas's opinion, for it violated the key constitutional requirement of governmental neutrality. "The First Amendment," Douglas reasoned, "leaves the Government in a position not of hostility to religion but of neutrality. . . . The First Amendment teaches that a government neutral in the field of religion better serves all religious interests."[101]

Justice Douglas, who earlier had expressed doubts about the case to Black,[102] would also express such doubts in his concurring opinion. Finding "no element of compulsion or coercion" in the state regulation nor any "effort at indoctrination" or "any element of proselytizing,"[103] Douglas asserted, "what New York does on the opening of its public schools is what we do when we open court."[104] He also argued that the same logic applies to Congress. Thus, wrote Douglas, "I cannot say that to authorize this prayer is to establish a religion in the strictly historic meaning of those words."[105]

He admitted, however, "My problem today would be uncomplicated but for *Everson v. Board of Education*.[106] Endorsing the dissent written by Justice Rutledge in *Everson*, Douglas maintained that *Everson* "seems in retrospect to be out of line with the First Amendment."[107] Yet, by basing his opinion in *Engel* on the issue of improper financial assistance to religion by the state, Douglas conceded that finding and holding the line between permissible and impermissible aid to religion was taxing, to say the least.

"Among the stupendous powers of the Supreme Court of the United States," a distinguished historian once wrote, "there are two which in logic may be independent and yet in fact are related. The one is the power . . . to interpret history. The other is the power . . . to make it."[108] The Roosevelt justices certainly exercised both powers; from *Cantwell* and *Everson* to *Engel* and beyond,[109] their jurisprudential efforts are still being felt today.[110]

Everson v. Board of Education, for instance, which is truly "a milestone decision,"[111] remains a seminal case; "one can plausibly view the modern jurisprudence of the religion clauses as a gradual unfolding of a few core ideas—the 'wall' of separation, governmental neutrality, the secular state—expressed in . . . *Everson*."[112] In the words of A. E. Dick Howard, Justice Black's majority opinion in *Everson* "remains the starting point for any consideration of the current Court's approach to religious liberty."[113] And due to the Court's use of Jefferson's metaphor, separation of church and state became "a stock phrase, an almost-hyphenated way of encapsulating an attitude toward a particular aspect of constitutional culture."[114] The Court's rulings on the religion clauses of the First Amendment, clauses that "have spawned debates as zealously contested as any in constitutional law,"[115] thus directly affected constitutional law, political thought and practice, and our popular culture.[116]

For almost half a century, the Court has tried to walk the constitutional straight and narrow in giving meaning to the establishment clause, which has not been easy given, inter alia, the fact that although the establishment clause "is commanding in tone and clear in syntax, it is utterly unclear in its intentions."[117] As we have seen, Justice Black, whose almost thirty-five years on the bench were marked by "an influence rare in the annals of the Court,"[118] purported to discover these intentions in both the language and history of the establishment clause, especially the history surrounding its adoption.[119] According to Black's most recent biographer, "Historical analogies studded his opinions as much as legal analyses. . . . To Black, history served as much as a precedent as any of the Court's prior rulings."[120] One easily can see this mode of analysis in his opinion in *Engel*, where no judicial precedents appear.[121]

There is, of course, nothing novel nor suspect about members of the Court seeking to anchor their opinions in history. Seeking such assistance is wise, since as Justice David Souter has acknowledged, "the constitutional language forbidding laws 'respecting an establishment of religion' is not pellucid."[122] However, a resort to history, contrary to what the justices often claim, "is seldom an answer in itself."[123]

Immediately following *Everson* and *McCollum*, the Court was charged with trying not simply to interpret or make history but, worse yet, to remake it.[124] And today, the debate over the history enveloping the establishment clause continues, both on and off the Court.[125] With respect to the history surrounding the adoption of the First Amendment, and especially the principles and purposes of the religion clauses, "a clear-cut resolution seems unlikely."[126]

However, some things, due to the work of the Roosevelt Court, are clear, not the least of which is the fact that the current Court, at least in its rhetoric, still proclaims allegiance to the principles and purposes of the establishment clause initially enunciated by the Roosevelt justices. In the words of Justice Souter, the Court "has long held that the First Amendment reaches more than classic, 18th century establishments."[127] Writing for the Court in another recent establishment clause case,[128] Justice Anthony Kennedy declared, "The lessons of the First Amendment are as urgent in the modern world as in the 18th century, when it was written."[129] Using language strikingly similar to Justice Black, Kennedy wrote, "One timeless lesson is that, if citizens are subjected to state-sponsored religious exercises, the State disavows its own duty to guard and respect that sphere of inviolable conscience and belief which is the mark of a free people."[130]

The Court in *Everson*, through the majority opinion of Justice Black, "announced a basic principle of constitutional law from which it has not strayed."[131] According to Justice Souter, *Everson* is the genesis of "a line of precedent from which there is no adequate historical case to depart."[132] Obviously, this claim invites dissent,[133] given that the quest (perhaps misconceived) for the one and true meaning of the establishment clause continues unabated.[134] With respect to the Roosevelt justices's development of a First Amendment jurisprudence of religion, one can question their logic, dispute their interpretation of history or reject their textual analysis. One cannot, however, deny the legacy left by their decisions.

ENDNOTES

1. John T. Noonan Jr., *The Believer and the Powers That Are* (New York: Macmillan Publishing Co., 1987), p. xiii.

2. Derek Davis, *Original Intent: Chief Justice Rehnquist and the Course of American Church/State Relations* (Buffalo, NY: Prometheus Books, 1991), p. 67.

3. *Cantwell v. Connecticut*, 310 U.S. 296 (1940).

4. Henry J. Abraham and Barbara A. Perry, *Freedom and the Court: Civil Rights and Liberties in the United States*, 7th ed. (New York: Oxford University Press, 1998) p. 236.

5. 310 U.S. 296, 305 (1940).

6. Ibid., p. 303.

7. *Abington School District v. Schempp*, 374 U.S. 203, 253–54 (1963) (Brennan, J., concurring).

8. See *Meyer v. Nebraska*, 262 U.S. 390 (1923). Also see *Hamilton v. Regents of the University of California*, 293 U.S. 245 (1934), where Justice Cardozo assumed "for present purposes that the religious liberty protected by the First Amendment against invasion by the nation is protected by the Fourteenth Amendment against invasion by states." Ibid., p. 265.

9. Davis, *Original Intent*, p. 67.

10. Leo Pfeffer, *This Honorable Court: A History of the Unites States Supreme Court* (Boston: Beacon Press, 1965), chapter 13.

11. Ibid., p. 346.

12. Michael E. Smith, "The Special Place of Religion in the Constitution," 1983 *Supreme Court Review*, pp. 83, 86.

13. *Davis v. Beason*, 133 U.S. 333 (1890).

14. Walter F. Murphy, James E. Fleming, and William F. Harris, II, *American Constitutional Interpretation* (Mineola, NY: The Foundation Press,

Inc., 1986), p. 1006.

15. Pfeffer, *This Honorable Court*, p. 347.

16. Ibid. See Fred Rodell, *Nine Men: A Political History of the Supreme Court of the United States from 1790 to 1955* (New York: Vintage Books, 1955); C. Herman Pritchett, *The Roosevelt Court: A Study in Judicial Politics and Values 1937-1947* (New York: Macmillan Company, 1948); C. Herman Pritchett, *Civil Liberties and the Vinson Court* (Chicago: University of Chicago Press, 1954); Charles A. Beard, *The Republic: Conversations on Fundamentals* (New York: Viking Press, 1943); *Murdock v. Pennsylvania*, 319 U.S. 105 (1943); *Prince v. Massachusetts*, 321 U.S. 158 (1944); *Marsh v. Alabama*, 326 U.S. 501 (1946); *Cantwell v. State of Connecticut*, 310 U.S. 296 (1940); *West Virginia State Board of Education v. Barnette*, 319 U.S. 624 (1943); *Minersville School Dist. v. Gobitis*, 310 U.S. 586 (1940).

17. *Jones v. Opelika*, 316 U.S. 584, 608 (1942) (Stone, C. J., dissenting).

18. See *Lee v. Weisman*, 505 U.S. 577 (1992); *Board of Education of Kiryas Joel Village School District v. Grumet*, 512 U.S. 687 (1994); *Rosenberger v. University of Virginia*, 515 U.S. 819 (1995).

19. Pritchett, *The Roosevelt Court*, p. 173.

20. Ibid., p. 129.

21. Derek Davis, *Original Intent*, p. 67.

22. *Everson v. Board of Education of Ewing Township*, 330 U.S. 1 (1947).

23. "Developments in the Law: Religion and the State," 100 *Harvard Law Review* 100 (1987): 1632.

24. 330 U.S. 1, 16 (1947) (Quoting *Reynolds v. U.S.*, 98 U.S. 145, 164 [1878]).

25. Ibid., p. 18. Writing one of the two biting dissents in *Everson*, Justice Robert H. Jackson stated that "the undertones of the opinion, advocating complete and uncompromising separation of Church from State, seems utterly discordant with its conclusion yielding support to their commingling in educational matters. The case which irresistibly comes to mind as the most fitting precedent is that of Julia who, according to Byron's reports, 'whispering "I will ne'er consent"–consented!'" Ibid., p. 19.

26. Mary Ann Glendon and Raul F. Yanes, "Structural Free Exercise," *Michigan Law Review* 90 (1991): 481.

27. 330 U.S. 1, 15–16 (1947).

28. A. James Reichley, *Religion in American Public Life* (Washington, DC: The Brookings Institution, 1985), p. 142.

29. Gerald T. Dunne, *Hugo Black and the Judicial Revolution* (New York: Touchstone: Simon & Schuster, 1977), pp. 264–66. Dunne states that Felix Frankfurter, Black's leading intellectual and doctrinal adversary on the bench, assisted Justices Jackson and Wiley Rutledge with their dissents, with Rutledge turning out eight drafts of his lengthy, influential dissent. Ibid., p. 266. According to a new biography of Black, his "discussion of the background of the First Amendment's establishment clause, but not its legislative history in Congress, came only in response to Rutledge's lengthy discussion." Roger K. Newman, *Hugo Black: A Biography* (New York: Pantheon Books, 1994), p. 362.

30. 330 U.S. 1, 8–11 (1947).

31. Laurence H. Tribe, *American Constitutional Law*, 2nd ed. (Mineola, NY: Foundation Press, Inc., 1988), p. 1160.

32. See Leonard W. Levy, *The Establishment Clause: Religion and the First Amendment*, 2nd ed., revised (Chapel Hill: University of North Carolina Press, 1994).

33. Rodell, *Nine Men*, p. 279.

34. 330 U.S. 1, 26 (1947) (Jackson, J., dissenting).

35. Ibid., pp. 26–27.

36. Ibid., p. 27.

37. See Howard Ball and Phillip J. Cooper, *Of Power and Right: Hugo Black, William O. Douglas, and America's Constitutional Revolution* (New York: Oxford University Press, 1992), pp. 246–7; see Jackson's dissent in *Zorach v. Clauson*, 343 U.S. 306, 325 (1952): "The day that this country ceases to be free for irreligion it will cease to be free for religion—except for the sect that can win political power. . . . We start down a rough road when we begin to mix compulsory public education with compulsory godliness. . . . The wall which the Court was professing to erect between Church and State has become even more warped and twisted than I expected. Today's judgment will be more interesting to students of psychology and of the judicial processes than to students of constitutional law."

38. Note, "Toward a Constitutional Definition of Religion," 91 *Harvard Law Review* 91 (1978): 1057–58.

39. 330 U.S. 1, 57 (1947) (Rutledge, J., dissenting).

40. Ibid., p. 31.

41. Ibid., pp. 31–32.

42. "No provision of the Constitution is more closely tied to or given content by its generating history than the religious clause of the First Amendment. It is at once the refined product and the terse summation of that history. . . . In the documents of the times, particularly of Madison, who was leader in the Virginia struggle before he became the Amendment's sponsor, but also in the writings of Jefferson and others and in the issues which engendered them is to be found irrefutable confirmation of the Amendment's sweeping content." Ibid., p. 33–34.

43. "This is Madison's complete, though not his only, interpretation of religious liberty. It is a broadside attack upon all forms of 'establishment' of religion, both general and particular, nondiscriminatory or selective. . . . [T]he Remonstrance is at once the most concise and the most accurate statement of the views of the First Amendment's author concerning what is 'an establishment of religion.'" Ibid., p. 37.

44. Ibid., pp. 31, 34.

45. 330 U.S. 1, 32, 40.

46. Ibid., p. 40.

47. Ibid., p. 63.

48. *McCollum v. Board of Education*, 333 U.S. 203 (1948).

49. Justice Stanley Reed was the only dissenter in *McCollum*. Justice Frankfurter, joined by Justices Jackson, Rutledge, and Burton, filed a concurring opinion, as did Justice Jackson. Justices Rutledge and Burton also joined the opinion written for the Court by Justice Black.

50. 333 U.S. 203, 210 (1948).

51. Ibid., p. 212.

52. Ibid., pp. 211, 212.

53. *Engel v. Vitale*, 370 U.S. 421 (1962).

54. 333 U.S. 203, 212 (1948).

55. Dunne, *Hugo Black and the Judicial Revolution*, pp. 264–68; Newman, *Hugo Black*, pp. 364–65; H. N. Hirsch, *The Enigma of Felix Frankfurter* (New York: Basic Books, Inc. 1981), pp. 192–93; James F. Simon, *The Antagonists: Hugo Black, Felix Frankfurter and Civil Liberties in Modern America* (New York: Touchstone: Simon and Schuster, 1989), pp. 182–83.

56. Dunne, *Hugo Black and the Judicial Revolution*, p. 270. See *McGowan v. Maryland*, 366 U.S. 420, 466-67 (1961) (Frankfurter, J., concurring).

57. Dunne, *Hugo Black and the Judicial Revolution*, p. 267.

58. See Newman, *Hugo Black*, pp. 364–65.

59. Hirsch, *The Enigma of Felix Frankfurter*, p. 193.

60. Henry J. Abraham, *Justices, Presidents, and Senators: A History of the U.S. Supreme Court Appointments from Washington to Clinton*, new and revised (Lanham: Rowman & Littlefield Publishers, Inc., 1999), p. 166.

61. See Dunne, *Hugo Black and the Judicial Revolution*, p. 267; See Newman, *Hugo Black*, p. 362; Hirsh, *The Enigma of Felix Frankfurter*, pp. 192–93; Mark Silverstein, *Constitutional Faiths: Felix Frankfurter, Hugo Black and the Process of Judicial Decision Making* (Ithaca, NY: Cornell University Press, 1984); *Adamson v. California*, 332 U.S. 46 (1947).

62. 366 U.S. 420 (1961) (Frankfurter, J., concurring).

63. 333 U.S. 203, 231.

64. Ibid.

65. Ibid.

66. Ibid., p. 214.

67. *Minersville School District v. Gobitis*, 310 U.S. 586 (1940).

68. *West Virginia State Board of Education v. Barnette* 319 U.S. 624 (1943).

69. 333 U.S. 203, 231 (1948) (Frankfurter, J., concurring). "Designed to serve as perhaps the most powerful agency for promoting cohesion among a heterogeneous democratic people, the public school must keep scrupulously free from entanglement in the strife of sects. The preservation of the community from divisive conflicts, of Government from irreconcilable pressures by religious groups, of religion from censorship and coercion however subtly exercised, requires strict confinement of the State to instruction other than religious, leaving to the individual's church and home, indoctrination in the faith of his choice." Ibid., pp. 216–17.

70. Ibid., p. 215.

71. Ibid.

72. Ibid., p. 232. Quoting from *Everson v. Board of Education*, 330 U.S. 1, 59 (1947) (Rutledge, J., dissenting).

73. Glendon and Yanes, "Structural Free Exercise," p. 488.

74. 333 U.S. 203, 236 (1948) (Jackson, J., concurring).

75. Ibid., 237.

76. Ibid., pp. 237–38.

77. Ibid. "If with no surer legal guidance we are to take up and decide every variation of this controversy, raised by persons not subject to penalty or tax but who are dissatisfied with the way schools are dealing with the problem, we are likely to have much business of the sort." Ibid., p. 238.

78. Ibid.

79. Abraham, *Justices, Presidents, and Senators*, p. 165.

80. 333 U.S. 203, 247 (1948) (Reed, J., dissenting).

81. Ibid., pp. 245–48.

82. Ibid., p. 256.

83. F. William O'Brien, *Justice Reed and the First Amendment: The Religion Clauses* (Washington, DC: Georgetown University Press, 1950), pp. 176–78.

84. 343 U.S. 306 (1952).

85. See Edward S. Corwin, "The Supreme Court as National School Board," *Law and Contemporary Problems* 14 (1949): 20. "[T]he decision [in *McCollum*] is seen to stem from an unhistorical conception of what is meant by 'an establishment of religion' in the First Amendment." Also John Courtney Murray, "Law or Prepossessions?" *Law and Contemporary Problems* 14 (1940): 22, 28: "The constitutional law written in the *Everson* and *McCollum* cases is obviously not . . . learned law"; to the extent that Justices Black and Rutledge were "essaying history, it is only in the Voltairean sense. The tricks they played on the dead are astonishing."

86. The Roman Catholic hierarchy in the United States, in a report released November 20, 1948, "The Christian in Action," argued that by its decisions in *Everson* and *McCollum*, the Supreme Court frustrated "the Christian education ideal" through the judicial "establishment of secularism." *New York Times*, November 21, 1948, as quoted in Milton R. Konvitz, "Separation of Church and State: The First Freedom," *Law and Contemporary Problems* 14 (1949): 45.

87. Abraham and Perry, *Freedom and the Court*, p. 273. In the words of Philip B. Kurland: "The immediate reaction to *Vitale* certainly was gross." "The Regents' Prayer Case," 1962 *Supreme Court Review* 1, 2.

88. 370 U.S. 421, 422 (1962): "Almighty God, we acknowledge our dependence upon Thee, and we beg Thy blessings upon us, our parents, our teachers and our Country."

89. *Engel v. Vitale*, 370 U.S. 421, 242 (1962). The case was decided by a six to one vote; Justices Frankfurter and Byron White did not take part in the case. The lone dissenter was Justice Potter Stewart.

90. 343 U.S. 306, 317-19 (Black, J., dissenting).

91. 370 U.S. 421, 425-27; see Newman, *Hugo Black*, p. 521.

92. Ibid., p. 425.

93. "It is a matter of history," Black declared, "that this very practice of establishing governmentally composed prayers for religious services was one of the reasons which caused many of our early colonists to leave England and seek religious freedom in America. . . . It is an unfortunate fact of history that when some of the very groups which had most strenuously opposed the established Church of England found themselves sufficiently in control of colonial governments in this country to write their own prayers into law, they passed laws

making their own religion the official religion of their respective colonies. . . . By the time of the adoption of the Constitution," Black concluded, "our history shows that there was a widespread awareness among many Americans of the dangers of a union of Church and State." Ibid., pp. 425, 427, 429.

94. *Engel v. Vitale*, 370 U.S. 421, 430-32 (1962).

95. Ibid., p. 434.

96. Ibid., p. 436.

97. Ibid., p. 435.

98. According to Black, "Our Founders were no more willing to let the content of their prayers and their privilege of praying whenever they pleased be influenced by the ballot box than they were to let these vital matters of personal conscience depend upon the succession of monarchs. The First Amendment was added to the Constitution to stand as a guarantee that neither the power nor the prestige of the Federal Government would be used to control, support or influence the kinds of prayer the American people can say." Ibid., p. 429.

99. "We are a religious people whose institutions presuppose a Supreme Being." *Zorach v. Clauson*, 343 U.S. 306, 313 (1952).

100. 370 U.S. 421, 439 (1962) (Douglas, J., concurring).

101. Ibid., p. 443.

102. See Ball and Cooper, *Of Power and Right*, pp. 248–49; also Melvin I. Urofsky, ed. *The Douglas Letters: Selections from the Private Papers of Justice William O. Douglas* (Bethesda, MD: Adler and Adler, 1987), p. 200.

103. 370 U.S. 421, 438, 439 (1962) (Douglas, J., concurring).

104. Ibid., p. 439.

105. Ibid., 442.

106. Ibid., p. 443. Also Michael E. Smith, "The Special Place of Religion in the Constitution," 1983 *Supreme Court Review*, 83, 86.

107. Ibid.

108. Mark DeWolfe Howe, *The Garden and The Wilderness: Religion and Government in American Constitutional History* (Chicago: University of Chicago Press, 1965), p. 3.

109. See *Abington School District v. Schempp*, 374 U.S. 203 (1963), and *Sherbert v. Verner*, 374 U.S. 398 (1963).

110. See *Lee v. Weisman*, 505 U.S. 577 (1992); *Board of Education of Kiryas Joel Village School District v. Grumet*, 512 U.S. 687 (1994); *Rosenberger v. University of Virginia*, 515 U.S. 819.

111. Paul G. Kauper, "Everson v. Board of Education: A Product of the Judicial Will," *Arizona Law Review* 15 (1973): 326.

112. Murphy, Fleming and Harris, *American Constitutional Interpretation*, p. 1006.

113. A. E. Dick Howard, "The Supreme Court and the Establishment of Religion," in *James Madison on Religious Liberty*, ed. Robert S. Alley (Buffalo, NY: Prometheus Books, 1985), p. 280.

114. Ira C. Lupu, "The Lingering Death of Separationism," *George Washington Law Review* 62 (1994): 230.

115. "Developments in the Law: Religion and the State," *Harvard Law Review* 100 (1987): 1609.

116. See Winnifred Fallers Sullivan, *Paying the Words Extra: Religious*

Discourse in the Supreme Court of the United States (Cambridge, MA: Harvard University Press, 1994); Michael W. McConnell, "Religious Freedom at a Crossroads," *University of Chicago Law Review* 59 (1992): 115; Kathleen M. Sullivan, "Religion and Liberal Democracy," *University of Chicago Law Review* 59 (1992): 195; Stephen L. Carter, *The Culture of Disbelief: How American Law and Politics Trivialize Religious Devotion* (New York: Basic Books, 1993).

117. Abraham and Perry, *Freedom and the Court*, p. 290.

118. Abraham, *Justices, Presidents, and Senators*, p. 162.

119. See Hugo L. Black, *A Constitutional Faith* (New York: Alfred A. Knopf, Inc.,1969), p. 8: "Thus, it is language and history that are the crucial factors which influence me in interpreting the Constitution."

120. Newman, *Hugo Black*, p. 507.

121. See Leo Pfeffer, *God, Caesar, and the Constitution; the Court as Referee of Church-State Confrontation* (Boston: Beacon Press, 1975), p. 199.

122. 505 U.S. 577, 620 (Souter, J., concurring).

123. Kurland, "The Regents' Prayer Case," 1962 *Supreme Court Review* 1, 22.

124. Corwin, "The Supreme Court as National School Board," *Law and Contemporary Problems* 14 (1949): 20. See, e.g., Kalper, "Everson v. Board of Education: A Product of the Judicial Will," *Arizona Law Review* 15 (1974): 307, 324; Glendon and Yanes, "Structural Free Exercise," *Michigan Law Review* 90 (1991): 477, 481; Smith, "The Special Place of Religion in the Constitution," 1983 *Supreme Court Review*, 83, 86; *Wallace v. Jaffree*, 472 U.S. 38, 91-114 (1985) (Rehnquist, J., dissenting).

125. See *Rosenberger v. University of Virginia*, 63 LW 4702 (1995); Levy, *The Establishment Clause-Religion and the First Amendment*; Daniel L. Dreisbach, *Real Threat and Mere Shadow: Religious Liberty and the First Amendment* (Westchester, IL: Crossway Books, 1987).

126. Tribe, *American Constitutional Law*, p. 1162.

127. 512 U.S. 687 (1994).

128. 505 U.S. 577 (1992).

129. Ibid., p. 592.

130. Ibid.

131. Ibid., p. 610.

132. Ibid.

133. See Ibid., p. 644: "Our Religion Clause jurisprudence has become bedeviled (so to speak) by reliance on formulaic abstractions that are not derived from, but positively conflict with, our long-accepted constitutional traditions." (Scalia, J., dissenting). Also *Board of Education of Kiryas Joel Village School District v. Grumet*, 512 U.S. 687 (1994) (Scalia, J., dissenting).

134. See 512 U.S. 687, 712: "It is always appealing to look for a single test, a Grand Unified Theory that would resolve all the cases that may arise under a particular Clause. . . . Experience proves that the Establishment Clause . . . cannot easily be reduced to a single test." (O'Connor, J., concurring). Dissenting in *Grumet*, Justice Scalia responded to O'Connor: "To replace *Lemon* with nothing is simply to announce that we are now so bold that we no longer feel the need even to pretend that our haphazard course of Establishment Clause decisions is governed by any principle." Ibid., p. 732 (Scalia, J., dissenting).

10

The Roosevelt Court and the Changing Nature of American Liberalism

An Uncertain Legacy

Harvey G. Hudspeth

The Evolution and the Irony of the Roosevelt Court

In terms of Supreme Court history, Franklin Delano Roosevelt must be viewed as either one of this country's great successes or one of this country's great failures. His success in remaking the Supreme Court of the "Nine Old Men" is, of course, legend. With the one obvious exception of President George Washington, FDR was able to appoint more justices to the high bench than any other chief executive. By his tenth year in office, in fact, Roosevelt had managed to either elevate or appoint all but one of the Court's sitting justices. This fact alone accounts for history's acknowledgment of Roosevelt as having made a major impact on both the Court and the Constitution. With that said, however, the question then arises: Exactly what impact did these changes ultimately produce in terms of overall American constitutionalism? In other words, what did the

Roosevelt revolution of 1937 achieve beyond the mere judicial sanctification of the programs of the Second New Deal?

The Roosevelt revolution is a well-known and often told story. Most scholars are aware of how the Court's "hot oil"[1] and "sick chicken"[2] decisions of 1935 all but crippled the early programs of the first New Deal. Equally established is the fact that following his landslide reelection bid of 1936, FDR then attempted to extend his mandate through his ill-fated "Court-packing plan" of 1937. Finally, we all are familiar with how Justice Owen Roberts's controversial "switch in time" decision in the *Parrish*[3] ruling of 1937 helped lead to the mass migration off the bench of all those "laissez faire, constitutionalist era" stalwarts who had refused to accept the new economic order of Roosevelt's New Deal.

On the day of the *Parrish* decision, March 29, 1937, the Court's composition had remained unchanged for a full half decade. Since March 1932, Chief Justice Charles Evans Hughes and his fellow economic moderate Owen Roberts had found themselves increasingly the swing votes in cases pitting the three Court liberals, Louis Brandeis, Harlan Fiske Stone, and Benjamin Cardozo against the conservative "Four Horsemen" bloc of Willis Van Devanter, James McReynolds, George Sutherland, and Pierce Butler. With Roberts's reluctant decision to join with Hughes in siding with the Court's liberals, the next two and one half years were to see a radical shift in court personnel. Within ten months of the *Parrish* decision, two of the Court's leading conservatives, Justices Van Devanter and Sutherland were to retire. They were soon followed by their liberal colleague, Louis Brandeis. At the same time, the death of liberal Justice Cardozo was to be ideologically balanced by the death of conservative Justice Butler. In their place, Franklin Roosevelt appointed men all known to be economic liberals—Hugo Black, Stanley Reed, Felix Frankfurter, William Douglas, and Frank Murphy. Consequently, by the end of 1939, the economic faction favoring government regulation of the economy held a solid Court majority of six justices.

With the retirement of Justice McReynolds fourteen months later in February 1941, not a single economic conservative remained to oppose the nation's move into state welfarism.[4] As the number of economic moderates and liberals on the Court rose from five in 1937 to nine in 1941, however, new issues were to arise that inevitably led to new divisions and new conflicts. In the end, the Roosevelt Court, under the nominal direction of Harlan Fiske Stone, and later Fred Vinson, was to enjoy no greater peace nor harmony than the Hughes Court before it. Furthermore, with liberalism's evolution, after 1937, from an economic to a social doctrine, especially with regard to organized labor, the Roosevelt Court was to find itself increasingly paralyzed and divided over issues that had been all but unheard of just one decade earlier. In the end, the Supreme Court of Franklin Delano Roosevelt was to fall apart just as quickly as it had first come together. By 1949, in fact, what had finally emerged as the "Roosevelt Court" only eight years earlier, was by that time referred to as the "Truman Court." Even before then, however, with the death of Chief Justice Stone in 1946 and the *United Mine Workers*[5] decision of 1947, the firm meaning of the term "Roosevelt Court" was lost altogether and the Supreme Court essentially became a no "justice's" land of philosophical disarray. For six brief years, however, between the final surrender of the Hughes Court in 1941 and the UMW ruling of 1947, the Roosevelt Court was a living albeit contradictory reality. The primary purpose here is to examine the ways in which the Roosevelt Court succeeded in repudiating the past while at the same time failing to leave a clear blueprint for the future.

Harlan F. Stone and the Roosevelt Court in Action: 1941-46

On July 1, 1941, Charles Evans Hughes, having presided over the demise, both in terms of policy and personnel, of the Nine Old Men, decided it was time for him to retire as Chief Justice of the United States. With the seat previously held by Justice

McReynolds as yet unfilled, Franklin Roosevelt now had the opportunity to place what would be the final touches on the Roosevelt Court. Consequently, on June 12, "as a reward for years of liberal service on a conservative court and in the interests of national unity,"[6] Roosevelt chose to elevate Associate Justice Harlan Fiske Stone to the position of Chief Justice. With sixteen years of judicial decisions to commend him and with the strong backing of Hughes, the former Coolidge attorney general and later ally of Holmes, Brandeis, and Cardozo had no trouble with his confirmation.[7] On July 3, 1941, just two days after Hughes had retired, Harlan F. Stone was confirmed as the twelfth chief justice of the United States.

In the meantime, Franklin Roosevelt had two associate positions to fill. On the same day that Stone was nominated for chief justice, Roosevelt nominated Attorney General Robert Jackson to succeed to the seat being vacated by Stone. At the same time, he also nominated South Carolina Senator James F. Byrnes to succeed to the seat previously vacated by Justice McReynolds. Neither man was to face any serious opposition; each had been considered for earlier appointments, and each had also been considered along with Douglas as strong potential running mates for Roosevelt in 1940.[8]

Jackson, as FDR's assistant attorney general, had served as Roosevelt's "gallant front-fighter on the Court-packing plan." Subsequently replacing first Reed as solicitor general and then Murphy as attorney general, Jackson had been considered along with Douglas and Black for the chief justice's position before Roosevelt finally settled on Stone, whose associate justice position Jackson was now to fill. At age sixty-eight, however, Stone was seen at best as a transitional figure; plus, there was much speculation that Jackson would ultimately come to succeed Stone as chief justice. Overcoming fierce opposition from Maryland Senator Millard Tydings, who claimed that Jackson's Justice Department had done little in response to what the senator considered libelous accusations that Tydings had personally benefited from a Works Project Administration project, Jackson nevertheless won easy Senate confirmation on July 7, 1941, just four days after Stone had taken the oath of office for chief justice.[9] In the meantime, James Byrnes, enjoying the benefit of senatorial courtesy, was to have his nomination confirmed by the Senate without being referred to committee.

A former congressman and United States senator since 1931, Byrnes by 1941 had risen to become de facto leader of the Senate, where he was able to push most of Roosevelt's war measures into law. Having earlier opposed many of the president's New Deal measures, as well as FDR's Court-packing plan, Byrnes nevertheless earned Roosevelt's respect for helping to stage manage his third-term nomination in 1940. When the Tennessee-born McReynolds retired a few months later, Roosevelt, at the urging of such southern and border state senators as Alben Barkley, Pat Harrison, and Carter Glass, repaid his debt by appointing Byrnes to the position and the Senate responded by confirming him on the very same day.[10]

On October 5, 1941, former Associate Justice Louis Brandeis died at age eighty-five. One day later, the United States Supreme Court convened for its fall 1941 session. At that time Chief Justice Stone and Associate Justices Jackson and Byrnes formally took their seats on a bench that now consisted of seven Democrats and two Republicans, only one of whom, Justice Roberts, did not owe his present position to Franklin Roosevelt. A few weeks later, however, Justice Byrnes, in penning the Court's unanimous verdict in the case of *Edwards v. California*,[11] was to help reveal the internal weaknesses and divisions that would ultimately come to rip the supposedly monolithic Franklin Roosevelt Court asunder.

In striking down a California statute making it a misdemeanor for anyone knowingly to bring into the state a nonresident "indigent person," the Court acted unanimously in overturning the 1837 Taney Court decision in *City of New York v. Miln*.[12] While unanimous in its holding, however, the Court here was seriously divided in its reasoning. Writing for a five man majority consisting of Stone, Roberts, Frankfurter, and Reed, Justice Byrnes was to assert that the statute in question was unconstitutional in that it violated Article 1, section 8—the commerce clause of the Constitution. Thus, in attempting to regulate the transportation of persons the Court's majority claimed that California had unconstitutionally interfered with Congress's authority over interstate commerce.

Later noting that Byrnes had used an analogy equating a state's authority over indigent people with that over diseased livestock, Justice Douglas, in a three-man concurrence with Black and Murphy argued instead that the statute in question was unconstitutional in that it violated Article 4—the privileges and immunities clause of the Constitution as well as the Fourteenth Amendment. Thus rather than merely interfering in interstate commerce, the state instead was guilty of the more serious offense of violating an individual's right to travel, a basic freedom guaranteed by the Constitution to all citizens.

In yet another separate opinion, Justice Jackson attempted to agree with both sides finding reliance on the commerce clause to be permissible, though unnecessarily narrow. With *Edwards*, though the Court was able to act unanimously to throw out an unconstitutional statute, the various reasons expressed for its action suggested a subtle turn in Court priorities. With the Court now thoroughly united in the matter of economic liberalism, the stage now seemed set for a shift in emphasis to social liberalism. And as time would soon show, adherence to economic liberalism did not always translate into full support of social liberalism. What had resulted in uneasy concurrence in *Edwards* later led to bitter dissent in other areas as the Roosevelt Court moved on beyond mere economics.[13]

Two weeks after the Court had issued its ruling in *Edwards*, the Japanese bombed Pearl Harbor and the United States found itself at war both in Europe and the Pacific. While President Roosevelt subsequently appointed Justice Roberts to head a commission to investigate the Pearl Harbor attack and

President Truman later sent Justice Jackson to assist in the prosecution of Nazi war criminals at Nuremberg, FDR's attempt to "borrow Justice Byrnes temporarily to aid in the revamping of the production organization" for an America at war proved to be a job too great for Byrnes to remain on the bench. Consequently, on October 3, 1942, after serving only one year on the bench, Byrnes resigned to become President Roosevelt's wartime director of economic stabilization. He would subsequently serve as secretary of state under Truman and as governor of South Carolina at the time of *Brown v. Board of Education*.[14] His resignation in 1942, however, was to have the more immediate effect of shifting the Court even further from economic to social liberalism.[15]

Perhaps no one was more aware of this development than Justice Frankfurter. Having in 1941 recommended that President Roosevelt appoint John Parker to the Court (thus reversing the Senate's prior rejection of Parker when he had been nominated by Herbert Hoover eleven years earlier), Frankfurter now lamented the departure of Byrnes for what he considered the accompanying loss of "that very rare faculty—sagacity, downright wisdom."

Having failed to obtain Parker and with Byrnes leaving, Frankfurter now sought to recruit another potential justice of like mind to the Court. Consequently, even before Byrnes's resignation from the bench, Frankfurter actively began to lobby for the nomination of United States Circuit Court Judge Learned Hand to succeed him. What was to follow would be an intense three-month campaign in which Frankfurter, in a series of letters and memoranda, portrayed Hand in the great tradition of Holmes, Brandeis, and Cardozo, and "the only lad who will create no headaches" for the White House.[16] Eventually, however, Frankfurter's efforts for the seventy-one-year-old jurist were to backfire. On January 11, 1943, Roosevelt was to instead nominate Wiley Blount Rutledge as his ninth and final appointee to the Court.

Formerly dean of the University of Iowa's School of

Law, the forty-eight-year-old Rutledge was at that time serving as associate justice of the United States Court of Appeals for the District of Columbia. Known as a "staunch believer in liberal interpretation of the Constitution's 'general welfare' clause," Rutledge had earlier gained fame as a critic of the old Supreme Court's opposition to child labor laws. Winning easy confirmation by the Senate on February 8,[17] he formally took his seat on the bench one week later and promptly became what Frankfurter had no doubt feared—"somewhat of a foursome with Justices Murphy, Black and Douglas."[18]

By early 1943 then, the final Supreme Court of Franklin Delano Roosevelt was firmly in place. Of the nine sitting justices, only Justice Roberts could still claim to have been free of any ties to Franklin Roosevelt and, given his prior forced conversion over *Parrish*, even he had difficulty in doing that. In the meantime, the depression that had necessitated that change had finally succumbed to war and both the nation and the Court were in the process of still further change. Former Justices Van Devanter and Brandeis had passed on in 1941 with former Justice Sutherland following suit just one year later.[19] Former Justice McReynolds and former Chief Justice Hughes would live on in retirement until their respective deaths in 1946 and 1948.[20] In the meantime, the Roosevelt Court was to devote itself to unfinished business.

Between Justice Rutledge's confirmation in 1943 and the Court's splintered decision in the *United Mine Workers'* case four years later, the Roosevelt Court as embodied first by Chief Justice Stone, and then by his Truman-appointed successor, Fred M. Vinson, was to become more and more fractionalized until finally it would evidence the same five to four vote divisions that had haunted the early Court of the Nine Old Men. Just as that previous Supreme Court had suffered through the transition from economic conservatism to economic liberalism, so too now would this Supreme Court of the "Nine Middle-Aged Men" suffer through a similar transition from economic liberalism to social liberalism. And in the end, the

Supreme Courts of Stone and Vinson would handle the transition no better (if not in fact actually worse) than the earlier Court of Hughes before them.

Just as ideological divisions and realignments had plagued the Court before the first Roosevelt appointment of Black, so now did they plague the Court after the final Roosevelt appointment of Rutledge. In attempting to fine-tune the economic reforms achieved after 1937, Rutledge was to join with his fellow justices Black, Douglas, and Murphy in forming a liberal bloc as solidly united as the conservative "Four Horsemen" bloc of Van Devanter, McReynolds, Sutherland, and Butler before it. Against them was pitted an increasingly conservative element made up of Frankfurter, Jackson, and Roberts who, in terms of analogy, succeeded to the minority position previously held by Brandeis, Stone, and Cardozo. At the same time, Stone as Chief Justice inherited Hughes's old role as leaning towards the minority, but nevertheless willing at times to join with the majority bloc. For his part, Reed was to, on more than one occasion, adapt to Roberts's old position as the crucial "switch in time" vote. The final result was to see the Court more thoroughly divided than at any time since the constitutional crisis of 1935–37.[21]

By 1945, the Court was clearly coming to loggerheads. Underneath the ideological underpinnings of its increasingly fractious opinions, the Court was exhibiting signs of internal animosities, which began spilling out with the *Jewell Ridge Coal Corp.*[22] decision of May 7, 1945. Here, in a case involving the United Mine Workers, the Court voted five to four in favor of the union's argument that its members were entitled to "portal to portal" pay. In seeking a rehearing, the coal company noted that Justice Black's former law partner had represented the union and that Black had improperly been a member of the five-man Court majority. While the Court customarily denied motions for rehearings without opinion, Chief Justice Stone here, aware of how strongly Jackson and Frankfurter felt on the matter, proposed a two-sentence opinion denying rehearing on the ground that the Court was "without authority . . . to pass upon the propriety of the participation by its members in the decision of cases brought . . . for review."[23]

While Jackson had been willing to accept this statement, Black declared that "any opinion which discussed the subject at all would mean a declaration of war." In response to what he considered to be Black's "bullying," Jackson then decided himself to write an opinion "to keep self-respect in the face of his threats." Jackson's opinion, concurred in by Frankfurter, concluded, "There is no authority known to me under which a majority of this Court has power under any circumstances to exclude one of its duly commissioned Justices from sitting or voting on any case."[24] From this altercation began the notorious Black-Jackson feud that came to characterize the final years of the Roosevelt Court. Ironically, had Black not participated in the *Jewell Ridge* decision, the resulting four to four vote would have had the effect of affirming the pro-UMW decision of the circuit court of appeals. Nevertheless, Black's actions here, by giving the Court's opinion the force of legal precedent, raised serious misgivings as to the former klansman's sense of judicial ethics. Thus was the opening scuffle that ultimately led to the Roosevelt Court's demise.[25]

All of this came during a period of great transition. On April 12, 1945, Franklin Delano Roosevelt, after leading the nation through twelve lengthy years of first depression and then war, died just three months into his fourth term as president. Two months later, having successfully prevented Roosevelt from making a clean sweep of Supreme Court appointments, and having inherited Justice Holmes's old title of "The Great Dissenter," Justice Owen J. Roberts retired from the bench, effective July 31. The new president, Harry S. Truman, selected Harold H. Burton as the first Republican nominee to the Court since Roberts himself had been chosen by Hoover fifteen years before.

A former mayor of Cleveland who had served as United States Senator from Ohio since 1941, Justice Burton was nominated to the Court by Truman on September 18 and was confirmed unanimously by the Senate just one day later. Considered by many at the time to be a "liberal Republican" and an "economic middle-roader," Burton was known "as a man with no causes or crusades to promote." Succeeding the Republican Roberts, he was also rightly expected to "fall in with the more moderate wing" of Stone, Frankfurter, and Jackson. As he formally took his seat on October 1, Burton consequently brought "no fundamental change in the alignment of the Court."[26]

Burton's appointment did, however, open public criticism as to the justices's pre-Court experiences. As the third U.S. Senator to be appointed to the bench in eight years,[27] Burton's appointment accentuated the fact that, with the exception of former circuit court judge Rutledge, no other sitting member of the Court had had prior judicial training. While this fact alone did little to hurt Burton's elevation, as the Stone Court entered into its final days and the Court's later difficulties became more pronounced, the character of the individual justices became more and more at issue with the public. With the advent to the Supreme Court of Fred M. Vinson (1946–53), the high bench's problems were to take on whole new dimensions.[28]

Fred Vinson and the Roosevelt Court in Decline: 1946–47

On April 22, 1946, the Supreme Court of Harlan Fiske Stone met for one final time. At age seventy-three, the chief justice had presided over the Court for roughly four years and ten months. On the day in question, he read brief dissents to majority opinions announced by justices Rutledge and Douglas respectively. With regard to the latter, a five-man majority opinion granting citizenship rights to an alien who had previously refused military service, Stone responded, "It's not the function of the Court to disregard the will of Congress on the exercise of its constitutional power." Staying one more case after that, Stone asked to be examined by awaiting physicians only to be assured that he was suffering merely from "a small case of indigestion." With that, Court was adjourned and the chief justice went home. Five hours later, Stone had expired—dead from a massive cerebral hemorrhage.[29]

With Stone's death, Harry Truman now had the opportunity to make his second appointment to the bench. With the year old animosity between Justices Black and Jackson a poorly kept secret, Truman judiciously avoided consulting any sitting member of the Roosevelt Court with regard to a possible successor. More importantly, with rumors abounding that both Black and Douglas would resign should Truman honor Roosevelt's reported promise of elevating Jackson to Stone's position, Truman seemed determined to avoid making contact with the Court altogether.

In view of the Court's recent decline in stature, Truman was no doubt driven by contemporary contrasts between Stone and his predecessor Hughes. As Frankfurter himself was to note, while "Stone used to fumble over things and allow talk to be too loose and confused," Hughes by contrast showed a rare combination of "executive competence—keeping things moving in an orderly way" and a "thoroughness of consideration at all matters no matter how complicated." Praising Hughes further for his "extraordinary qualities, his intellectual powers, and his tolerance of contrary view," Frankfurter noted that when Hughes presided at Court conferences, "the atmosphere was free, but whatever inhibition was felt was due not to Hughes's restriction of discussion, but derived from the influence of his intrinsic authority."[30]

With that contrast in mind, and more important, in view of the present Court difficulties resulting from the lack of strong leadership, President Truman now looked for a "jurist who might be able to bring harmony out of dissonance" and "stand at the balancing center of gravity" so as to bring order to a "divided and disorganized Court." Consequently, "after weeks of searching," Truman's "middle-of-the-road" secretary of the

Treasury, Fred Vinson "seemed . . . to be just the man for the job." Consequently, on June 6, 1946, Vinson was nominated to be the thirteenth chief justice of the United States. Two short weeks later, he was confirmed by the Senate. Four days after that, he actively took over his duties as chief justice.[31]

What neither Truman nor Vinson apparently understood, however, was the true extent to which the Court at this time was divided. In terms of ideology, Justice Jackson would explain the recent Court years as

> a struggle between the ideas of Chief Justice Stone, as a liberal of one school, and Mr. Justice Black, as a liberal of an entirely different school. Chief Justice Stone was a good deal of a liberal in the Holmes tradition. That is to say, he didn't agree with a good many of the legislative experiments that were going on, but he thought that the people would only learn that they wouldn't work by trying them and that they had a right to experiment. Mr. Justice Black had a different view, as his opinions will indicate. He was strongly in favor of some of the social reforms and would interpret the Constitution and text of acts to further the ends that he had in view. That is the school of thought that has been characterized as "judicial activism."[32]

Stone himself had lamented this ideological difference. Toward the end of his life as he found himself increasingly under siege by Black and his fellow activists, the chief justice was to dolefully reminisce:

> My more conservative brethren in the old days enacted their own economic prejudice into law. What they did placed in jeopardy a great and useful institution of government. The pendulum has now swung to the other extreme and history is repeating itself. The Court is now in as much danger of becoming a legislative Constitution-making body, enacting into law its own predilections, as it was then. The only difference is now the interpretations of statutes whether "over-conservative" or "over-liberal" can be corrected by Congress.[33]

Beyond mere ideology, however, the divisions within the Court at this point transcended politics for the more disruptive issue of personalities. Jackson's ally Frankfurter was a source of much of this internal friction. With a talent for manipulating men of lesser intelligence, Frankfurter could never admit that his colleagues had minds of their own. Consequently, his tendency of treating many of them as though they were first-year law students was to become a source of great aggravation, especially after the first flag salute case (*Minersville School District v. Gobitis*[34]) of 1940. Having initially induced a unanimous Court to join him in ruling that a state could compel its citizens to salute the American flag,[35] Frankfurter was to face a revolt three years later in the second flag salute case (*West Virginia Board of Education v. Barnette*[36]) of 1943. Having grown "disillusioned" over Frankfurter as a result of his initial ruling, Douglas, Black, and Murphy (whom Frankfurter had come to label "the Axis") were to break with him in *Barnette*. *Gobitis*, consequently, was overruled and Frankfurter found himself permanently alienated from the Court's liberal faction.[37]

The Court's problems over Jackson, however, were to prove to be even stronger. Having privately split with Black over the *Jewell Ridge* decision of 1945, Jackson was to spend most of the next year as the government's special prosecutor at Nuremberg, a position he did not finally return from until after Vinson's appointment as Chief Justice in 1946. Even before he had returned, however, Jackson made it clear what to expect in terms of the new Court by making public his charges against Black.

Black had attacked him, he raged. And now that the Chief Justice appointment was settled, Jackson was determined to lash right back. "It is high time," he trumpeted, "that Congress has the facts. If war is declared on me, I propose to wage it with the weapons of an open warrior, not those of a stealthy assassin." Recounting the earlier controversy over *Jewell Ridge*, Jackson went on to assert that Black had waged a subtle war in Washington to keep him from getting the chief justiceship and Black had used contacts from within the press to further his aims. Addressing his complaints to the judiciary committees of both houses of Congress, Jackson concluded with the statement: "It is desirable to get the controversy all back of us now so that he [Vinson] can take up his tasks without a cloud hanging over the Court."[38]

Neither the controversy nor the cloud, however, drifted away any time soon. While the Court was closed for the summer, tourists would flock to the Supreme Court building in Washington "looking as if they expected to find the justices clubbing each other with baseball bats." It was soon plain that the controversy arising out of Jackson's attack would not blow over in a few days—or even in a few weeks. Coming as a result of a deep-seated feud which had long soiled the Court with internal turmoil, the Jackson/Black feud now had brought the Supreme Court of Fred Vinson "into public disgrace."[39]

To most observers, the Court's main problem at that time "was the justices' continual and active politicking around Washington." While James Byrnes may have left the Court to return full-time to politics in 1942, many of his former colleagues preferred to combine the two worlds with the unfortunate result of engendering further personal antagonisms within the Court. Thus, Frankfurter had maintained his ties to the White House as a personal adviser to Roosevelt, while Jackson "hoped for a bigger political plum." At the same time, Black was making speeches before the National Citizens Political Action Committee and Murphy lobbied for an ambassadorship or even a position in the cabinet. Douglas, however, was perhaps the most political of all. Having previously been considered for vice-president in 1940 and 1944, he now looked to 1948 for a possible run for the presidency.[40]

This was the Supreme Court that Fred Vinson inherited when he took his seat as chief justice in June of 1946. If Truman had hoped he would be able to return the Court to the discipline of the Hughes era, however, he was to be sorely disappointed. A former congressman from Kentucky whom

Roosevelt had appointed associate justice of the United States Court of Appeals for the District of Columbia, Vinson had subsequently served as director of the war-time Office of Economic Stabilization and then briefly as Harry Truman's secretary of the Treasury. For all of his prior training, however, Vinson was known more as a "skillful politicker rather than a jurist." In replacing the liberal Republican Stone, he was to have little impact on the Court's ideological balance. More importantly, as far as Frankfurter was concerned, the new chief justice seemed "to have the confident air of a man who does not see the complexities of problems and blithely hits the obvious points" while precluding the "thoroughness of consideration" that had earlier been so masterfully exhibited by Hughes.[41]

Frankfurter went on to note early attempts by both Black and Douglas to win Vinson over to their side. Noting Reed's comment comparing the new chief justice to "a new girl at school when every boy is courtin' her," Frankfurter went on to muse how he could never understand how a person such as Vinson could "go through life with a vast experience . . . and still remain as ingenuous" as he apparently was.[42] Such was the case that in November 1946, just five months after Vinson took office, the legal scholar and Vinson confidant C. Herman Pritchett was to observe: "Poor Fred Vinson is certainly foolin' himself by his idea as to what is smoothness. . . . The nice man is going to have an awakening sooner than he thinks." With the case of *United States v. United Mine Workers of America* set for argument just two months away in January, "Poor Fred Vinson" was to "have an awakening" even sooner than that.

For all intents and purposes, the Roosevelt Court came to an end on March 6, 1947, the day the Supreme Court of Fred L. Vinson handed down its decision in the case of *United States v. United Mine Workers of America*. Publishing a study of the incident one year later, Professor Pritchett was to observe that the Court's decision "was about as bitter a pill as a Court, generally sympathetic to labor and ardently believing in strict adherence to constitutional procedure in criminal cases, could have been called on to swallow."[43] As it had previously demonstrated in *Jewell Ridge*, the Roosevelt Court by a narrow five to four margin was firmly committed to the cause of organized labor. In the 1945 case of *Hunt v. Crumboch*, it even went so far as to sanction a labor union's efforts to force an employer out of business. As Pritchett, however, was to observe, it was the UMW case that would ultimately prove to be the Court's undoing. In the end, the Court which came into being with the *Parrish* case decision enforcing minimum wage and maximum hour statutes ultimately came apart over John L. Lewis.[44]

In 1946, John L. Lewis, president of the United Mine Workers and one of the most powerful labor leaders in America, ordered a nation-wide strike in the nation's bituminous coal mines. On May 21 of that year, the government on President Truman's orders had taken possession of the mines in order to keep them in operation. On May 24, an agreement was reached between the government and Lewis setting both wages and working conditions to cover the period of government possession. In October, however, Lewis asserted that the contract was subject to termination under a provision of the National Bituminous Coal Wage Agreement of 1945 and on November 15, he gave the government five days notice that the contract was to be terminated. At this point, Lewis added that unless the government agreed to reopen certain terms of the contract, he would strike the mines, whether they were government operated or not.

Considering this a threat, Truman responded by ordering Attorney General Tom Clark to "fight John L. Lewis on all fronts." Consequently, on November 18, the government obtained an order from the District Court temporarily restraining Lewis' call for a strike. Lewis, however, ignored this order and on December 4, he was found guilty of contempt and both he and the union were fined over $3,500,000. Calling a temporary end to the strike three days later, Lewis appealed immediately to the Supreme Court for relief. As Pritchett was to note one year later, Lewis was to catch an already fractured "liberal Court completely unprepared" and fractured it even further.

Thirty years later, a retired William Douglas was to note the animosity surrounding the case. Asserting what he claimed to be an occasional Court tendency to disregard "high principles and standards of justice and equality" so as to allow "government or individuals to get after a person or a class of people," Douglas claimed that the "1947 case was supercharged with feelings about John L. Lewis and led . . . to extreme strictures on his union." Noting that the case had come "in a blaze of anti-Lewis public sentiment" and, that "Vinson was convinced that . . . Lewis was 'too big for his britches,'" Douglas was to conclude that March 6, 1947 "was a bad day for law." In the end, he condemned both the late chief justice's "complete dedication to finding or fashioning some law to put John L. Lewis 'in his place,'" and his former colleagues for allowing "passion" to send them "pell-mell to a public stand against . . . Lewis."[45]

In the end, the district court's verdict against Lewis was upheld, but the original fine was ordered reduced to $700,000. Douglas was unable to determine "[H]ow our Court had the power to set a fine in a criminal case which it had never heard at the trial level." More to the point, the Lewis decision had the unfortunate effect of splitting the Court even further "into splinter groups." Frankfurter and Jackson succeeded in "finding a purely judicial hook—maintenance of respect for the courts"—on which the chief justice as well as justices Reed and Burton were willing to allow Lewis to be "snagged." Rutledge and Murphy, on the other hand in their dissent were to "stick to the doctrines of old liberalism and deny the government's right to coercion" altogether. At the same time, however, Douglas and Black, also in dissent, were to "assist in judicial formulation of a new public policy for dealing with crucial conflicts between strong unions and the public interest" while at the same time insisting "that judicial enforcement of that policy should avoid any taint of retaliatory action."

Thus to a Court formally versed in an "old liberalism . . . familiar only with a weak labor movement, which needed protection if it was to survive, "the *Lewis* decision had the effect of separating old theories from new realities and further divided and weakened an already comatose Court. Having initially won the battle for economic liberalism in 1937, the post-*Parrish* liberalism of the post-*Parrish* Court was to mount its horse and ride off "in all directions."[46]

Aftermath and Conclusions—The Final Demise and Legacy of the Roosevelt Court: 1947–49

Writing just seven months after the *Lewis* decision, Pritchett was to observe that two and one half years after his death, Franklin Roosevelt's appointees still dominated the Supreme Court and "presumably will continue to do so for some time." With regard to its previous two terms, however, he questioned whether it was still proper "to term the current Court the 'Roosevelt Court.'" Noting that even then, the "temper of the Court was already changing," Pritchett contended that "a swing to the right is apparent in many fields." While Pritchett's conclusion that "the Roosevelt Court came to an end on that Thursday in March 1947, when the *Lewis* decision was handed down,"[47] may be a subject to debate, the fact of the matter is that from 1947 on, the days when any sort of Rooseveltian majority was to hold sway over the Court were at best numbered.

By the summer of 1949, the Court had managed to regain a little of its former stature. A "sad-faced Chief Justice Vinson . . . a formidable poker player, above-all a man of diplomacy," was said to be at the helm of a Court consisting of Hugo Black, "an ex-police court judge . . . now rated as one of the best-read, hardest working, most learned justices on the Court"; Stanley Reed, "massive and heavy-jowled . . . writer of pedestrian opinions, rated as an able lawyer"; Felix Frankfurter, though at age 66, the "oldest in years . . . a bouncing, argumentative, brilliant little man planted firmly on the roost of his vast knowledge of the law"; William Orville Douglas, "the justice with the cowlick and the friendly grin," at age 50 "the Court's youngest," yet "an assertive, restless, billy-be-damned man"; Frank Murphy "with a starched, far-off look . . . a man of humanitarian impulses without the intellectual drive and capacity to make himself highly effective"; Robert Jackson "with his open-work, Dutch expression . . . an eloquent, incisive writer who, when he dissents, dissents in vitriol"; Wiley Rutledge "rocklike . . . large, dignified, and pedagogical . . . a liberal in the tradition of the Midwest"; and finally Harold Burton, "with an air of avuncular interest . . . an amiable man, out-paced by his hard-running colleagues, generally regarded as the least effective justice on the court."[48]

Thus, eight full years after Franklin Roosevelt named seven of the nine justices to the United States Supreme Court, seven of its nine members remained Roosevelt appointees. "Since 1937," one observer noted,

> the Nine had taken themselves pretty well out of the headlines, but they had made news nonetheless. Closer to the tradition of Holmes and Brandeis than to that of Hughes, they had plowed under old and respected landmarks; they had overturned, altogether, some thirty previous decisions of the Supreme Court; they had struck out boldly, sometimes brashly, into new grounds. Other courts had split more violently, but no court had quarreled so continuously and rambunctiously with itself. Whereas in the Twenties and Thirties, the courts found themselves in solid agreement some eighty percent of the time, seventy percent of the time this term the court had found itself split.[49]

Reviewing the previous twelve years which had followed *Parrish*, this same observer noted that the present Court

> had not got in spectacular knockdown fights with other branches of government, as for example, had their predecessors, the Nine Old Men. That Court, dominated by McReynolds, Van Devanter, Sutherland, and Butler, defiantly stood against a social revolution. This court in contrast was part of the revolution.[50]

"In the twelve years," he continued,

> only two congressional measures—neither of them major—had been declared unconstitutional. The court merely nibbled around the edge of the big, still unresolved questions, leaving it to time and changing customs to determine the ultimate shape of things. The nibbling was deliberate and not the result of timidity. Rebutting by implication their immediate predecessors, the present justices insisted that it was Congress's job to legislate, not the Court's.[51]

And so it went. As had been noted so many times before,

> the justices were nine broiling brooks in search of a new main stream. Running down one side of the hill were Frankfurter, Jackson, Burton and Vinson. Running down the other side, a more precipitous slope, were Black, Douglas, Murphy and Rutledge. Reed ran back and forth. . . . The Frankfurter group thought the Court should stay in the well-defined grooves, left by precedent. Only then, they believed would the people have any idea of what to expect from justice. . . . The Black group cared less for precedent, more for a flexible legal logic in a world in a state of flux.[52]

Quoting Justice Douglas, it was noted that the Black group "would not stand in the way of legislation leading toward the welfare state." Addressing a CIO convention in 1948, Douglas asserted, "The human welfare state is the greatest invention of the Twentieth Century." Later noting the Court's current trend, Douglas contended that "[I]t is better that we make our own history than be governed by the dead. We too must be dynamic components of history." Enthusiastically proclaiming that "[s]uch a doctrine made for exciting legal history," the observer was to conclude that "[i]t also made for some difficulty in knowing what the bright young court would do next."[53]

Unfortunately the "bright young court" would do nothing. In 1949, the Court, in the case of *Lincoln Federal Labor Union v. Northwestern Iron and Metal Company*,[54] did formally overrule the Fuller Court's 1908 antilabor ruling in *Adair v. United States*.[55] Before year's end, however, the Court's composition was drastically altered by the untimely deaths of first Justice Murphy (on July 16)[56] and then Justice Rutledge (on September 10).[57] In their place, in the space of six weeks, President Truman was able to name his third and fourth appointees to the Court. Naming Attorney General Tom Clark (of *U.S. v. UMW* notoriety) on August 2 to succeed Murphy, Truman subsequently nominated Sherman Minton to succeed Justice Rutledge on September 15. By October 12, both men had joined their fellow Truman appointees, Vinson and Burton on the bench and the Supreme Court of Franklin Roosevelt formally gave way to that of Harry Truman. Looking back on this Court thirty years later, retired Justice William O. Douglas would opine that "[u]nder Truman, the Court sank to its lowest professional level until the Burger Court arrived." While conceding that Truman's appointees "would be called liberal on economic issues," Douglas nevertheless faulted them for reflecting what he considered to be "the small-town attitude of conformity more than the emerging urban consciousness of the need for diversity."[58]

Speaking "from the viewpoint of one who believes that the judiciary should be alert to construe the Constitution and laws of the United States as providing a strong arsenal for protection of the individual,"[59] Douglas thus reflected the change in judicial emphasis that had taken place a dozen years after economic liberalism's breakthrough in *Parrish*. As has been seen, with the demise of the Nine Old Men and the triumph of government regulation of commerce, the post-

Roosevelt Court was finally free to pursue other areas of judicial interest. With economic liberalism a constitutional given by 1949, the Truman-dominated Court of Fred M. Vinson and all of the other Courts that were to follow were to shift their attention to the struggle over social liberalism.

This however, brings us back to the premise of this chapter. While Franklin Roosevelt was successful in remaking the Court into a bastion of state welfarism, his seeming indifference to the emerging emphasis towards social liberalism left in his wake a Supreme Court which was just as badly divided in 1947 as it had been a full decade earlier. Ironically, it took later justices such as Earl Warren and William Brennan, appointees of Republican Dwight Eisenhower, as well as later Kennedy and Johnson appointees such as Arthur Goldberg, Abe Fortas, and Thurgood Marshall, to help Roosevelt holdovers Douglas and Black achieve their goals. With the subsequent advent of the Burger and, later, Rehnquist Courts, however, social liberalism gradually gave way to social conservatism.[60]

The rise of social conservatism, however, did not necessarily, at least initially, mean a return to economic conservatism. With Roosevelt's justices all now dead, the concept of economic liberalism lives on. As the Burger Court after 1986, became the Rehnquist Court and social liberalism succumbed to the doctrine of social conservatism, the judicial decisions made with *Parrish* and all of the rest of the Roosevelt Court's landmark economic decisions remain as if etched in stone and as sacrosanct as the Fourteenth Amendment and the Bill of Rights before them. In the half century since these decisions were made, Court adherence to economic liberalism has been reflected in a number of different opinions offered by various justices reflecting all ends of the political spectrum.

As the chief justice of this new conservative Court as well as the chief architect of this new social conservatism, William Rehnquist perhaps better than any other jurist reflects the persistent and final triumph of economic liberalism as Roosevelt's legacy in constitutional law. In a biting dissent in the 1988 case of *Riley v. National Federation of the Blind*,[61] wherein the Court invalidated a North Carolina statute setting a three-tiered schedule for establishing "reasonable fees" that a professional fundraiser could charge for his services, the chief justice noted that the Court had acted out of a First Amendment regard that the statute in question was unlawful in that it was based on "the paternalistic premise that charities' speech must be regulated for their own benefit."[62] With that however, in the best tradition of Brandeis, Holmes, and Frankfurter, the former Jackson law clerk was to continue:

> All economic regulation of this sort is "paternalistic" in the sense that it prevents parties who wish to contract with one another from entering into a contract on precisely the terms that they would choose. But ever since *West Coast Hotel Company v. Parrish* . . . finally overruled *Lochner v. New York* . . . and *Adkins v. Children's Hospital* . . . paternalism has been a perfectly acceptable motive for legislative regulation of this sort.[63]

And so it is, nearly six full decades after Franklin Roosevelt brought economic liberalism to the forefront of constitutional thought, the conservative appointees of Richard Nixon and Ronald Reagan continue to pay homage to his Court. With the Court's recent decision, however, in the May 1995, case of *United States v. Lopez*,[64] a fifty-eight-year trend toward unlimited federal power may actually be on the verge of redefinition. In a narrow five to four vote reversal of the Gun-Free School Zones Act of 1990, the Supreme Court, for the first time since 1937, actually voted to limit the application of the heretofore seemingly unlimited commerce clause so as to prevent direct federal intervention in the area of state-run local schools. At this point, however, only time will tell whether *Lopez* represents a "constitutional moment" of historic importance or only a "constitutional minute" of fleeting significance.[65] Whatever its shortcomings in defining the Constitution's commitment to social liberalism, however, the

Roosevelt Court does at least have sixty years of nearly unabated economic liberalism to stand as part of its undeniable legacy to this nation's constitutional landscape.

ENDNOTES

1. *Panama Refining Co. v. Ryan*, 293 U.S. 389 (1935).
2. *Schechter Poultry Corp. v. United States*, 295 U.S. 495 (1935).
3. *West Coast Hotel Co. v. Parrish*, 300 U.S. 379 (1937).
4. Kermit Hall, ed., *The Oxford Companion to the Supreme Court of the United States* (New York: Oxford University Press, 1992), p. 986.
5. *United States v. United Mine Workers of America*, 330 U.S. 258 (1947).
6. "Whispers in the White House," *Time*, March 10, 1941, pp. 14–15.
7. "High Bench Echoes," *Newsweek*, June 16, 1941, p. 22; "Full Bench," *Newsweek*, June 23, 1941, p. 18.
8. James A. Farley, *Jim Farley's Story, The Roosevelt Years* (New York: McGraw-Hill Book Co., Inc., 1948), p. 301.
9. Phillip B. Kurland, "Transcript of Taped Interview of Robert Jackson," in *The Justices of the United States Supreme Court, 1789-1969: Their Lives and Opinions*, ed. Leon Friedman and Fred L. Israel (New York: Chelsea House Publishers, 1969) vol. 4, pp. 2562–63. See also William O. Douglas, *The Court Years: 1939-1975, The Autobiography of William O. Douglas* (New York: Random House, 1980), p. 28; "Congressional Record Citation to Nomination Confirmation of Robert H. Jackson to be Associate Justice of the Supreme Court of the United States," *The Supreme Court of the United States, Hearings and Reports on Successful and Unsuccessful Nominations of Supreme Court Justices by the Senate Judiciary Committee, 1916 - 1975*, vol. 4, pp. 47–51, 60–1, 64, 68.
10. James F. Byrnes, *All in One Lifetime* (New York: Harper & Brothers, 1958), pp. 129–32. See also David E. Lilienthal, *The Journals of David E. Lilienthal: the TVA Years* (New York: Harper and Row, 1964), pp. 285–86; Douglas, p. 26; Raymond Moley, *The First New Deal*, (New York: Harcourt, Brace, & World, Inc., 1966), pp. 365–69; *Time*, January 11, 1943, p. 20.
11. 314 U.S. 160 (1941).
12. 11 Peters 102 (1837).
13. *Edwards v. California*, 314 US 160 (1941). See also Byrnes, pp. 140–41; Douglas, p. 27.
14. 349 U.S. 294 (1954).
15. Byrnes, pp. 147–57. See also Douglas, p. 253; *Time*, January 11, 1943, p. 20.
16. *Roosevelt and Frankfurter: Their Correspondence, 1928–1945*, ann. by Max Freeman, (Boston: Little, Brown, & Co., 1967), pp. 580–81, 670–76. See also Joseph Lash, ed., *From the Diaries of Felix Frankfurter* (New York: W.W. Norton & Co, Inc., 1975), p. 239.

17. "Everybody's Justice," *Time*, January 18, 1943, p. 191; *US News*, February 19, 1943, p. 66.

18. Douglas, pp. 27–28.

19. Preface, 312 United States Reports (1940); Preface, 314 United States Reports (1941); Preface, 317 United States Reports (1942).

20. Preface, 329 United States Reports (1946); Preface, 335 United States Reports (1947-1948).

21. "The Judiciary," *Time*, June 27, 1949, vol. 53–2, p. 19.

22. *Jewell Ridge Coal Corp. v. Local No. 6167*, 325 U.S. 897 (1945).

23. *Jewell Ridge Coal Company v. Local No. 6167, UMW*, 325 US 161 (1945); rehearing denied, 325 US 897 (1945). See also C. Herman Pritchett, *The Roosevelt Court: A Study in Judicial Politics and Values, 1937–1947* (New York: MacMillan Co., 1948), p. 27. Douglas, pp. 29–31.

24. 325 U.S. 897 (1945).

25. Ibid.

26. "Roberts Dissenting," *Time*, July 16, 1945, pp. 16–17; "People of the Week," *US News*, September 28, 1945, pp. 81–84; Pritchett, pp. 9–14.

27. The other two senators were Hugo Black (D-AL) and James Byrnes (D-SC).

28. "Even Stephen," *Time*, June 17, 1946, pp. 18–19; Lash, pp. 263–65.

29 "The Case Should be Stayed," *Time*, April 29, 1946, p. 28.

30. Lash, pp. 274–75; "Even Stephen," *Time*, June 17, 1946, p. 18.

31. Harry S. Truman, *Memoirs by Harry S. Truman, 1946–1952: Years of Trial and Hope* (New York: Doubleday & Company, Inc., 1956), pp. 552–54.

32. Kurland, p. 2564.

33. Alpheus Thomas Mason, "Harlan Fiske Stone," *The Justices of the United States Supreme Court 1789-1969*, vol. 3, p. 2235.

34. *Minersville School District v. Gobitis*, 310 U.S. 586 (1940).

35. Ibid.

36. *West Virginia Board of Education v. Barnette*, 319 U.S. 624 (1943).

37. Ibid. See also Douglas, pp. 43–45; Melvin Urofsky, ed., *The Douglas Letters: Selections from the Private Papers of Justice William O. Douglas* (Bethesda, MD: Adler & Adler, 1987), pp. 73–75.

38. "Wrath Without Dignity," *Time*, June 17, 1946, pp. 18–19. See also Hugo Black and Elizabeth Black, *The Memoirs of Hugo L. Black and Elizabeth Black* (New York: Random House, 1986), p. 72.

39. Ibid.

40. "Feud Continued," *Time*, June 17, 1946, p. 21. See also Lash, pp. 274–76, 286–87, 303–04, 306, 307–11.

41. Ibid.

42. Ibid. See also "Even Stephen," *Time*, June 17, 1946, p. 18.

43. Pritchett, pp. 232–36, 273.

44. Ibid. See also *Hunt v. Crumboch*, 325 U.S. 821 (1945); *United States v. United Mine Workers*, 330 U.S. 258 (1947).

45. Pritchett, pp. 232–36, 273. See also Douglas, pp. 102, 139, 246.

46. Pritchett, pp. 232–36, 273. See also "Grand Right and Left," *Time*, July 2, 1945, p. 16.

47. Pritchett, p. xiv.

48. "The Living Must Judge," *Time*, June 27, 1949, pp. 16–19. See also Milton R. Konvitz, "Value of Judgments," *The Saturday Review of Literature*, September 18, 1946, p. 15.

49.Konvitz, p. 15

50. Ibid.

51. Ibid.

52. Ibid.

53. Ibid.

54. *Lincoln Federal Labor Union v. Northwestern Iron and Metal Company*, 335 U.S. 525 (1949).

55. 208 U.S. 161 (1908).

56. "Death of an Apostle," *Time*, August 1, 1949, p. 12; "Promise Kept," *Time*, August 8, 1949, pp. 10–11.

57. "Death of a Scholar," *Time*, September 19, 1949, pp. 26–27.

58. Douglas, p. 425.

59. Ibid.; Merle Miller, *Plain Speaking: An Oral Autobiography of Harry S. Truman* (New York: Berkley Publishers Corporation, 1973), pp. 144–45, 225–26.

60. See Vincent Blasi, ed., *No Burger Court* (New Haven, CT: Yale University Press, 1983).

61. *Riley, District Attorney of the Tenth Prosecutorial District of North Carolina v. National Federation of the Blind of North Carolina*, 487 U.S. 781, 808 (1988).

62. Ibid., p. 809.

63. Ibid.

64. 514 U.S. 549 (1995).

65. "A Gun Ban is Shot Down," *Time*, May 8, 1995, p. 85. See also "The Limits of Commerce," *Newsweek*, May 8, 1995, p. 72; "After 58 Years, the Court Says No," *US News and World Report*, May 8, 1995, p. 15. "A Long-Anticipated Right Turn," *US News and World Report*, July 10, 1995, p. 9.

CULTURAL CHRONOLOGY

Mar	1933	FDR inaugurated
Jan	1934	Court upholds Minnesota Mortgage Moratorium Act
Mar	1934	Court upholds New York milk price control law
Jan	1935	Court strikes down "hot oil" provision of National Industrial Recovery Act
May	1935	Court strikes down portion of National Recovery Act, limits president's removal power, and strikes down Railroad Retirement Act
Oct	1935	New Supreme Court building opens in Washington, D.C.
Jan	1936	Court strikes down Agricultural Adjustment Act
May	1936	Court strikes down Bituminous Coal Act, and strikes down Municipal Bankruptcy Act
June	1936	Court strikes down New York minimum wage law for women

Nov	1936	FDR defeats Alfred Landon for second term
Feb	1937	FDR submits Judicial Reform Act to Congress
Mar	1937	FDR gives national radio address on "Court-packing" plan
Mar	1937	Court upholds Washington State minimum wage law ("switch in time that saved nine")
Apr	1937	Court upholds National Labor Relations Act
May	1937	Court upholds Social Security Act
May	1937	Justice Van Devanter announces retirement
July	1937	Senate rejects Judicial Reform Act
Aug	1937	FDR nominates Senator Hugo L. Black for Court
Jan	1938	Justice Sutherland retires; FDR nominates Solicitor General Stanley Reed
Jan	1938	Justice Cardozo dies; FDR nominates Felix Frankfurter
Feb	1939	Justice Brandeis retires; FDR nominates William O. Douglas

Nov	1939	Justice Butler dies; FDR nominates Attorney General Frank Murphy
Nov	1940	FDR defeats Wendell Willkie for unprecedented third term
Feb	1941	Justice McReynolds retires; FDR nominates Senator James Brynes
June	1941	Chief Justice Charles Evans Hughes retires; FDR nominates Justice Harlan Fiske Stone as Chief Justice, and selects Attorney General Robert H. Jackson to replace Stone
Oct	1942	Justice Brynes resigns from Court; FDR nominates Wiley B. Rutledge
Nov	1944	FDR defeats Thomas E. Dewey for fourth term
April	1945	FDR dies in Warm Springs, Georgia

BIOGRAPHICAL DIGEST

168 Days (1938). Initial, influential account of the battle over the Court between FDR and Congress. Written by noted Washington journalists Joseph Alsop and Turner Catledge.

Adamson v. California (1947). By a vote of five to four, the Court rejected the total incorporation thesis of Justice Black, and accepted instead the selective incorporation approach of Justice Frankfurter (concerning the Bill of Rights and Fourteenth Amendment).

Ashwander v. Tennessee Valley Authority (1936). Upheld Tennessee Valley Authority Act in an opinion by Chief Justice Hughes, with a critical concurrence by Justice Brandeis concerning judicial review and governmental power.

Black, Hugo L. (1886-1971). First nominee to the Court of FDR in 1937. Justice Black served until his death in September 1971 and authored numerous landmark decisions during his tenure.

"Black Monday" (1935). On May 27, 1935 the Supreme Court delivered three unanimous rulings voiding critical elements of FDR's New Deal program, including the National Recovery Act.

Brandeis, Louis D. (1856-1941). First Jewish member of the Court, selected by Woodrow Wilson in 1916. Author of the "Brandeis brief," and leading First Amendment jurist.

Butler, Pierce (1866-1939). Nominated for the Court in 1923 by President Harding, serving until his death in 1939. Wrote Court's opinion in controversial *Tipaldo* case in 1936. Member of the Four Horsemen.

Byrnes, James F. (1882-1972). Was selected by FDR for Court seat in 1941, and resigned sixteen months later. He served in both chambers of Congress before joining the Court, and was governor of South Carolina afterward.

Cantwell v. Connecticut (1940). Major First Amendment free exercise clause ruling involving Jehovah's Witnesses. Court incorporated/absorbed free exercise clause into Fourteenth Amendment in opinion by Justice Roberts.

Cardozo, Benjamin N. (1870-1938). Appointed by President Hoover in 1932 and served until his death in 1938. Noted author and jurist in pre-Court days. Wrote the Court's opinion upholding Social Security Act in 1937.

Carter v. Carter Coal Co. (1936). Court strikes down Bituminous Coal Conservation Act of 1935 by five to four vote. Justice Sutherland's opinion strongly relies on the Tenth Amendment.

"Court-Packing" Plan (1937). In February and March of 1937, FDR unveils plan to "reform" the federal judiciary and enlarge membership on the Supreme Court. Measure was personal and political debacle for the president.

Douglas, William O. (1898-1980). FDR appointed Douglas to the Court in 1939. Douglas has the longest tenure in the history of the Court, serving until 1975, and authored more opinions than any justice in the Court's history.

Everson v. Board of Education of Ewing Township (1947). The Court's initial major ruling on the establishment clause. By a five to four vote, the Court announced a "high wall of separation" between church and state.

Frankfurter, Felix (1902-1965). FDR's third nominee to the Court, serving from 1939-62. Frankfurter was a leading advocate of principled judicial restraint.

Gilbert, Cass (1859-1934). Architect of the "marble temple," the new building for the Supreme Court that opened in the fall of 1935, after Gilbert's death. His son completed the project.

Home Building and Loan Associates v. Blaisdell (1934). Upheld 1933 Minnesota Mortgage Moratorium law by a five to four vote. This case reflected the divisions within the Court regarding New Deal era legislation.

Hughes, Charles Evans (1862-1948). Appointed to Court by President Taft in 1910, and made chief justice by Hoover in 1930 after leaving the Court in 1916 for failed presidential race against Wilson. Author of crucial Court decisions, including *Parrish* in 1937. Resigned from the Court in 1941.

Humphrey's Executor v. United States (1935). Court unanimously restricts removal power of the president with respect to certain officials. Part of the "Black Monday" rulings toward FDR and the New Deal.

Jackson, Robert H. (1892-1954). Appointed to the Court by FDR in 1941, and served until his death following *Brown* in 1954. Wrote key dissent in *Everson*. Allies' chief prosecutor at Nuremberg war crimes trial following World War II.

Kiyoshi Hirabayashi v. United States (1943). Unanimous decision affirming government's authority to enact wartime curfew order for Japanese Americans. Justice Stone authored opinion for the Court.

McReynolds, James C. (1862-1946). Woodrow Wilson nominee in 1914, and served until 1941, bitter at FDR's third election. Trenchant critic of the New Deal; key member of the Four Horsemen.

Minersville School District v. Gobitis (1940). The Court's first "flag salute case," upholding the conviction of Jehovah's Witnesses for failure to salute the flag in public school. Court's opinion was written by Justice Felix Frankfurter; sole dissenter was Justice Harlan Fiske Stone.

Morehead v. New York ex rel. Tipaldo (1936). Court nullifies New York State minimum wage law for women. Justice Butler writes for a five to four Court.

Murphy, Frank (1890-1949). Was nominated by FDR in 1940, after having served as governor of Michigan and U.S. attorney general. Wrote critical dissent in *Korematsu.*

New Deal (1930s). FDR's plan for national recovery and restoration. An approach to governmental intervention, especially in the economy. Most often associated with FDR's first two presidential terms.

"Nine Old Men" (1936). Sobriquet that was placed on the Court in the 1930s. Title of sensationalistic book written by journalists Drew Pearson and Robert S. Allen, published in late October 1936.

Panama Refining Co. v. Ryan (1935). Supreme Court voids the "hot oil" provision of the NIRA. Opinion for the Court written by Chief Justice Hughes.

National Labor Relations Board v. Jones and Laughlin Steel Corp. (1937). The Court sustained the National Labor Relations Act of 1935. Opinion was written by Chief Justice Charles Evans Hughes, and marked the beginning of a new era of jurisprudence.

Railroad Retirement Board v. Alton Railroad Co. (1935). Invalidated the Railroad Retirement Act; another "Black Monday" ruling.

Reed, Stanley (1884-1980). Was the second nominee to the Court of FDR. His tenure lasted from 1938 to 1957. Reed was solicitor general of the United States at the time of his appointment.

Roberts, Owen J. (1875-1955). Nominated by President Hoover in 1930, and tenure lasted until 1945. Wrote the Court's opinion in *U.S. v. Butler* striking down Agricultural Adjustment Act.

Rutledge, Wiley B. (1894-1949). Appointed to Court in 1943, died suddenly in 1949. Was President Roosevelt's final nominee to the Court.

Schechter Poultry Corp. v. United States (1935). Struck down the National Industrial Recovery Act of 1933, which was the first major New Deal law passed by Congress.

Steward Machine Co. v. Davis (1937). By five to four margin, Court upheld the Social Security Act of 1935, the centerpiece of the New Deal. Majority opinion written by Justice Cardozo.

Stone, Harlan Fiske (1872-1946). Appointed to the Court by fellow Amherst alum Calvin Coolidge in 1925, and chosen as chief justice in 1941 by FDR. Collapsed in Court's courtroom on April 22, 1946, while announcing a dissent, and died later that evening.

Sutherland, George (1862-1942). Selected for Court in 1922 by President Harding, and retired in 1938. Only member of Court from Utah. Member of the Four Horsemen.

"Switch in Time That Saved Nine" (1937). The change in the Court's jurisprudence, particularly as witnessed in the *Parrish* and *Jones and Laughlin* decisions in the spring of 1937. Helped to defeat FDR's Court-packing plan.

Toyosaburo Korematsu v. United States (1944). Court validates forced removal of Japanese Americans from sensitive military areas on West Coast. Justice Black writes opinion for the six to three Court.

United States v. Butler (1936). Court overturns major New Deal statute, Agricultural Adjustment Act. Opinion by Justice Owen Roberts.

United States v. Carolene Products Co. (1938). Otherwise insignificant case that contains probably the most famous footnote in Court's history, the famous "Footnote Four" by Justice Stone, which advocated different levels of judicial review for different kinds of laws.

United States v. Curtiss-Wright Corp. (1936). Court grants expansive authority to chief executive in realm of foreign policy. Justice Sutherland develops "sole organ" thesis concerning presidential power.

United States v. Darby Lumber Co. (1941). The Court upheld the Fair Labor Standards Act of 1938. A key ruling on the power of Congress to regulate interstate commerce, the decision marked the nadir of the Tenth Amendment.

Van Devanter, Willis (1859-1941). Was selected for Court by President Taft in 1911, and served until 1937. Leader of the "Four Horsemen," and first of the quartet to resign.

West Coast Hotel v. Parrish (1937). Court sustains Washington State minimum wage law in the famous "switch in time that saved nine." Chief Justice Hughes wrote for a five to four Court.

West Virginia Board of Education v. Barnette (1943). Court's second "flag salute case." Overruled *Gobitis* on free speech grounds, in opinion by Justice Robert Jackson. Critical dissent by Justice Frankfurter.

BIBLIOGRAPHY

Abraham, Henry J. "Hugo Black as Great Justice." In *Great Justices of the U.S. Supreme Court*, edited by William D. Pederson and Norman W. Provizer. New York: Peter Lang Publishing, Inc., 1993.

——. *Justices and Presidents: A Political History of Appointments to the Supreme Court*. New York: Oxford University Press, 1974.

——. *Justices, Presidents, and Senators: A History of the U.S. Supreme Court Appointments from Washington to Clinton*. Lanham: Rowman & Littlefield Publishers, Inc., 1999.

Ackerman, Bruce A. "Transformative Appointments." *Harvard Law Review* 101 (April 1988): 1164–84.

——. *We the People: Foundations*. Cambridge: The Belknap Press of Harvard University Press, 1991.

Alsop, Joseph, and Turner Catledge. *The 168 Days*. Garden City, NY: Doubleday, Doran and Co., 1938.

Baker, Leonard. *Back to Back: The Duel Between FDR and the Supreme Court*. New York: Macmillan, 1967.

Ball, Howard, and Phillip J. Cooper. *Of Power and Right: Hugo Black, William O. Douglas, and America's Constitutional Revolution*. New York: Oxford University Press, 1992.

Barber, James David. *The Presidential Character: Predicting Performance in the White House*, 5th ed. Englewood Cliffs, NJ: Prentice-Hall, 2001.

Biles, Roger. *The South and the New Deal*. Lexington: University Press of Kentucky, 1994.

Brinkley, Alan. *Liberalism and Its Discontents*. Cambridge, MA: Harvard University Press, 1998.

Burns, James MacGregor. *Roosevelt the Lion and the Fox*. New York: Harcourt, Brace and World, 1956.

Caldeira, Gregory A. "Public Opinion and the U.S. Supreme Court: FDR's Court-Packing Plan." *American Political Science Review* 81 (December 1987): 1139–53.

Cardozo, Benjamin N. *The Nature of the Judicial Process*. New Haven, CT: Yale University Press, 1921.

Dunne, Gerald T. *Hugo Black and the Judicial Revolution*. New York: Simon and Schuster, 1977.

Friedel, Frank. *Franklin D. Roosevelt: A Rendezvous with Destiny*. Boston: Back Bay Books, 1990.

Genovese, Michael A. *The Power of the American Presidency 1789-2000*. New York: Oxford University Press, 2001.

Goodwin, Doris Kears. *No Ordinary Time*. New York: Simon and Schuster, 1994.

Greenstein, Fred I., ed. *Leadership in the Modern Presidency*. Cambridge, MA: Harvard University Press, 1988.

Hamilton, Virginia Van Der Veer. *Hugo Black The Alabama Years*. Baton Rouge: Louisiana State University Press, 1972.

Hargrove, Erwin C. *The President as Leader: Appealing to the Better Angels of Our Nature*. Lawrence: University Press of Kansas, 1998.

Hirsch, H. N. *The Enigma of Felix Frankfurter*. New York: Basic Books Inc, 1981.

International Yearbook, Editor and Publisher. New York: Editor and Publisher, 1937.

Jackson, Robert H. *The Struggle for Judicial Supremacy: A Study of a Crisis in American Power Politics*. New York: Vintage Books, 1941.

Kammen, Michael. *A Machine That Would Go of Itself: The Constitution in American Culture*. New York: Alfred A. Knopf, 1987.

Kernell, Samuel. *Going Public: New Strategies of Presidential Leadership*, 3rd ed. Washington DC: Congressional Quarterly Inc., 1997.

Leuchtenburg, William E. *Franklin Roosevelt and the New Deal, 1932-1940*. New York: Harper and Row, 1963.

——. *In the Shadow of FDR: From Harry Truman to George Bush*, 3rd ed. Ithaca, NY: Cornell University Press, 2001.

——. *The Supreme Court Reborn: The Constitutional Revolution in the Age of Roosevelt*. New York: Oxford University Press, 1995.

Levinson, Sanford. *Constitutional Faith*. Princeton, NJ: Princeton University Press, 1988.

Levy, Leonard. *The Religion Clauses*. New York: Macmillan, 1986.

Mason, Alpheus Thomas. *Free Government in the Making: Readings in American Political Thought*. New York: Oxford University Press, 1965.

——. *Harlan Fiske Stone: Pillar of the Law*. New York: Viking, 1956.

——. *The Supreme Court from Taft to Warren*. New York: W.W. Norton & Co., 1964.

McCloskey, Robert G. *The American Supreme Court*, 2nd ed. Chicago: The University of Chicago Press, 1960.

Murphy, Walter F., James E. Fleming, and Sotirios A. Barber. *American Constitutional Interpretation*, 2nd ed. Westbury: The Foundation Press, 1995.

Nelson, Michael. "The President and the Court: Reinterpreting the Court-packing Episode of 1937." *Political Science Quarterly* 101 (Summer 1988): 267–93.

Neustadt, Richard E. *Presidential Power and The Modern Presidents*. New York: The Free Press, 1990.

Newman, Roger K. *Hugo Black: A Biography*. New York: Pantheon Books, 1994.

O'Brien, David M. *Storm Center: The Supreme Court in American Politics*, 5th ed. New York: W.W. Norton & Co., 2000.

Pearson, Drew, and Robert S. Allen. *The Nine Old Men*. Garden City, NY: Doubleday, Doran & Co., Inc., 1936.

Perry, Barbara A. *The Priestly Tribe: The Supreme Court's Image in the American Mind* Westport: Praeger, 1999.

Pfeffer, Leo. *This Honorable Court: A History of the United States Supreme Court*. Boston: Beacon Press, 1965.

Pritchett, C. Herman. *The Roosevelt Court: A Study in Judicial Politics and Values, 1933-1947*. New York: The Macmillan Company, 1948.

Roosevelt, Franklin D. "Reorganizing the Federal Judiciary." In *Free Government in the Making: Readings in American Political Thought*, 3rd ed. edited by Alpheus T. Mason. New York: Oxford University Press, 1965.

Schlesinger, Arthur M. Jr. *The Politics of Upheaval*. Boston: Houghton Mifflin, 1960.

Scigliano, Robert. *The Supreme Court and the Presidency*. New York: The Free Press, 1971.

Silverstein, Mark. *Constitutional Faiths: Felix Frankfurter, Hugo Black and the Process of Judicial Decision Making*. Ithaca, NY: Cornell University Press, 1984.

Skowronek, Stephen. *The Politics Presidents Make: Leadership from John Adams to Bill Clinton*, Cambridge, MA: Belknap Press of Harvard University Press, 1997.

Thompson, Kenneth W., ed. *Ten Presidents and the Press*. Lanham, MD: University Press of America, 1983.

Tugwell, Rexford G. *FDR: The Architect of an Era*. New York: Macmillan, 1967.

White, Graham J. *FDR and the Press*. Chicago: University of Chicago Press, 1979.

White, Theodore H. *America in Search of Itself: The Making of the President 1956-1980*. New York: Harper and Row, 1982.

LIST OF EDITORS AND CONTRIBUTORS

Henry J. Abraham is James Hart Professor of Government and Foreign Affairs, emeritus at the University of Virginia in Charlottesville. He is the author of numerous works, including *The Judicial Process: An Introductory Analysis of the Courts of the Unites States, England, and France*; *Freedom and the Court: Civil Rights and Liberties in the United States*; and *Justices, Presidents, and Senators: A History of the U.S. Supreme Court Appointments from Washington to Clinton*.

William D. Bader is an attorney in Charlottesville, Virginia. He is a long-time student of the Supreme Court, especially Associate Justice Felix Frankfurter.

Roger W. Corley is professor of history, emeritus at Northwest Missouri State University in Maryville, Missouri. Professor Corley's areas of interest include American political history and twentieth-century presidential history.

James C. Duram is professor of history in the Department of History at Wichita State University in Wichita, Kansas. He is the author of many scholarly publications, including books on Norman Thomas, Associate Justice William O. Douglas, and President Eisenhower.

Kenneth M. Holland is professor of political science at the University of Memphis in Memphis, Tennessee. He is the author of numerous articles, and has authored or edited several books, including *Landmark Laws on the Environment*; *Federalism and the Environment*; *Judicial Activism in Comparative Perspective*; and *The Political Role of Law Courts in Modern Democracies*.

Harvey G. Hudspeth is professor of history and history program coordinator in the Department of Social Science at Mississippi Valley State University in Itta Benna, Mississippi. His teaching and research interests include American politics, the American presidency, and modern American political history.

Donald W. Jackson is Herman Brown Professor of Political Science in the Department of Political Science at Texas Christian University in Fort Worth, Texas. He is the author or editor of numerous publications, including *Presidential Leadership and Civil Rights Policy*, and *The United Kingdom Confronts the European Convention on Human Rights*. His particular interests are civil rights policy and transnational human rights.

Elaine T. King is director of the Office of Information Resources at Louisiana State University Medical Center, Shreveport, Louisiana. She is a student of the Supreme Court and southern political history.

James L. Moses is assistant professor of history at Arkansas Tech University in Russellville, Arkansas. His teaching interests include American constitutional history, and twentieth century American political, social, and cultural history. He has several publications to his credit including articles on William O. Douglas, and the politics of 1968. He is currently working on *Political Justice: William O. Douglas, the Supreme Court, and American Presidential Politics*.

William D. Pederson is professor of political science at Louisiana State University-Shreveport. He has authored and edited numerous publications, and is chair of the American studies program, editor of the *International Abraham Lincoln Journal*, and holds the American studies chair in liberal arts.

Barbara A. Perry is Carter Glass Professor of Government and chair in the Department of Government at Sweet Briar College in Lynchburg, Virginia. She was a Judicial Fellow (1994-95) at the U.S. Supreme Court, where she received the Tom C. Clark Award. Her books include *The Priestly Tribe: The Supreme Court's Image in the American Mind*, and *A "Representative" Supreme Court? The Impact of Race, Religion, and Gender on Appointments*.

James W. Riddlesperger Jr is professor and chair of political science in the Department of Political Science at Texas Christian University in Fort Worth, Texas. He is the author or editor of several publications, and his particular interest is the American presidency and presidential transitions.

Stephen K. Shaw is professor of political science and dean of the School of Arts, Humanities, and Social Sciences at Northwest Nazarene University in Nampa, Idaho. He is the author of *The Ninth Amendment: Preservation of the Constitutional Mind*, and several other scholarly publications. His teaching and research interests include the American presidency, constitutional law, and political extremism.

Frank J. Williams is chief justice of the Rhode Island State Supreme Court, and has edited several scholarly publications with William D. Pederson and other scholars. He is chair of the Lincoln Forum, president of the Ulysses Grant Foundation, and is a nationally recognized scholar on the Lincoln presidency.

INDEX